Garfield at large

BY JIM DAVIS

Ballantine Books • New York

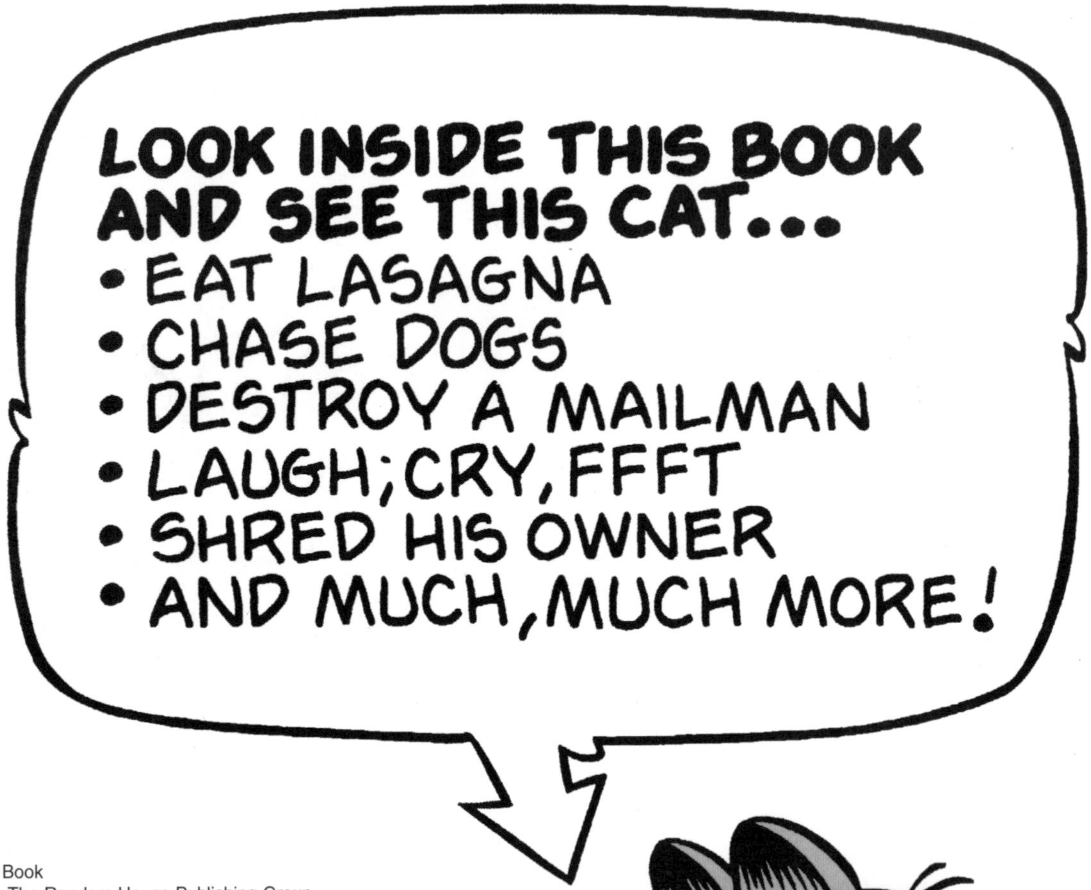
LOOK INSIDE THIS BOOK AND SEE THIS CAT...
• EAT LASAGNA
• CHASE DOGS
• DESTROY A MAILMAN
• LAUGH; CRY, FFFT
• SHRED HIS OWNER
• AND MUCH, MUCH MORE!

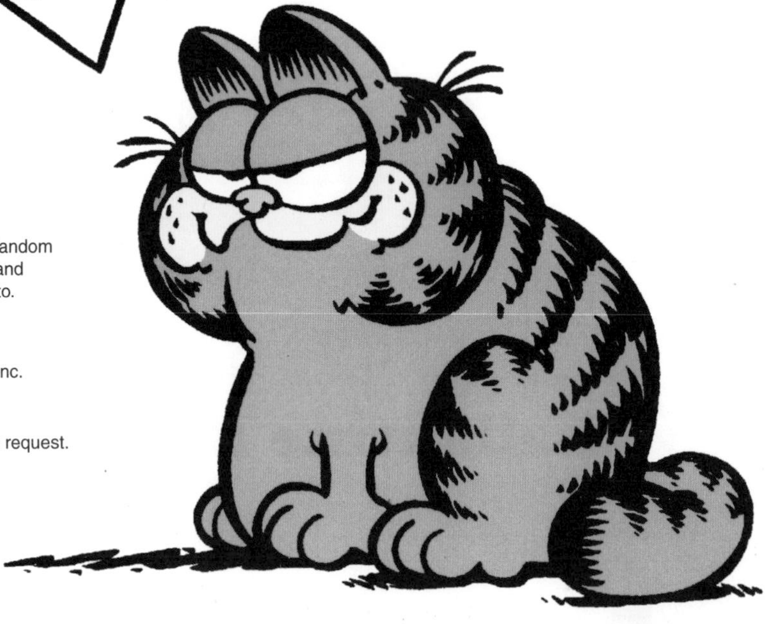

A Ballantine Book
Published by The Random House Publishing Group

Published in the United States by Ballantine Books, an imprint of The Random House Publishing Group, a division of Random House, Inc., New York, and simultaneously in Canada by Random House of Canada Limited, Toronto. Originally published in slightly different form by The Random House Publishing Group, a division of Random House, Inc., in 1980.

Ballantine and colophon are registered trademarks of Random House, Inc.

www.ballantinebooks.com

A Library of Congress card number is available from the publisher upon request.

ISBN 0-345-44382-9

Manufactured in China

First Colorized Edition: June 2001

9 8 7 6

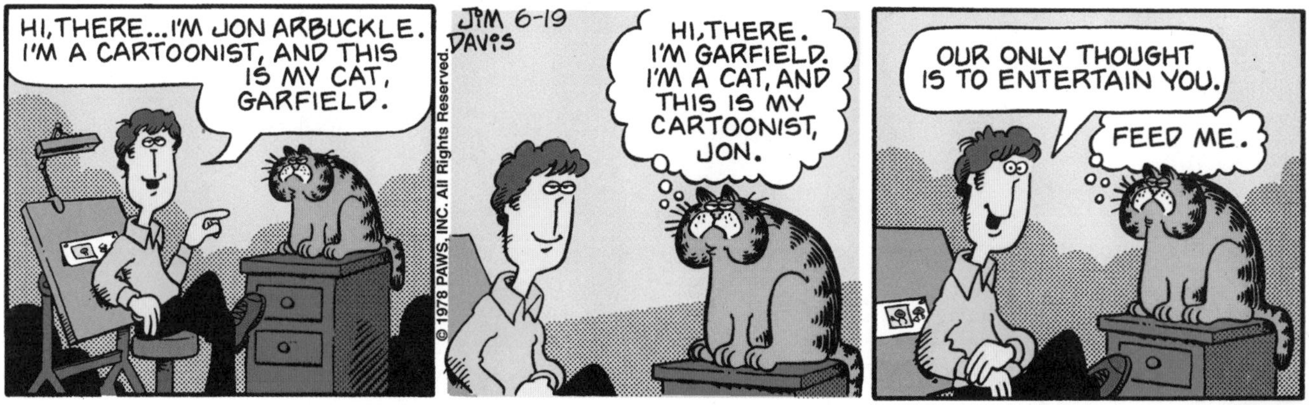
HI, THERE... I'M JON ARBUCKLE. I'M A CARTOONIST, AND THIS IS MY CAT, GARFIELD.
JIM DAVIS 6-19
© 1978 PAWS, INC. All Rights Reserved.
HI, THERE. I'M GARFIELD. I'M A CAT, AND THIS IS MY CARTOONIST, JON.
OUR ONLY THOUGHT IS TO ENTERTAIN YOU.
FEED ME.

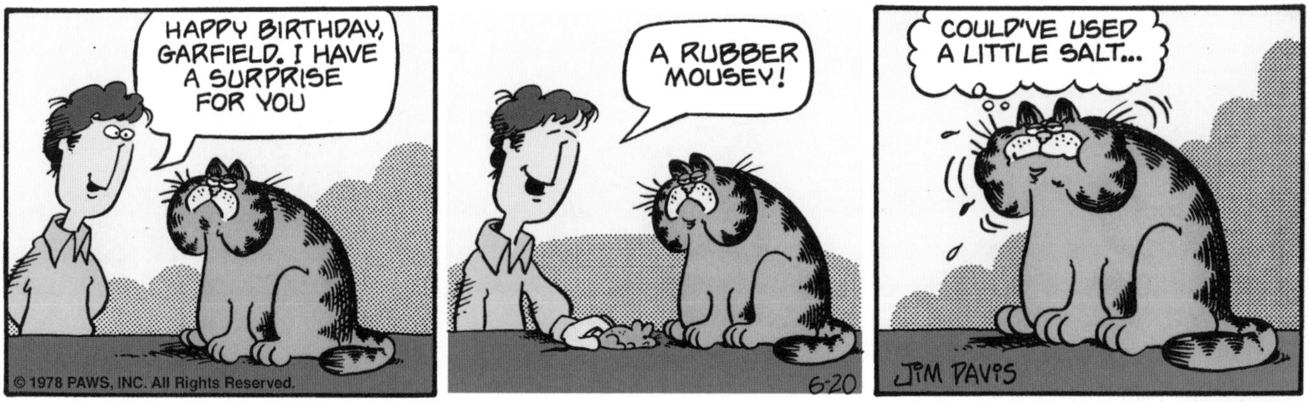
HAPPY BIRTHDAY, GARFIELD. I HAVE A SURPRISE FOR YOU
© 1978 PAWS, INC. All Rights Reserved.
A RUBBER MOUSEY!
6-20
COULD'VE USED A LITTLE SALT...
JIM DAVIS

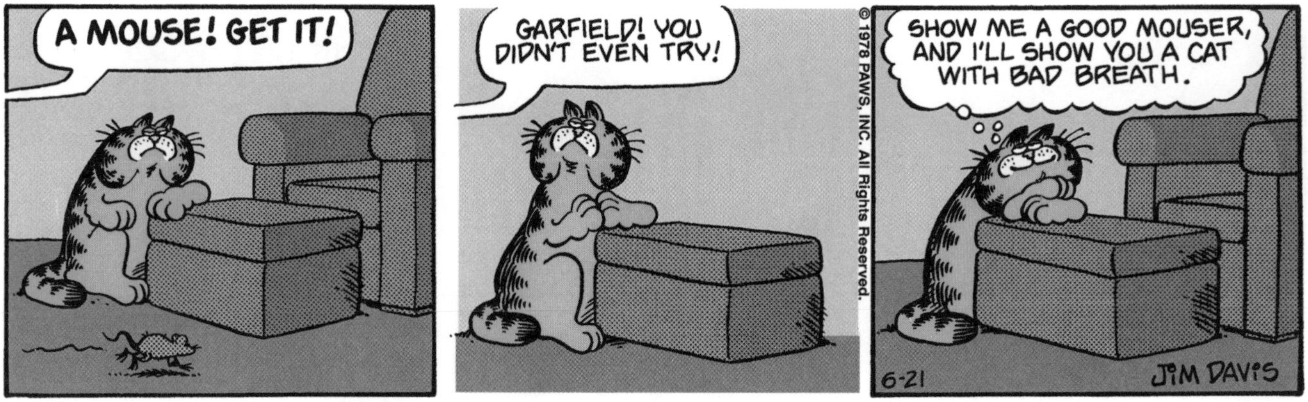
A MOUSE! GET IT!
GARFIELD! YOU DIDN'T EVEN TRY!
© 1978 PAWS, INC. All Rights Reserved.
SHOW ME A GOOD MOUSER, AND I'LL SHOW YOU A CAT WITH BAD BREATH.
6-21
JIM DAVIS

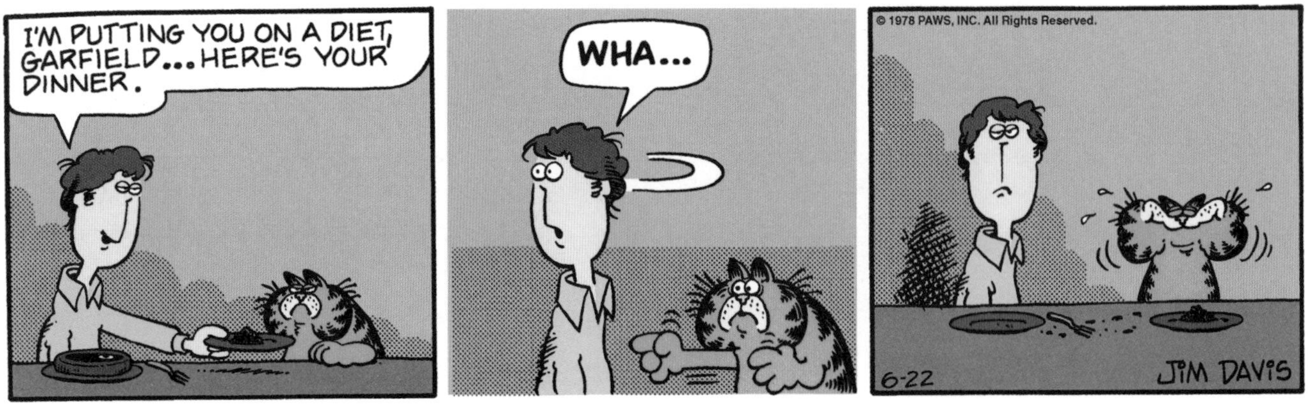
I'M PUTTING YOU ON A DIET, GARFIELD... HERE'S YOUR DINNER.
WHA...
© 1978 PAWS, INC. All Rights Reserved.
6-22
JIM DAVIS

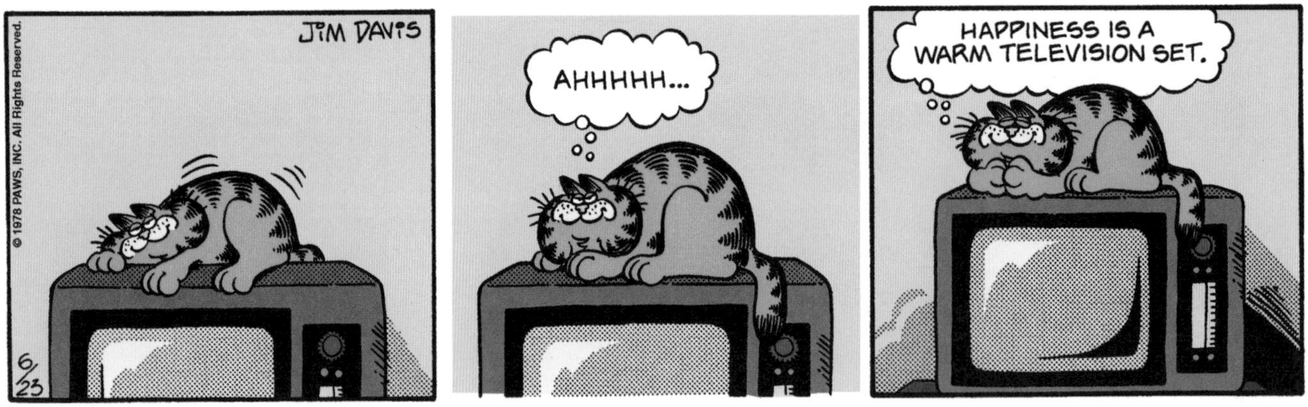
JIM DAVIS
© 1978 PAWS, INC. All Rights Reserved.
6/23
AHHHHH...
HAPPINESS IS A WARM TELEVISION SET.

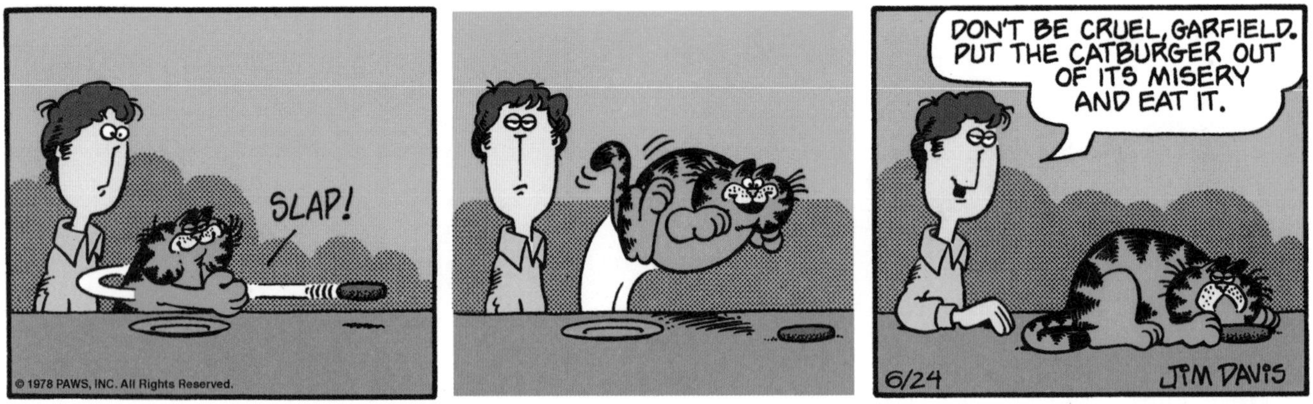
SLAP!
© 1978 PAWS, INC. All Rights Reserved.
DON'T BE CRUEL, GARFIELD. PUT THE CATBURGER OUT OF ITS MISERY AND EAT IT.
6/24
JIM DAVIS

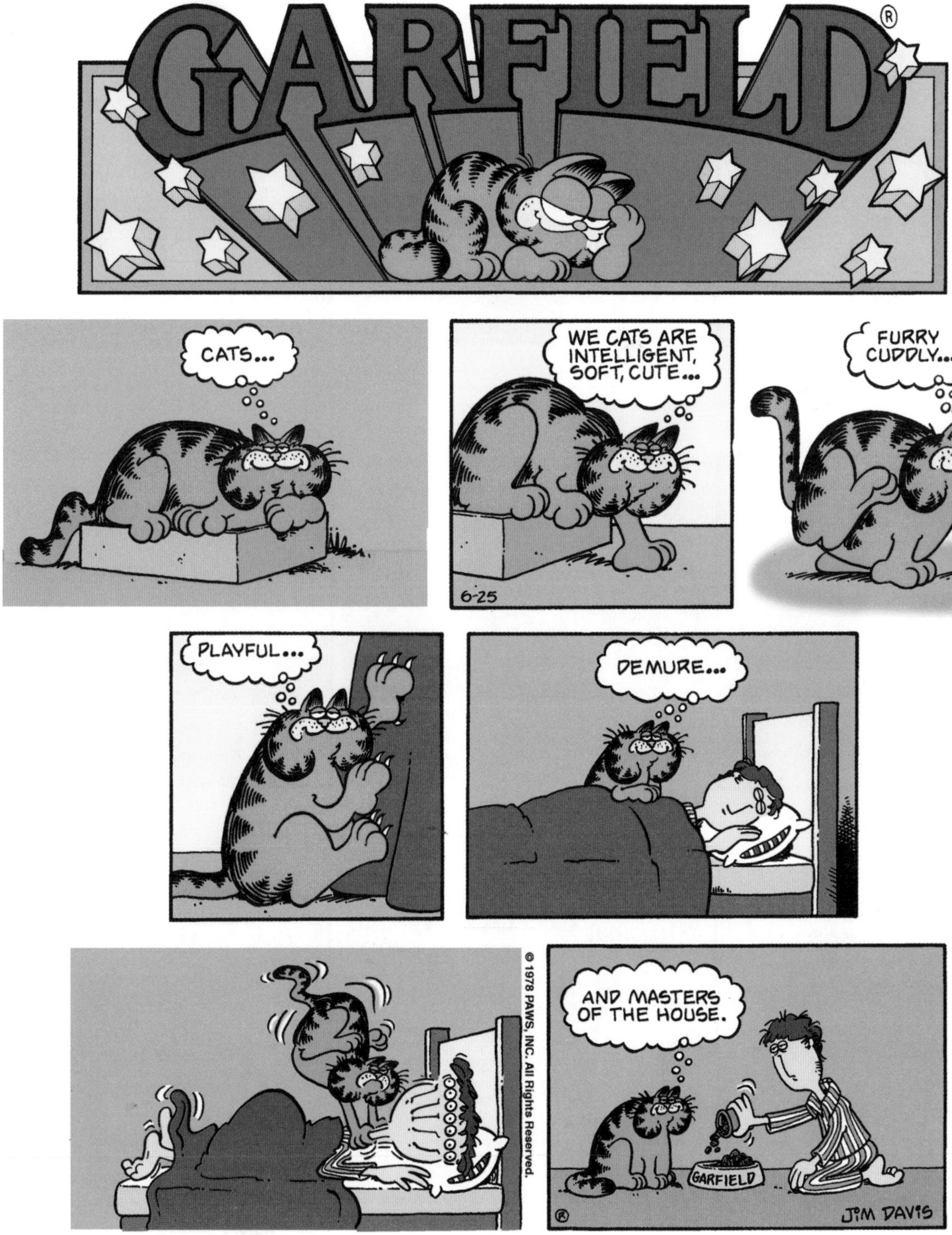
GARFIELD®
CATS...
WE CATS ARE INTELLIGENT, SOFT, CUTE...
FURRY CUDDLY...
6-25
PLAYFUL...
DEMURE...
© 1978 PAWS, INC. All Rights Reserved.
AND MASTERS OF THE HOUSE.
GARFIELD
®
JIM DAVIS

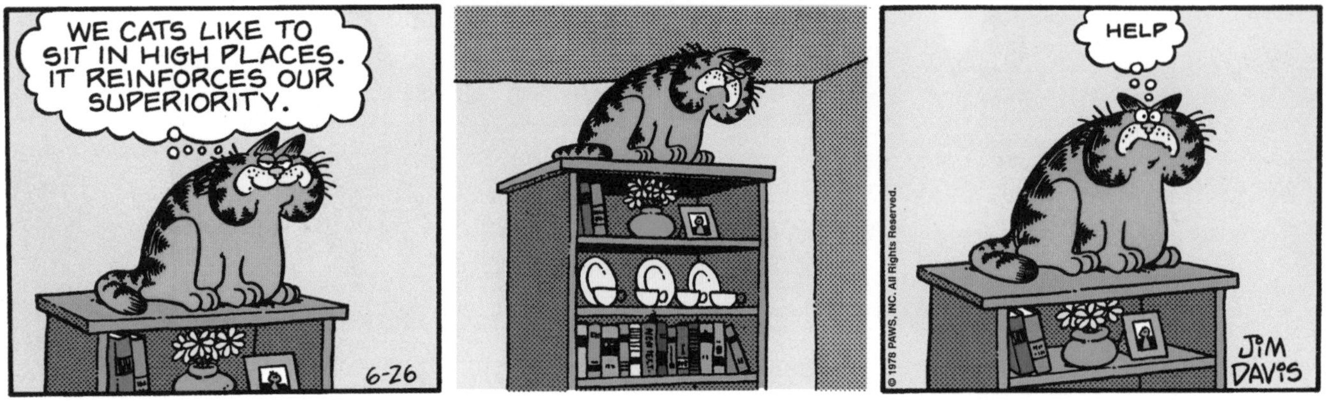
WE CATS LIKE TO SIT IN HIGH PLACES. IT REINFORCES OUR SUPERIORITY.
6-26
HELP
© 1978 PAWS, INC. All Rights Reserved.
JIM DAVIS

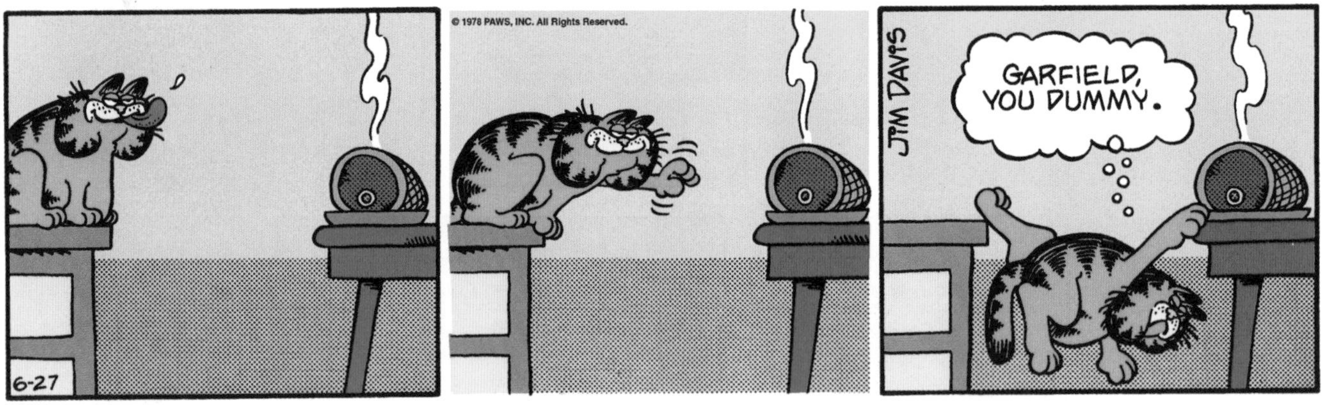
6-27
© 1978 PAWS, INC. All Rights Reserved.
JIM DAVIS
GARFIELD, YOU DUMMY.

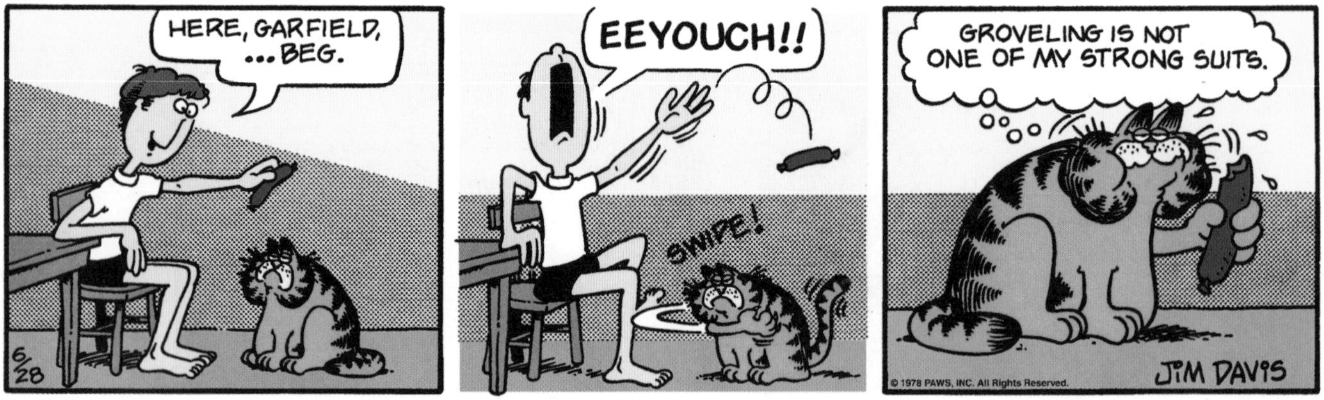
HERE, GARFIELD, ...BEG.
6/28
EEYOUCH!!
SWIPE!
GROVELING IS NOT ONE OF MY STRONG SUITS.
© 1978 PAWS, INC. All Rights Reserved.
JIM DAVIS

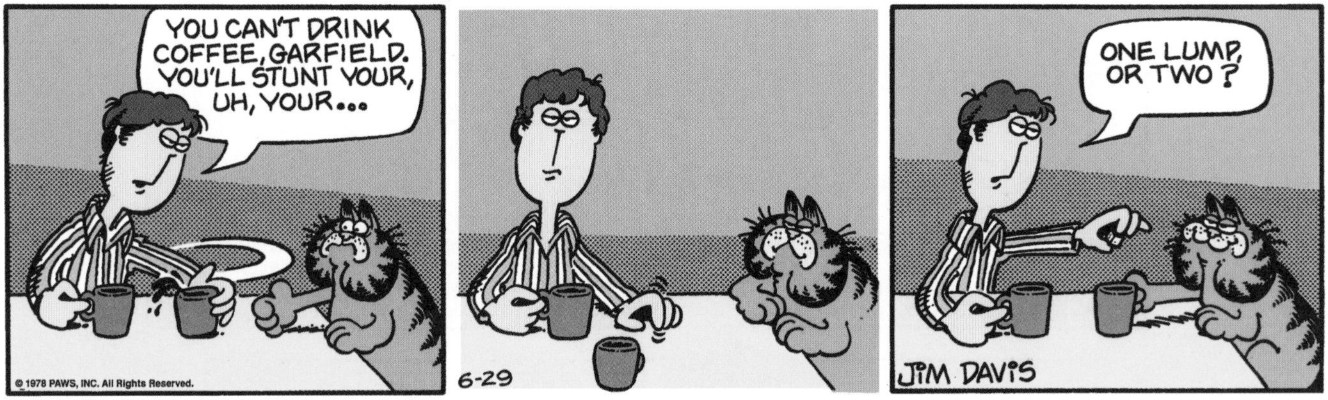
YOU CAN'T DRINK COFFEE, GARFIELD. YOU'LL STUNT YOUR, UH, YOUR...
ONE LUMP, OR TWO?
© 1978 PAWS, INC. All Rights Reserved.
6-29
JIM DAVIS

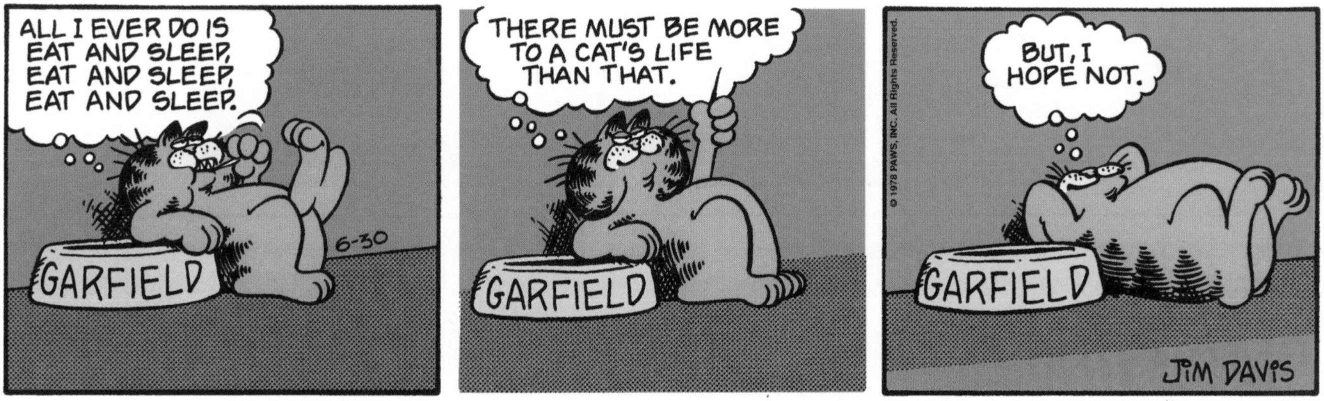
ALL I EVER DO IS EAT AND SLEEP, EAT AND SLEEP, EAT AND SLEEP.
GARFIELD
6-30
THERE MUST BE MORE TO A CAT'S LIFE THAN THAT.
GARFIELD
© 1978 PAWS, INC. All Rights Reserved.
BUT, I HOPE NOT.
GARFIELD
JIM DAVIS

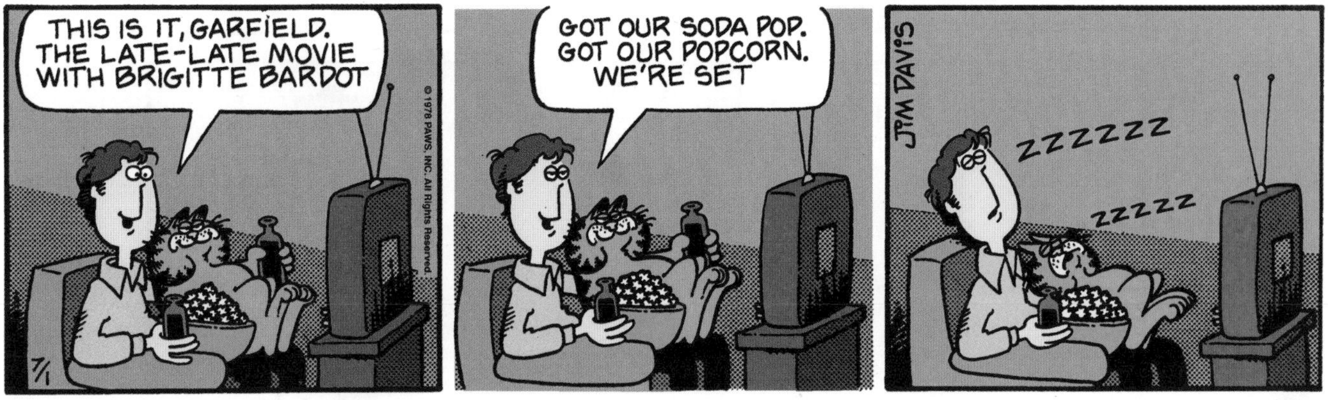
THIS IS IT, GARFIELD. THE LATE-LATE MOVIE WITH BRIGITTE BARDOT
© 1978 PAWS, INC. All Rights Reserved.
7/1
GOT OUR SODA POP. GOT OUR POPCORN. WE'RE SET
JIM DAVIS
ZZZZZZ
ZZZZZ

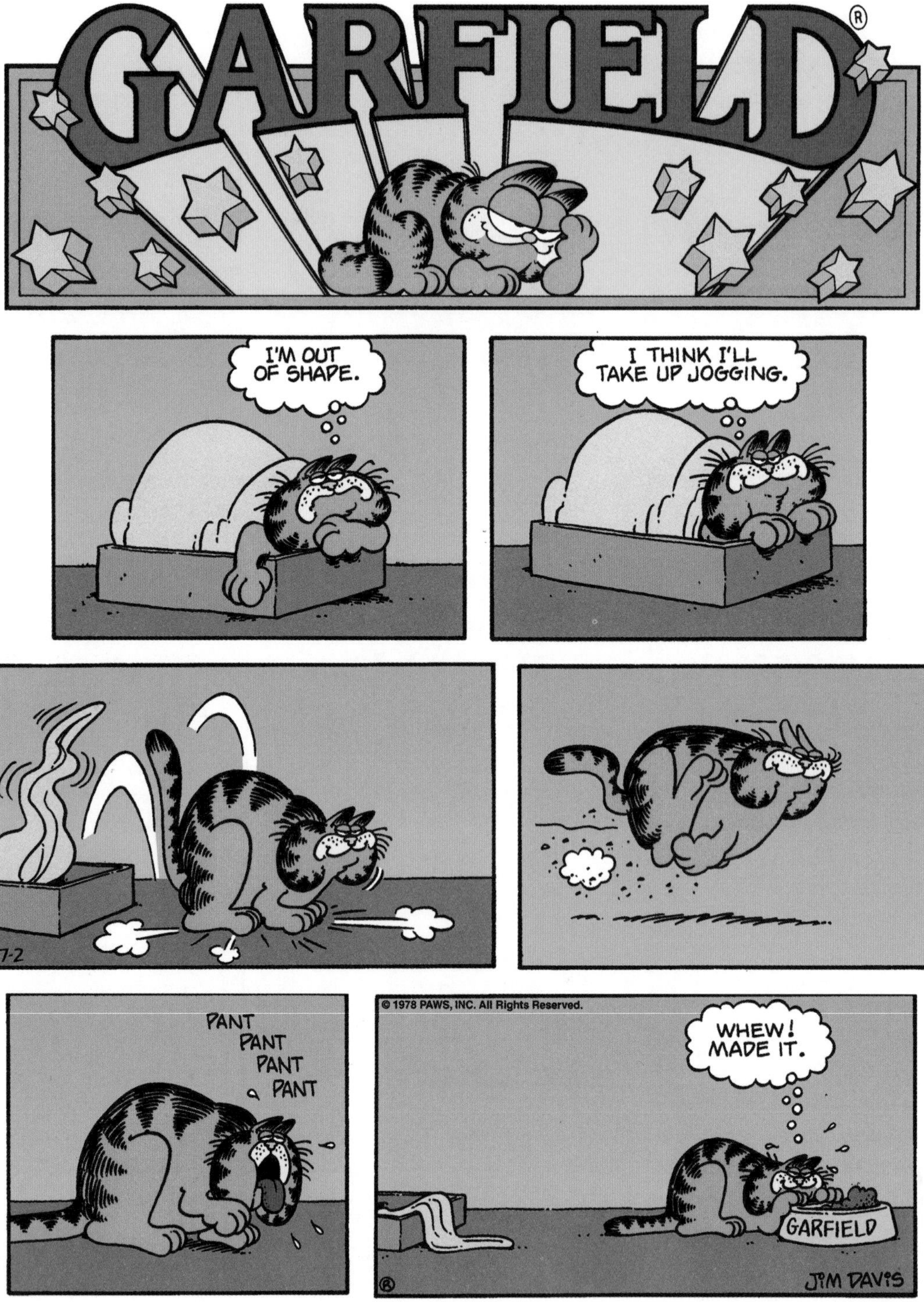
GARFIELD
I'M OUT OF SHAPE.
I THINK I'LL TAKE UP JOGGING.
7-2
PANT PANT PANT PANT
© 1978 PAWS, INC. All Rights Reserved.
WHEW! MADE IT.
GARFIELD
JIM DAVIS

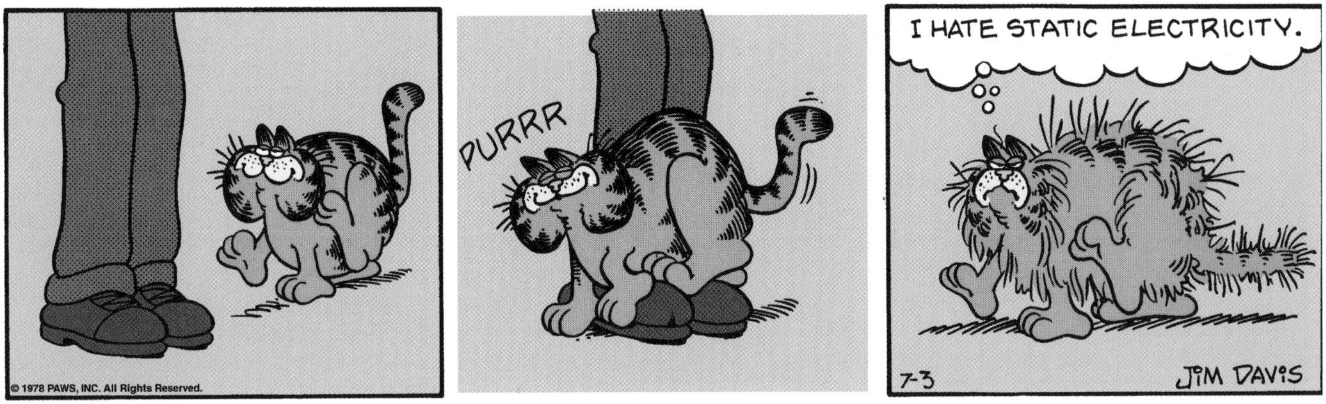
© 1978 PAWS, INC. All Rights Reserved.
PURRR
I HATE STATIC ELECTRICITY.
7-3
JIM DAVIS

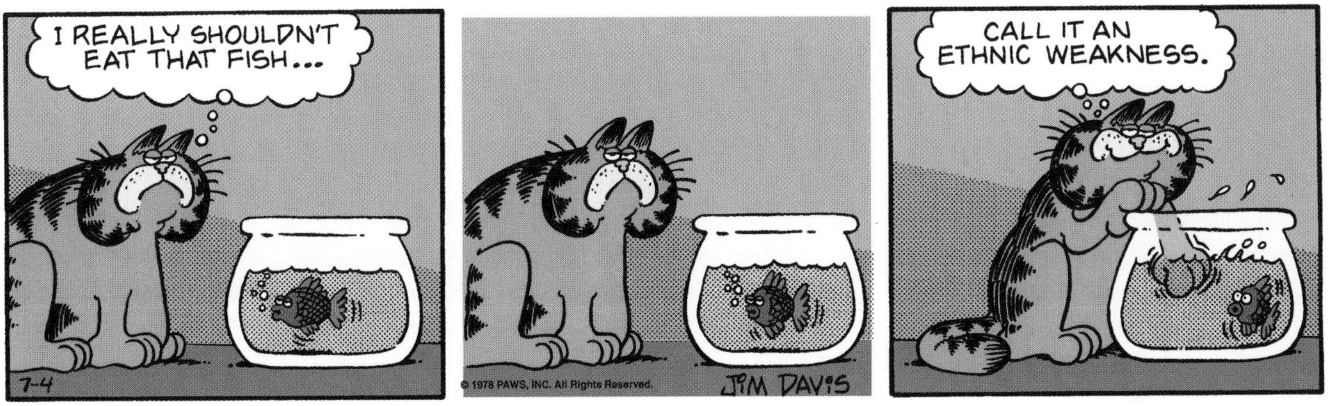
I REALLY SHOULDN'T EAT THAT FISH...
7-4
© 1978 PAWS, INC. All Rights Reserved.
JIM DAVIS
CALL IT AN ETHNIC WEAKNESS.

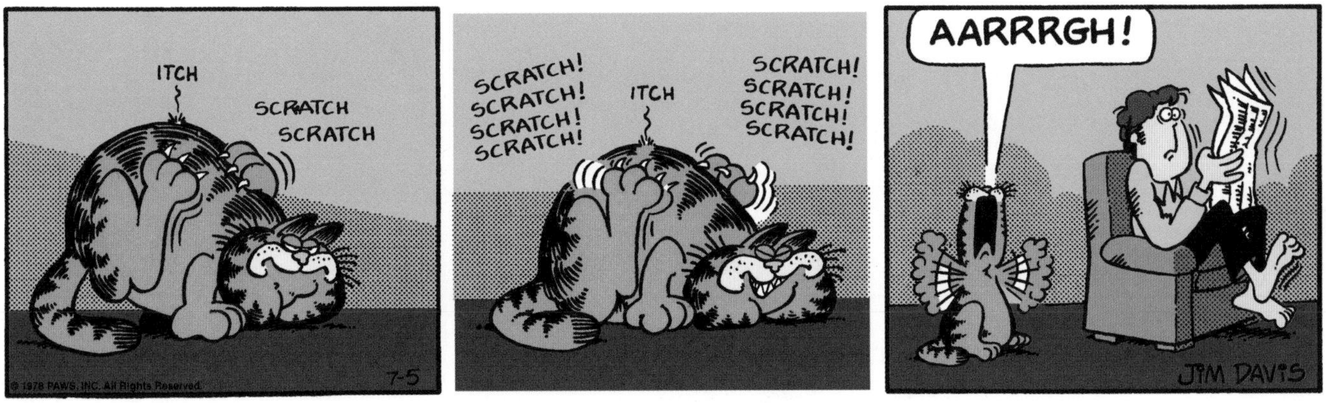
ITCH
SCRATCH SCRATCH
© 1978 PAWS, INC. All Rights Reserved.
7-5
SCRATCH! SCRATCH! SCRATCH! SCRATCH!
ITCH
SCRATCH! SCRATCH! SCRATCH! SCRATCH!
AARRRGH!
JIM DAVIS

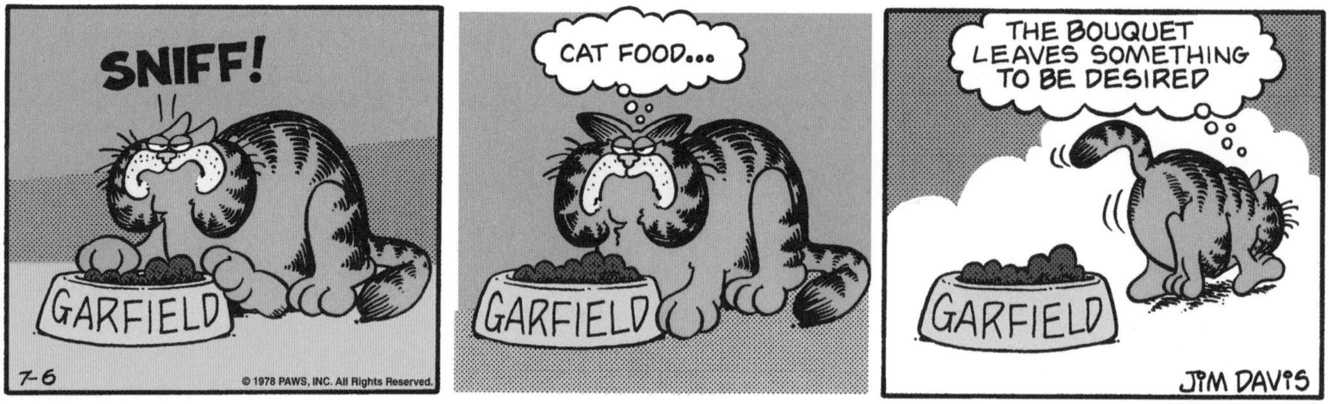
SNIFF!
GARFIELD
7-6
© 1978 PAWS, INC. All Rights Reserved.
CAT FOOD...
GARFIELD
THE BOUQUET LEAVES SOMETHING TO BE DESIRED
GARFIELD
JIM DAVIS

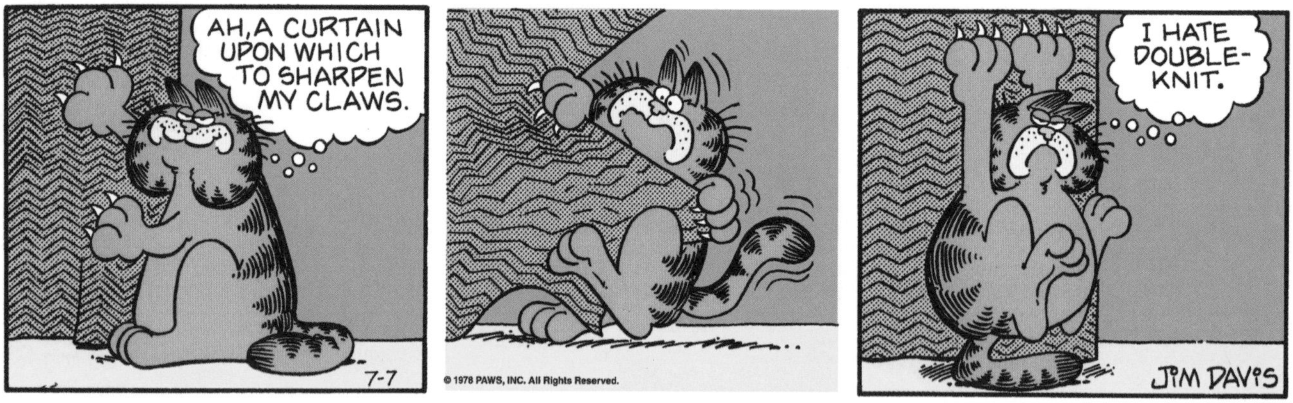
AH, A CURTAIN UPON WHICH TO SHARPEN MY CLAWS.
7-7
© 1978 PAWS, INC. All Rights Reserved.
I HATE DOUBLE-KNIT.
JIM DAVIS

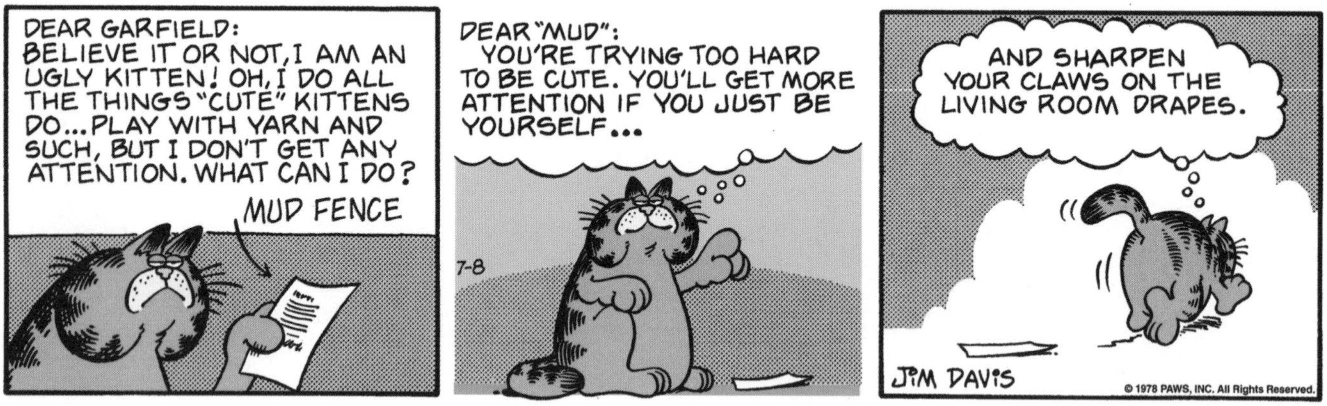
DEAR GARFIELD: BELIEVE IT OR NOT, I AM AN UGLY KITTEN! OH, I DO ALL THE THINGS "CUTE" KITTENS DO...PLAY WITH YARN AND SUCH, BUT I DON'T GET ANY ATTENTION. WHAT CAN I DO?
MUD FENCE
DEAR "MUD": YOU'RE TRYING TOO HARD TO BE CUTE. YOU'LL GET MORE ATTENTION IF YOU JUST BE YOURSELF...
7-8
AND SHARPEN YOUR CLAWS ON THE LIVING ROOM DRAPES.
JIM DAVIS
© 1978 PAWS, INC. All Rights Reserved.

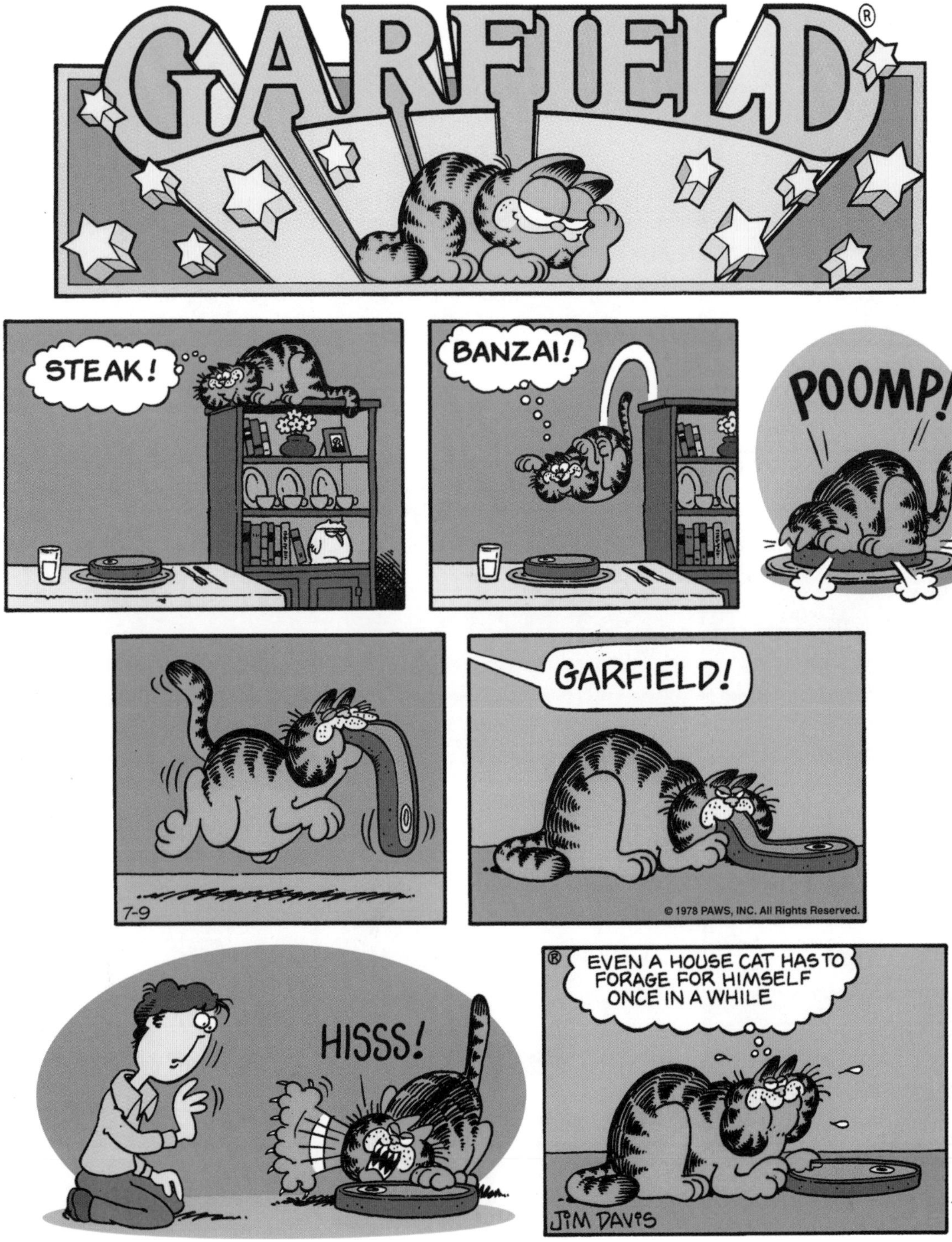
GARFIELD®
STEAK!
BANZAI!
POOMP!
7-9
GARFIELD!
© 1978 PAWS, INC. All Rights Reserved.
HISSS!
®
EVEN A HOUSE CAT HAS TO FORAGE FOR HIMSELF ONCE IN A WHILE
JIM DAVIS

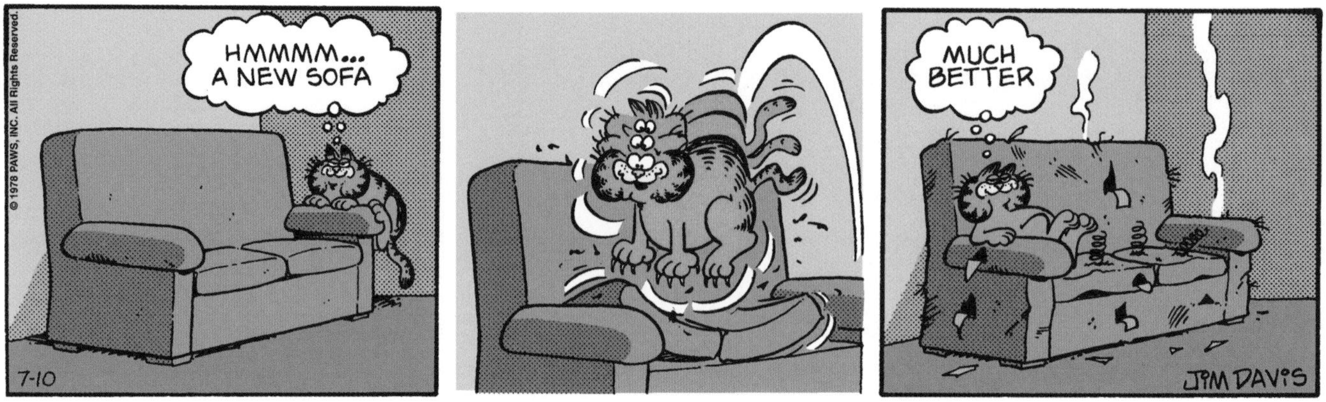
© 1978 PAWS, INC. All Rights Reserved.
HMMMM... A NEW SOFA
7-10
MUCH BETTER
JIM DAVIS

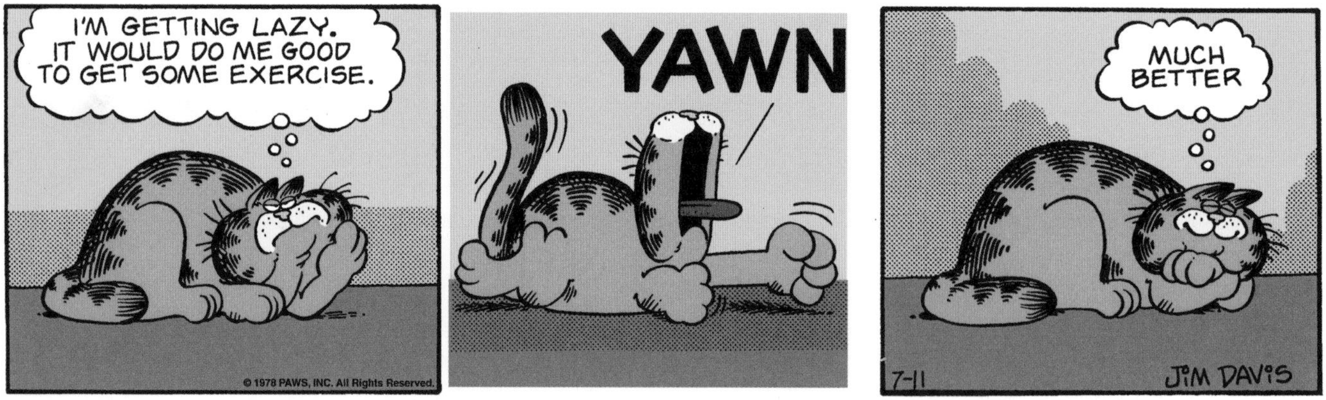
I'M GETTING LAZY. IT WOULD DO ME GOOD TO GET SOME EXERCISE.
© 1978 PAWS, INC. All Rights Reserved.
YAWN
MUCH BETTER
7-11
JIM DAVIS

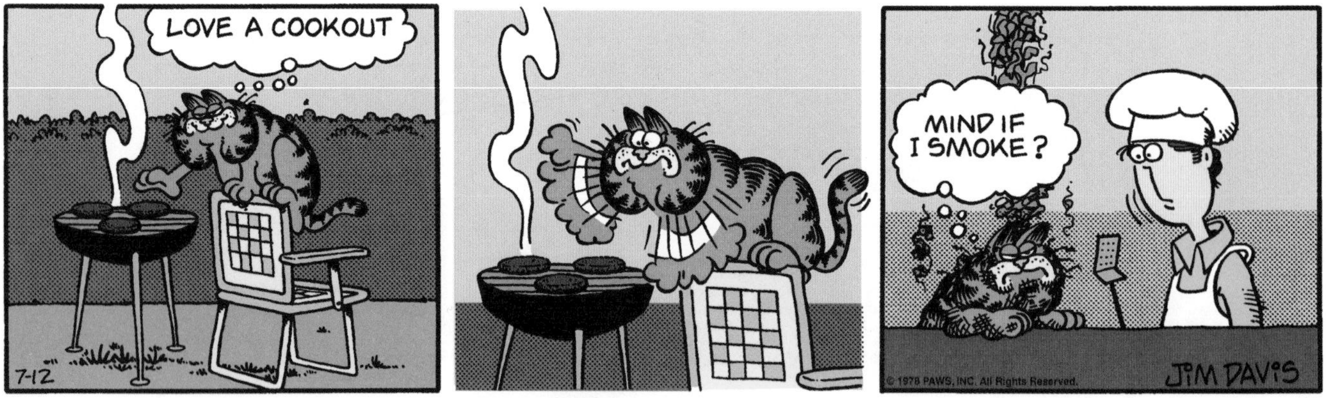
LOVE A COOKOUT
7-12
MIND IF I SMOKE?
© 1978 PAWS, INC. All Rights Reserved.
JIM DAVIS

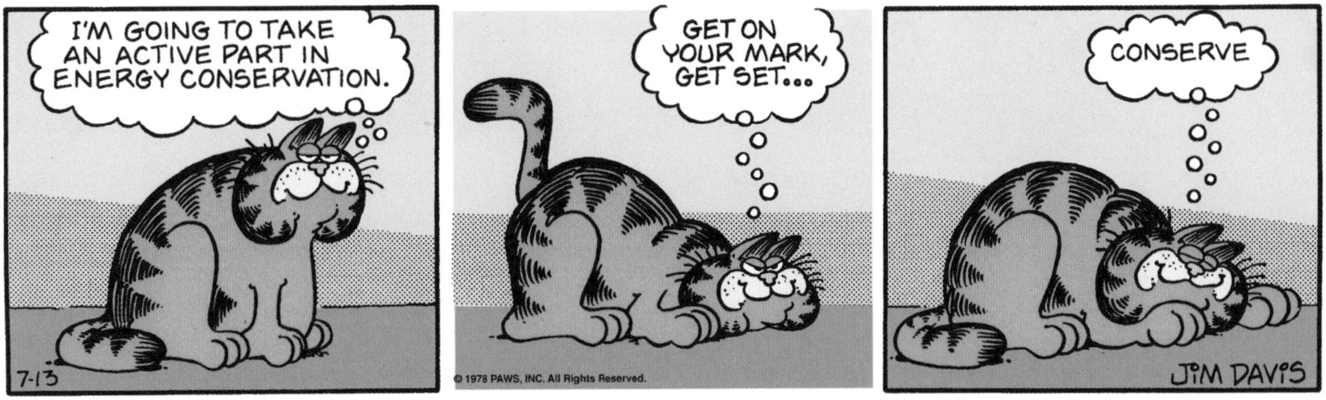
I'M GOING TO TAKE AN ACTIVE PART IN ENERGY CONSERVATION.
7-13
GET ON YOUR MARK, GET SET...
© 1978 PAWS, INC. All Rights Reserved.
CONSERVE
JIM DAVIS

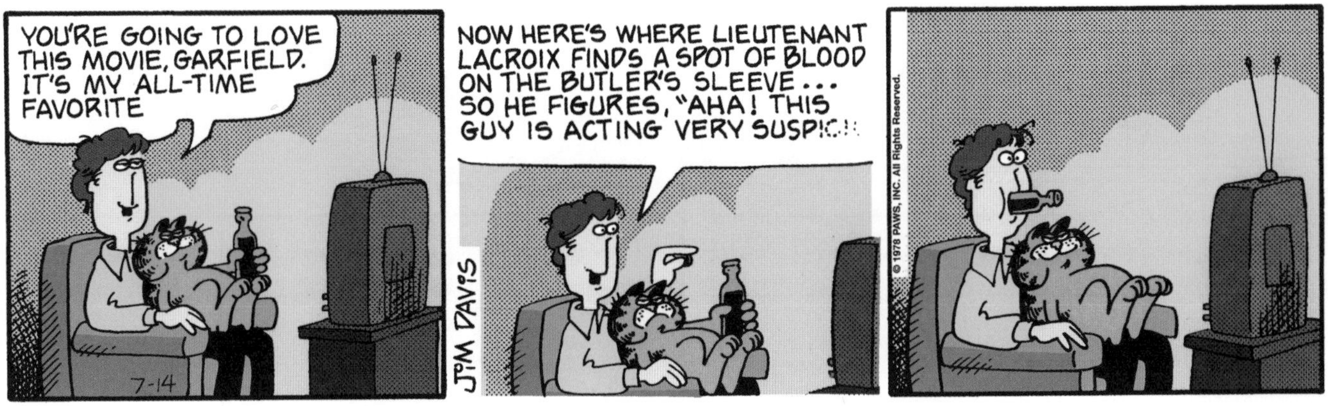
YOU'RE GOING TO LOVE THIS MOVIE, GARFIELD. IT'S MY ALL-TIME FAVORITE
7-14
NOW HERE'S WHERE LIEUTENANT LACROIX FINDS A SPOT OF BLOOD ON THE BUTLER'S SLEEVE... SO HE FIGURES, "AHA! THIS GUY IS ACTING VERY SUSPIC
JIM DAVIS
© 1978 PAWS, INC. All Rights Reserved.

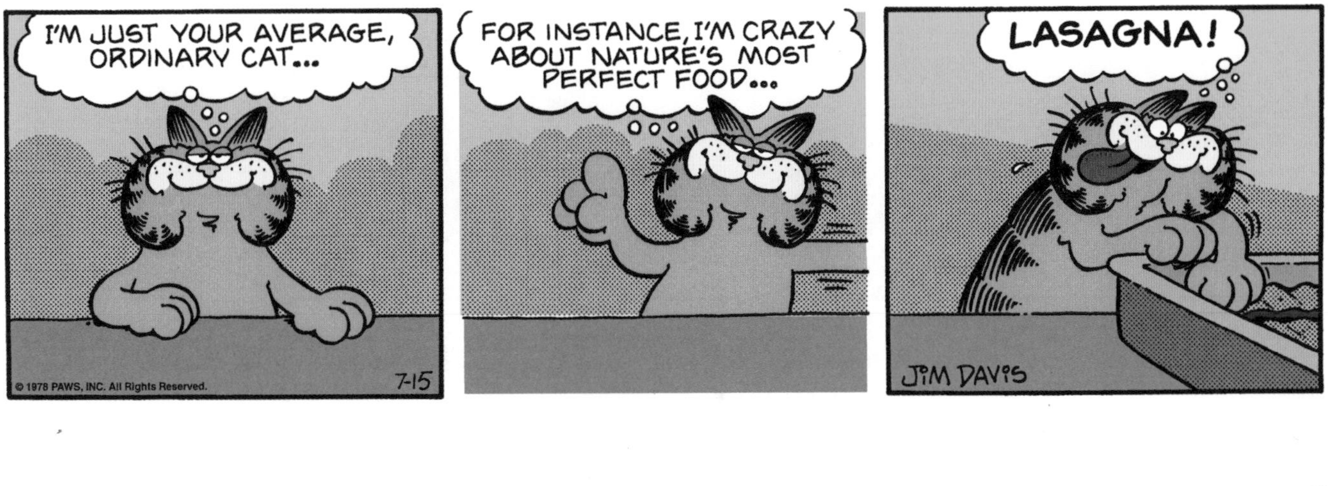
I'M JUST YOUR AVERAGE, ORDINARY CAT...
© 1978 PAWS, INC. All Rights Reserved.
7-15
FOR INSTANCE, I'M CRAZY ABOUT NATURE'S MOST PERFECT FOOD...
LASAGNA!
JIM DAVIS

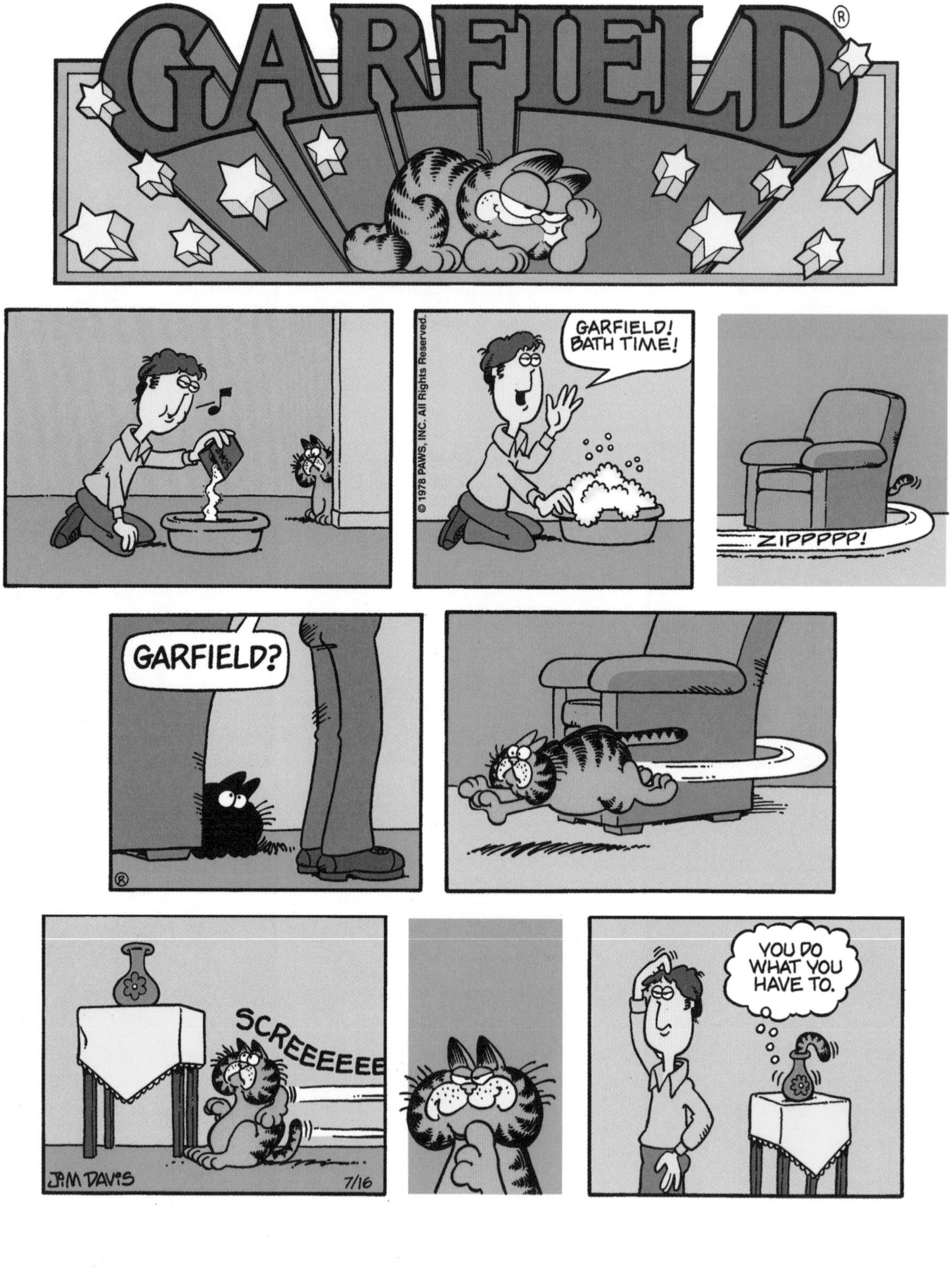
GARFIELD®
© 1978 PAWS, INC. All Rights Reserved.
GARFIELD! BATH TIME!
ZIPPPPPP!
GARFIELD?
SCREEEEEEE
JIM DAVIS
7/16
YOU DO WHAT YOU HAVE TO.

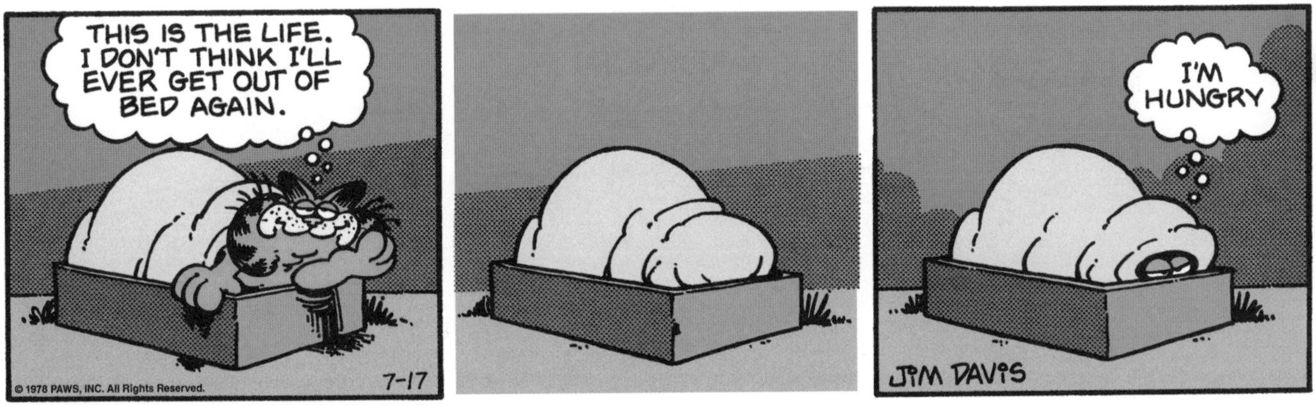
THIS IS THE LIFE. I DON'T THINK I'LL EVER GET OUT OF BED AGAIN.
© 1978 PAWS, INC. All Rights Reserved.
7-17
I'M HUNGRY
JIM DAVIS

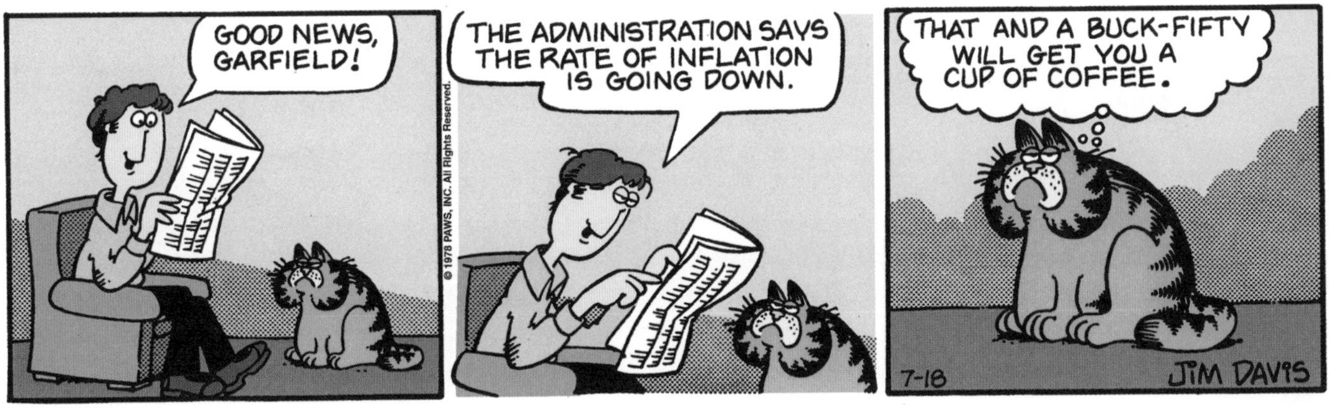
GOOD NEWS, GARFIELD!
© 1978 PAWS, INC. All Rights Reserved.
THE ADMINISTRATION SAYS THE RATE OF INFLATION IS GOING DOWN.
THAT AND A BUCK-FIFTY WILL GET YOU A CUP OF COFFEE.
7-18
JIM DAVIS

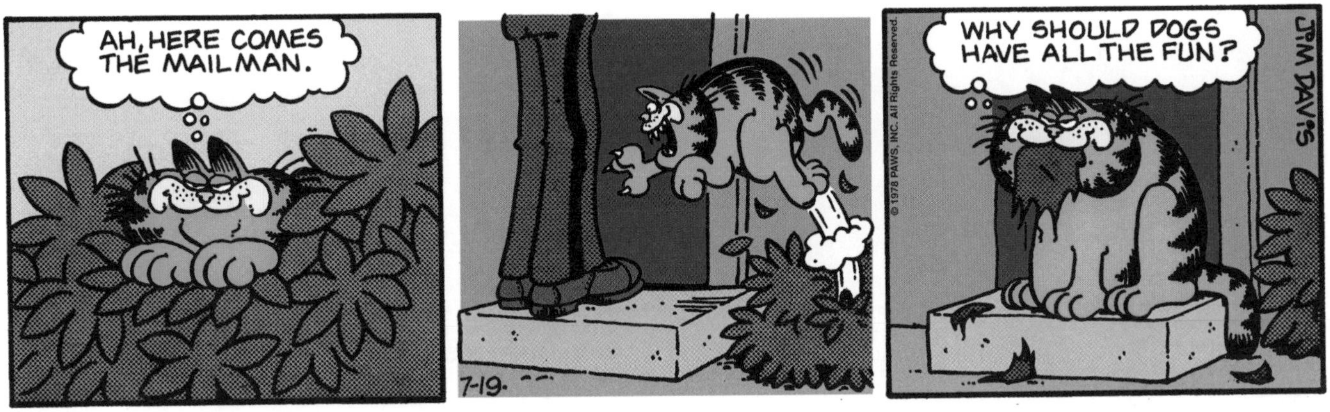
AH, HERE COMES THE MAILMAN.
7-19
© 1978 PAWS, INC. All Rights Reserved.
WHY SHOULD DOGS HAVE ALL THE FUN?
JIM DAVIS

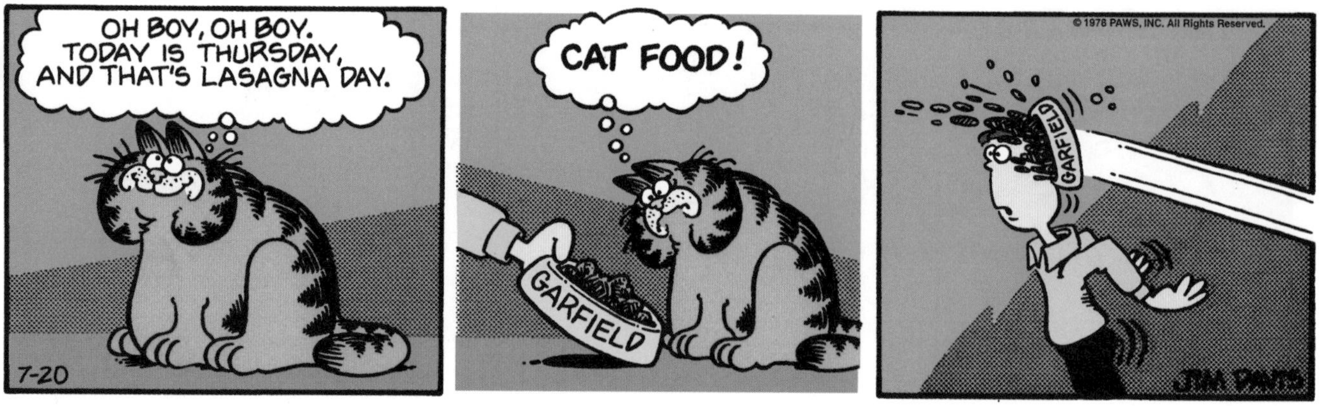
OH BOY, OH BOY. TODAY IS THURSDAY, AND THAT'S LASAGNA DAY.
7-20
CAT FOOD!
GARFIELD
© 1978 PAWS, INC. All Rights Reserved.
GARFIELD
JIM DAVIS

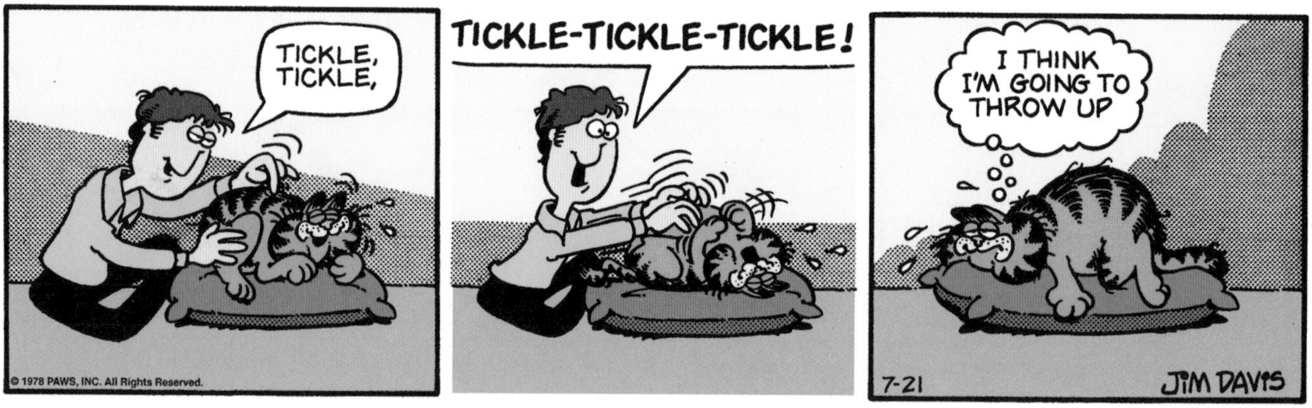
TICKLE, TICKLE,
© 1978 PAWS, INC. All Rights Reserved.
TICKLE-TICKLE-TICKLE!
I THINK I'M GOING TO THROW UP
7-21
JIM DAVIS

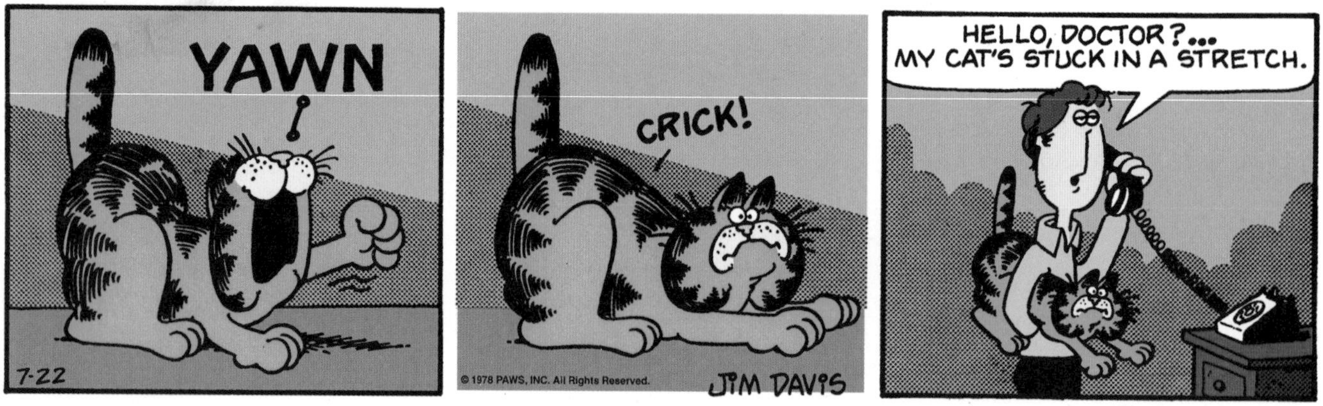
YAWN
7-22
CRICK!
© 1978 PAWS, INC. All Rights Reserved.
JIM DAVIS
HELLO, DOCTOR?... MY CAT'S STUCK IN A STRETCH.

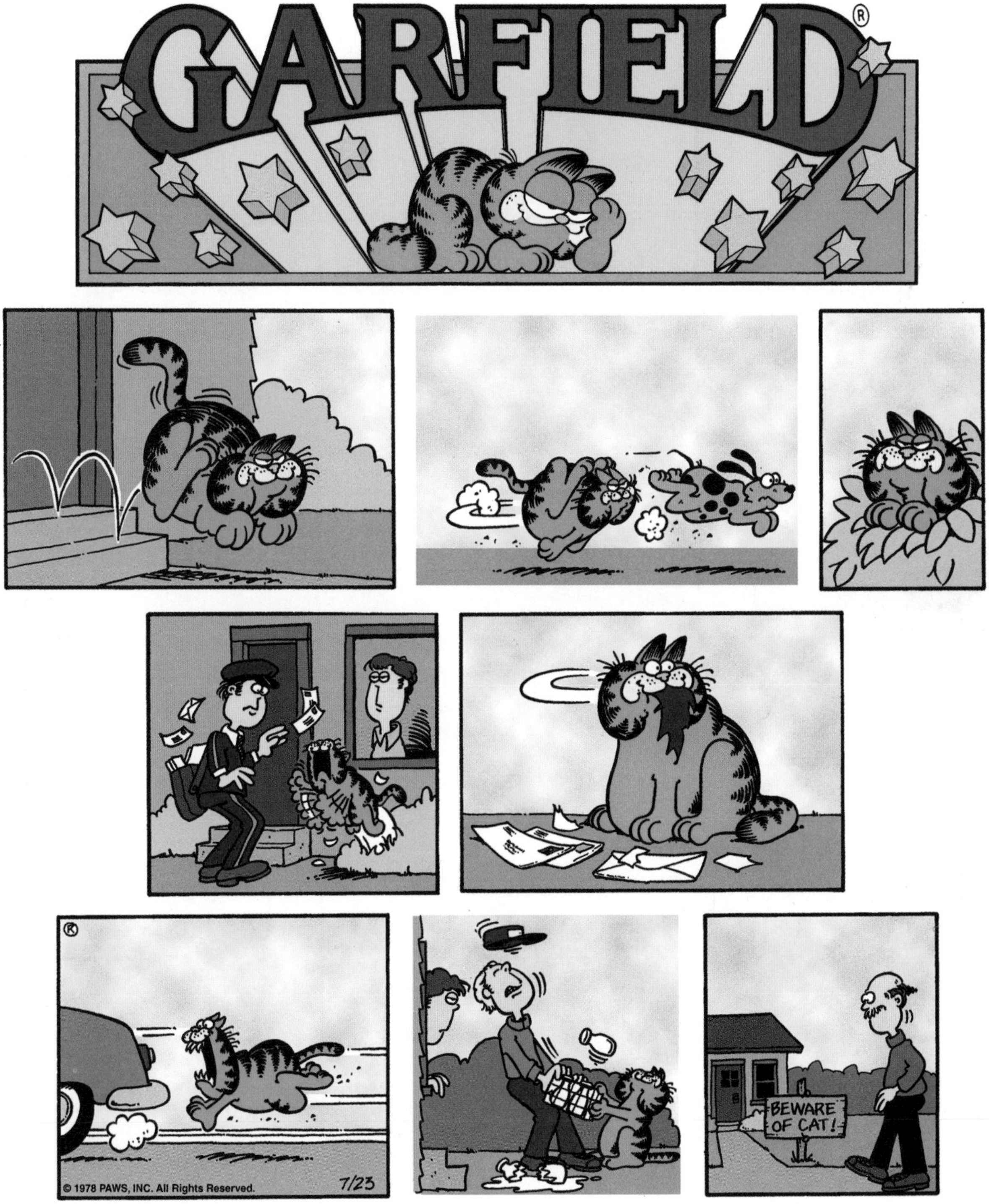
GARFIELD®
BEWARE OF CAT!
© 1978 PAWS, INC. All Rights Reserved.
7/23

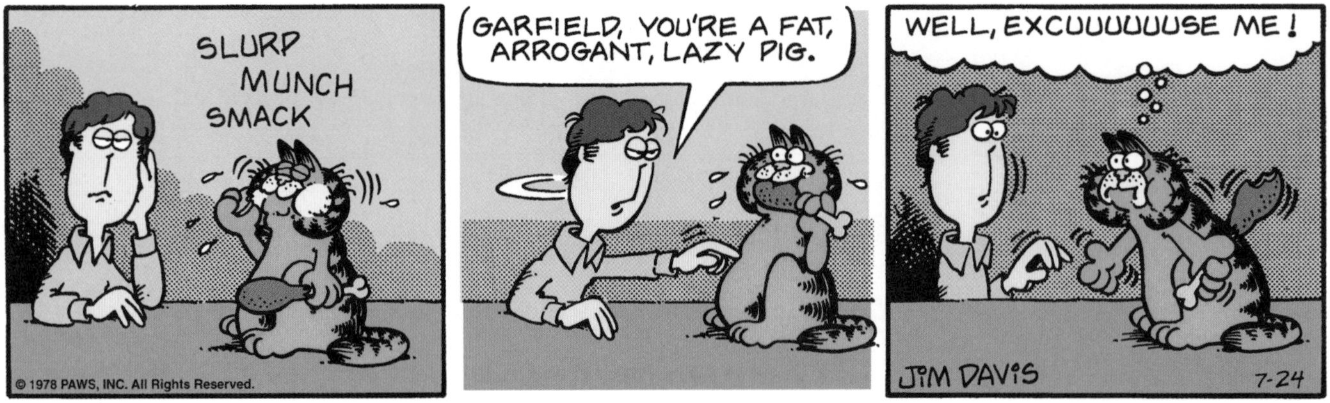
SLURP
MUNCH
SMACK
© 1978 PAWS, INC. All Rights Reserved.
GARFIELD, YOU'RE A FAT, ARROGANT, LAZY PIG.
WELL, EXCUUUUUUSE ME!
JIM DAVIS
7-24

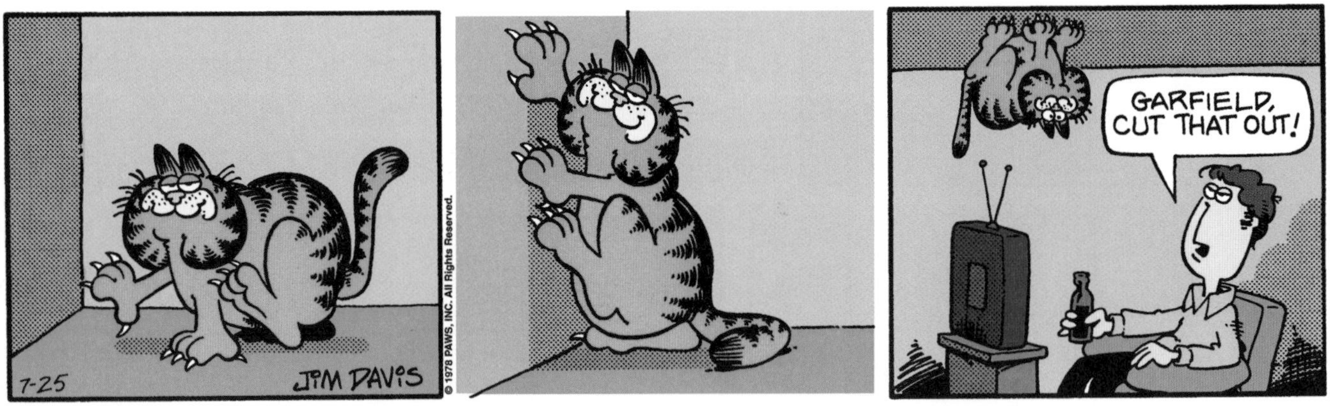
7-25
JIM DAVIS
© 1978 PAWS, INC. All Rights Reserved.
GARFIELD, CUT THAT OUT!

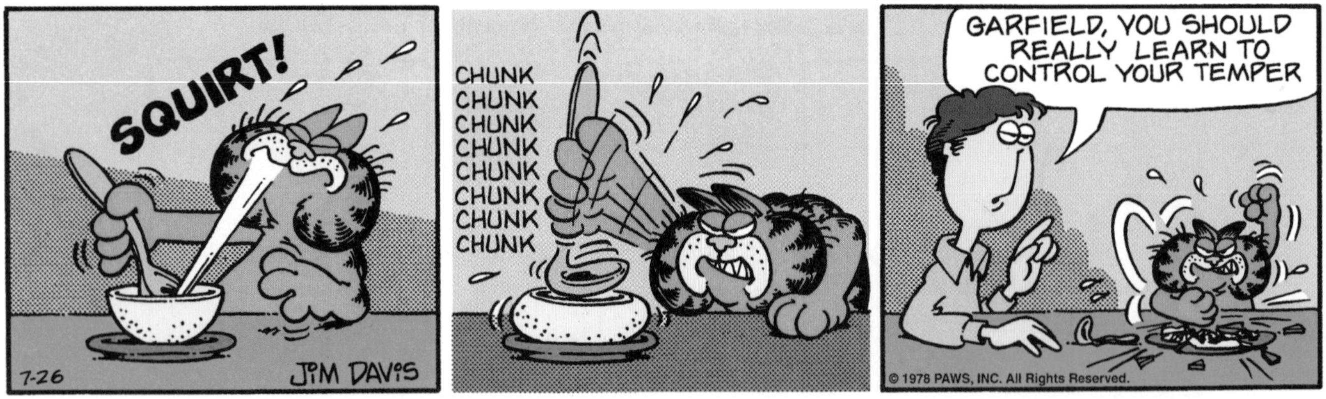
SQUIRT!
7-26
JIM DAVIS
CHUNK
CHUNK
CHUNK
CHUNK
CHUNK
CHUNK
CHUNK
CHUNK
GARFIELD, YOU SHOULD REALLY LEARN TO CONTROL YOUR TEMPER
© 1978 PAWS, INC. All Rights Reserved.

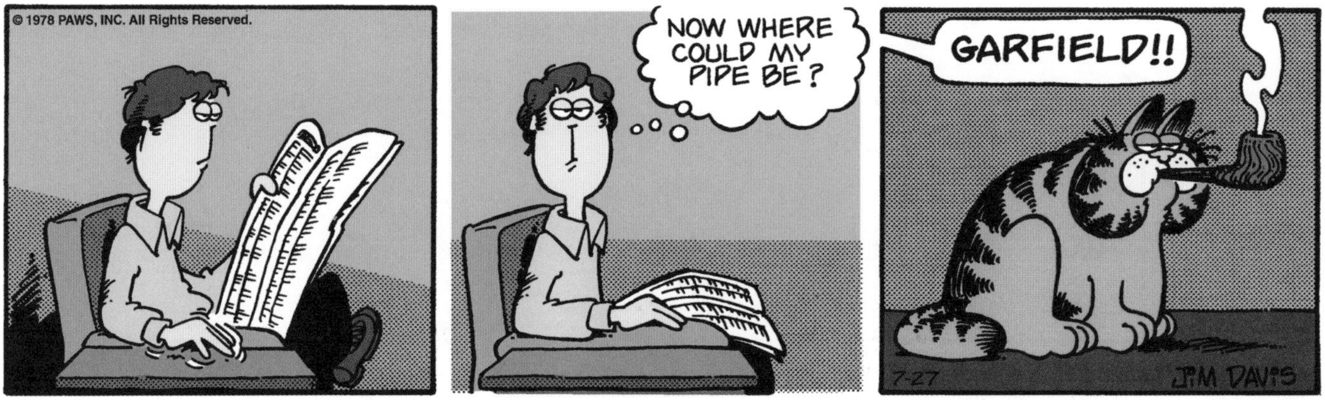
© 1978 PAWS, INC. All Rights Reserved.
NOW WHERE COULD MY PIPE BE ?
GARFIELD!!
7-27
JIM DAVIS

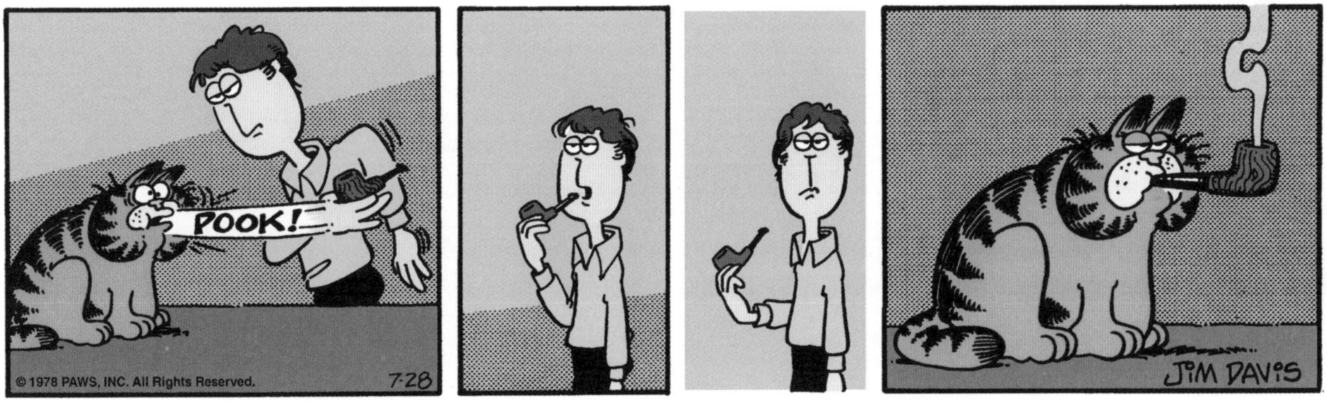
POOK!
© 1978 PAWS, INC. All Rights Reserved.
7-28
JIM DAVIS

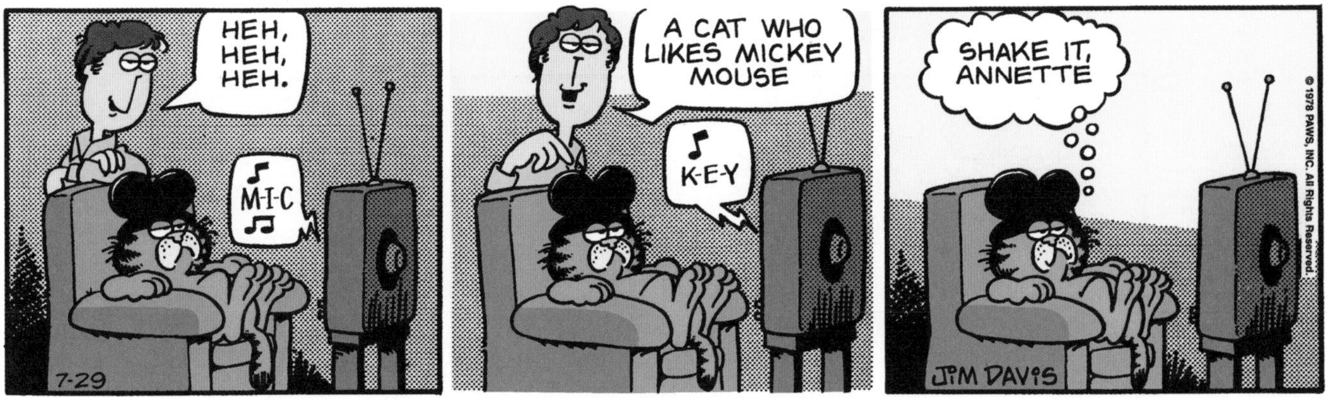
HEH, HEH, HEH.
M-I-C
7-29
A CAT WHO LIKES MICKEY MOUSE
K-E-Y
SHAKE IT, ANNETTE
© 1978 PAWS, INC. All Rights Reserved.
JIM DAVIS

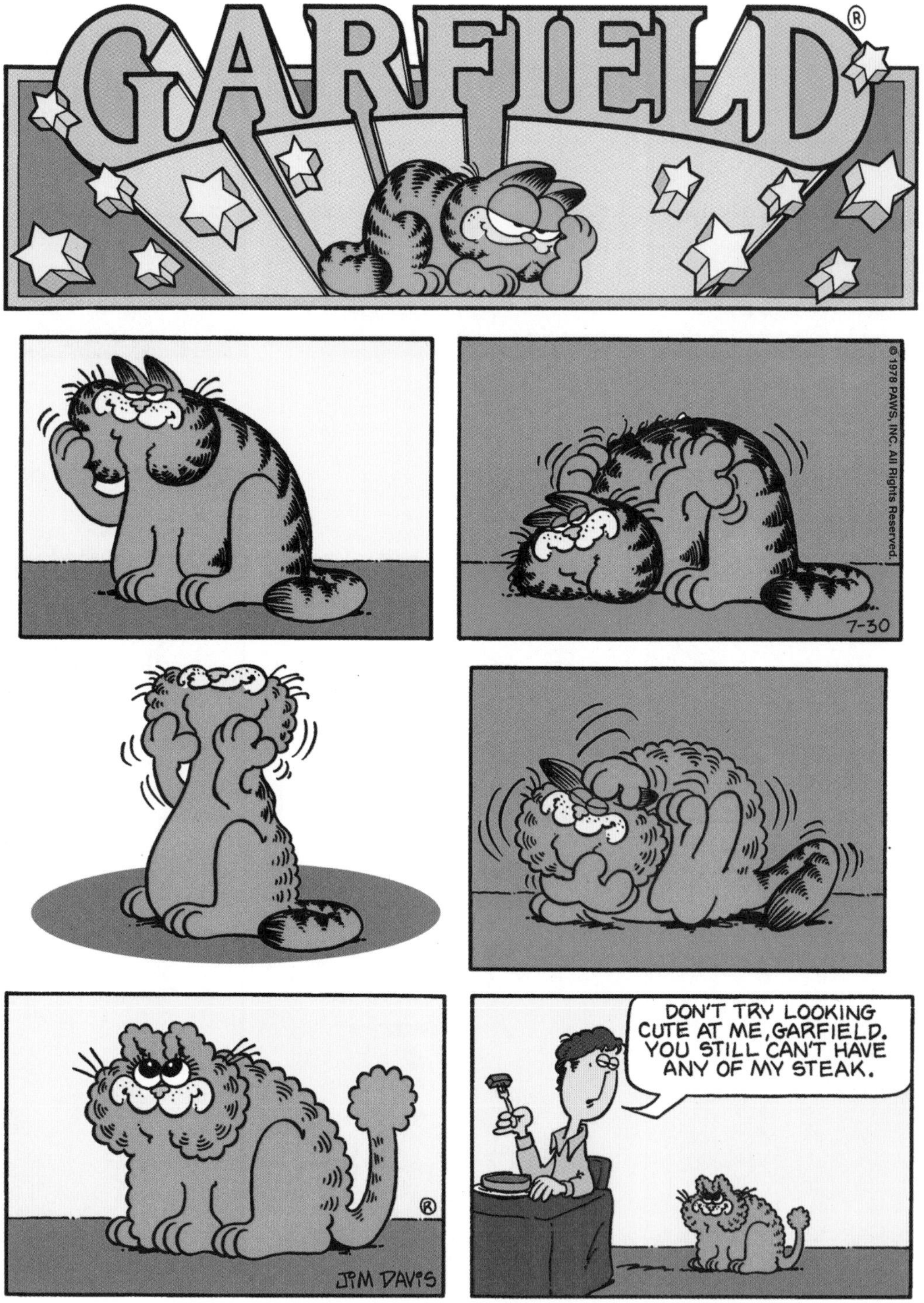
GARFIELD®
© 1978 PAWS, INC. All Rights Reserved.
7-30
DON'T TRY LOOKING CUTE AT ME, GARFIELD. YOU STILL CAN'T HAVE ANY OF MY STEAK.
JIM DAVIS

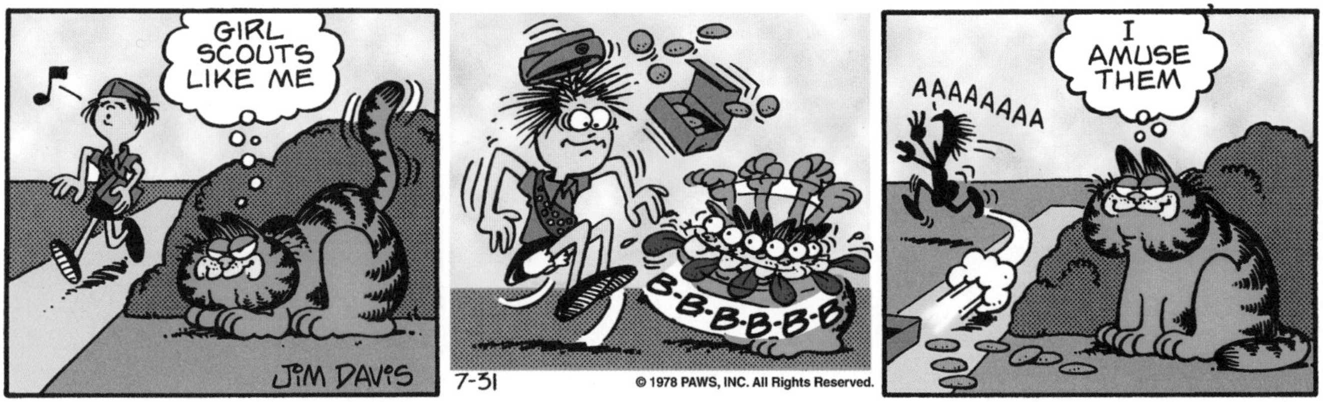
GIRL SCOUTS LIKE ME
JIM DAVIS
B-B-B-B-B-B-B
7-31
© 1978 PAWS, INC. All Rights Reserved.
AAAAAAAA
I AMUSE THEM

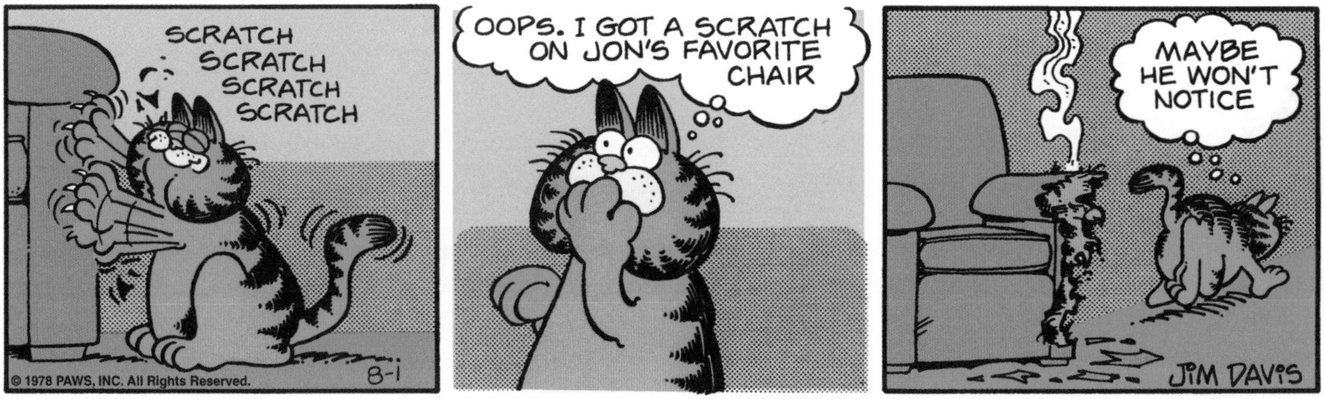
SCRATCH SCRATCH SCRATCH SCRATCH
© 1978 PAWS, INC. All Rights Reserved.
8-1
OOPS. I GOT A SCRATCH ON JON'S FAVORITE CHAIR
MAYBE HE WON'T NOTICE
JIM DAVIS

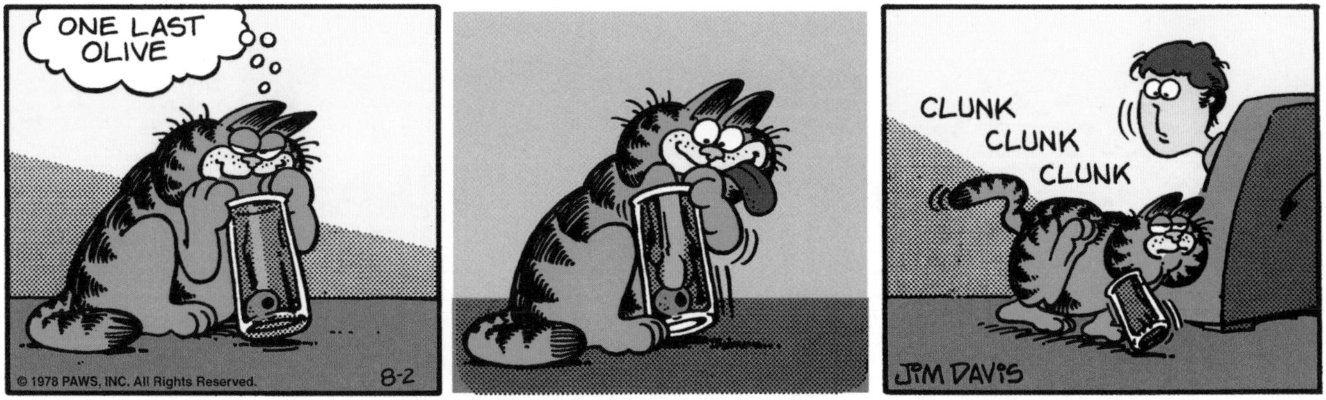
ONE LAST OLIVE
© 1978 PAWS, INC. All Rights Reserved.
8-2
CLUNK CLUNK CLUNK
JIM DAVIS

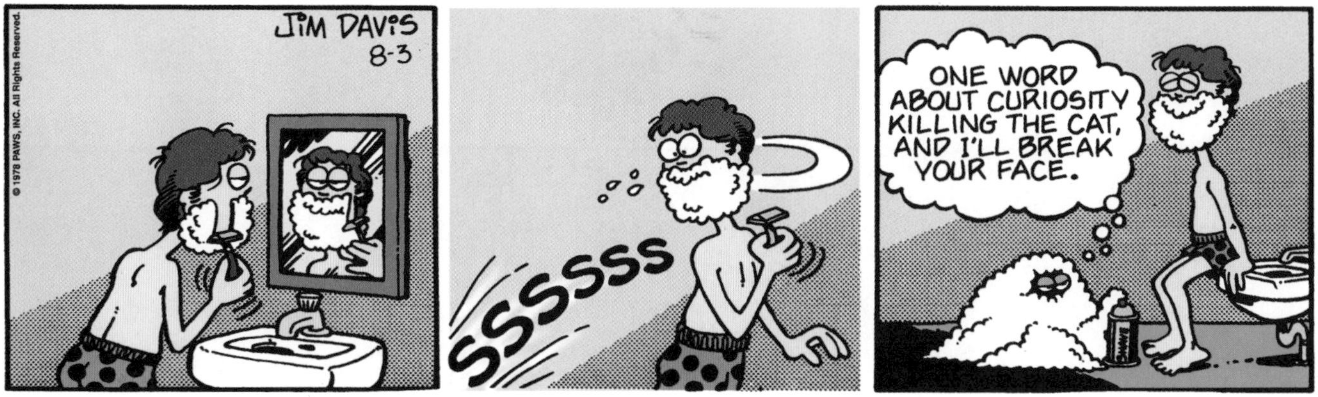
JIM DAVIS
8-3
© 1978 PAWS, INC. All Rights Reserved.
SSSSSS
ONE WORD ABOUT CURIOSITY KILLING THE CAT, AND I'LL BREAK YOUR FACE.

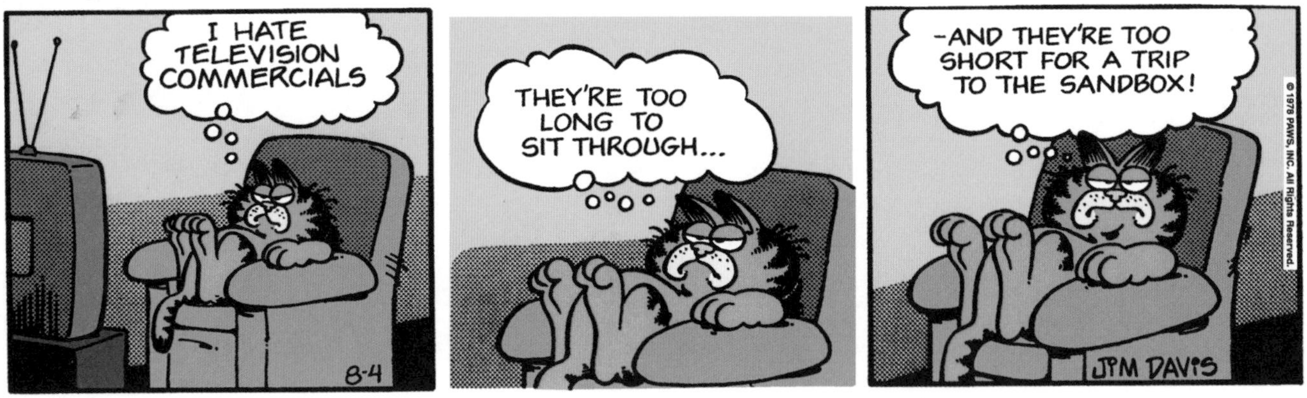
I HATE TELEVISION COMMERCIALS
8-4
THEY'RE TOO LONG TO SIT THROUGH...
-AND THEY'RE TOO SHORT FOR A TRIP TO THE SANDBOX!
© 1978 PAWS, INC. All Rights Reserved.
JIM DAVIS

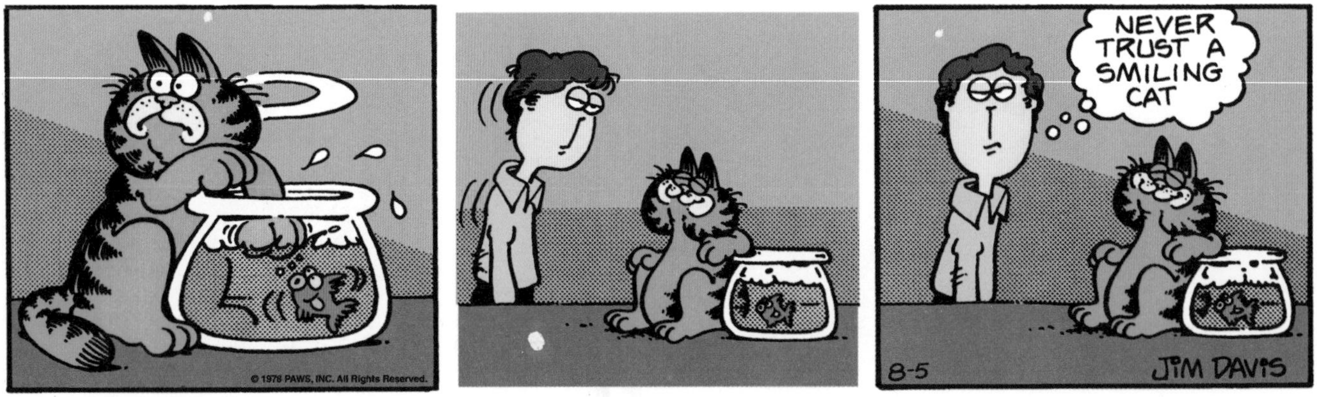
© 1978 PAWS, INC. All Rights Reserved.
NEVER TRUST A SMILING CAT
8-5
JIM DAVIS

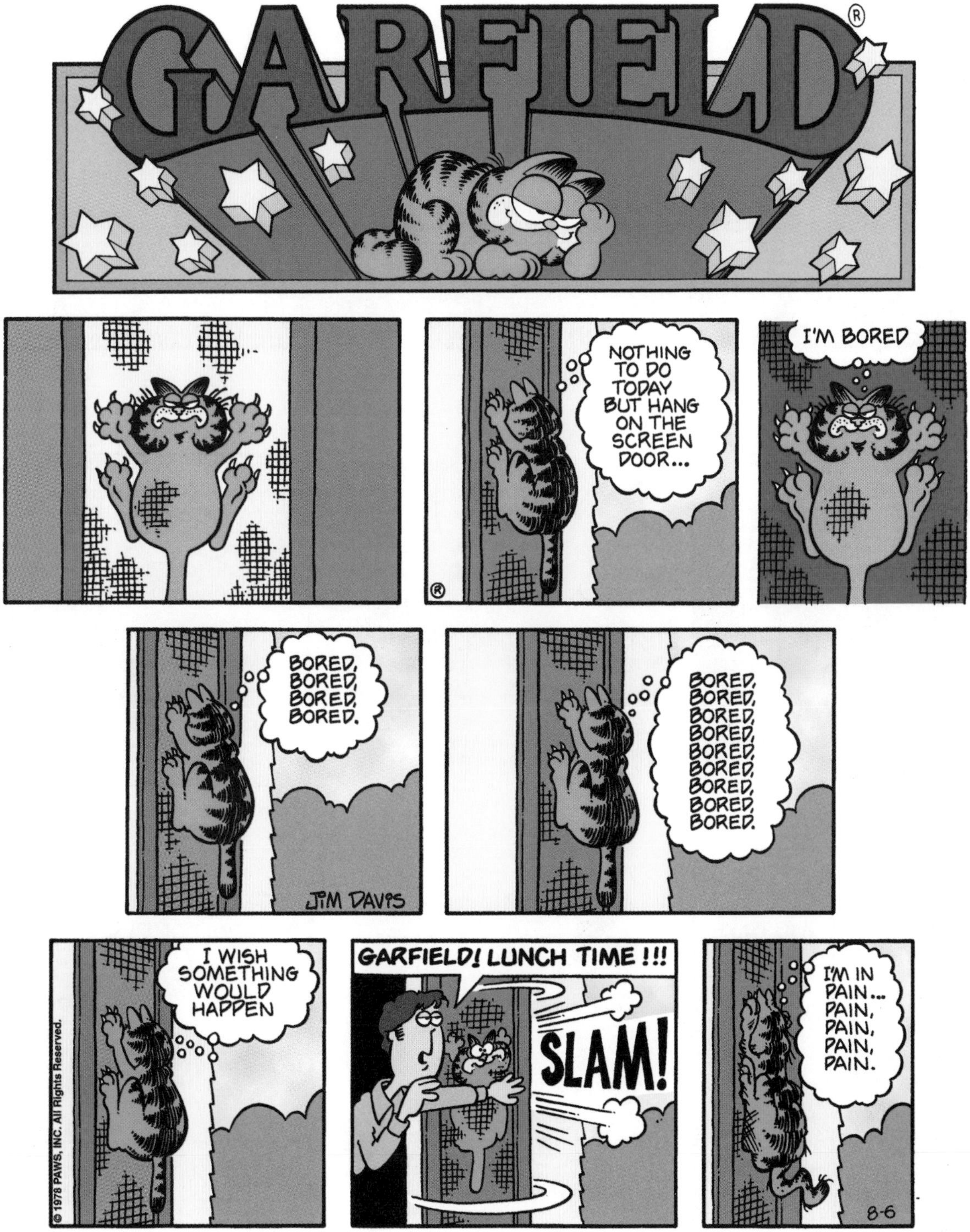
GARFIELD®
NOTHING TO DO TODAY BUT HANG ON THE SCREEN DOOR...
I'M BORED
BORED, BORED, BORED, BORED.
BORED, BORED, BORED, BORED, BORED, BORED, BORED, BORED, BORED.
JIM DAVIS
I WISH SOMETHING WOULD HAPPEN
GARFIELD! LUNCH TIME!!!
SLAM!
I'M IN PAIN... PAIN, PAIN, PAIN, PAIN.
8-6
© 1978 PAWS, INC. All Rights Reserved.

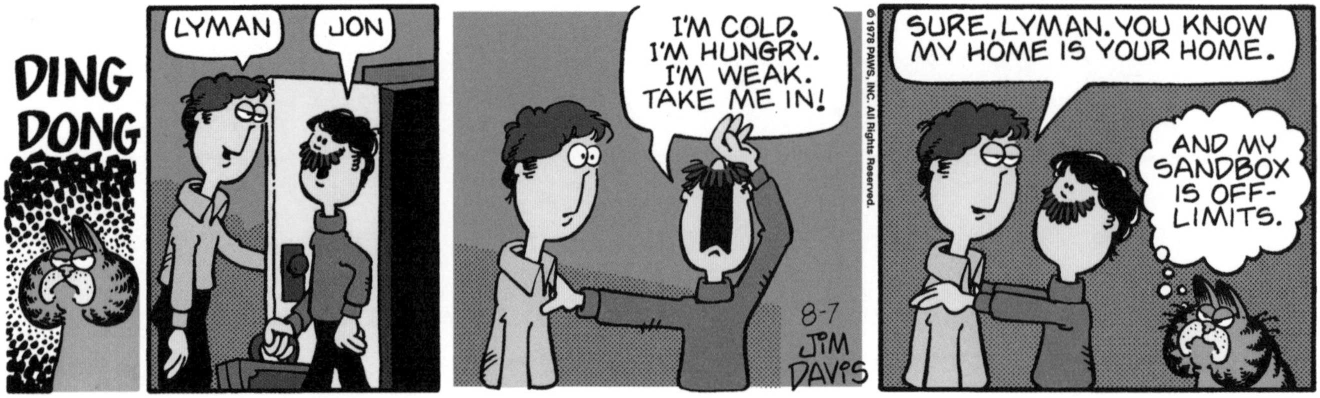
DING DONG
LYMAN
JON
I'M COLD. I'M HUNGRY. I'M WEAK. TAKE ME IN!
© 1978 PAWS, INC. All Rights Reserved.
8-7
JIM DAVIS
SURE, LYMAN. YOU KNOW MY HOME IS YOUR HOME.
AND MY SANDBOX IS OFF-LIMITS.

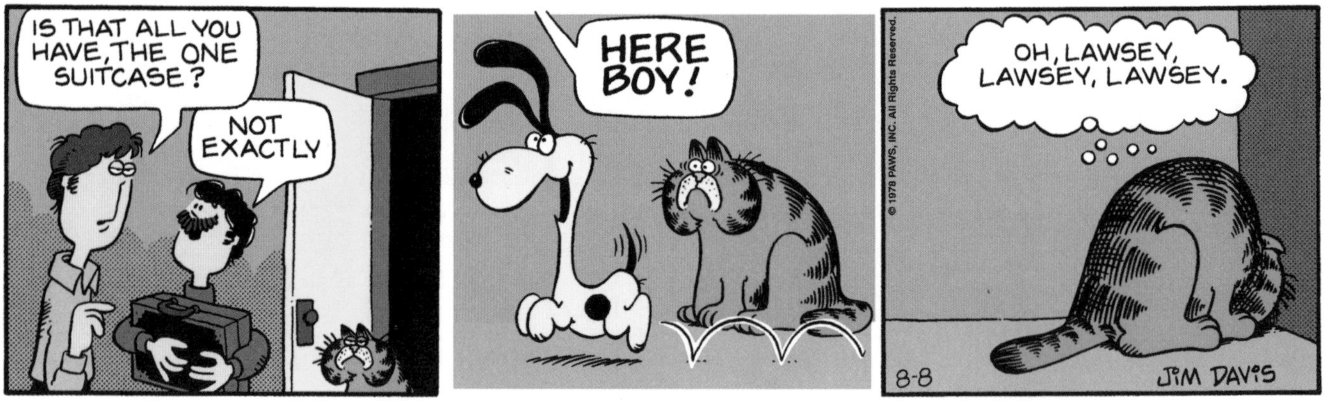
IS THAT ALL YOU HAVE, THE ONE SUITCASE?
NOT EXACTLY
HERE BOY!
© 1978 PAWS, INC. All Rights Reserved.
OH, LAWSEY, LAWSEY, LAWSEY.
8-8
JIM DAVIS

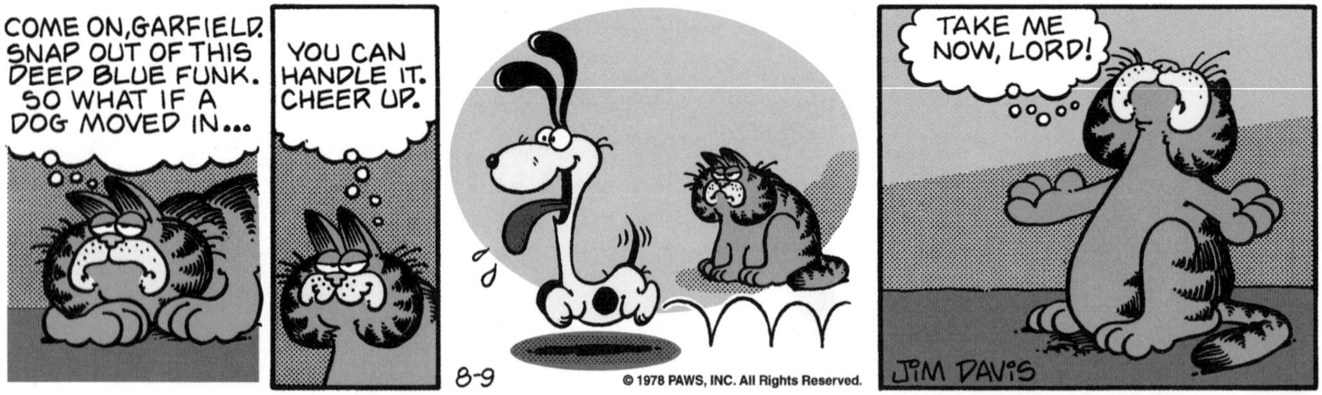
COME ON, GARFIELD. SNAP OUT OF THIS DEEP BLUE FUNK. SO WHAT IF A DOG MOVED IN...
YOU CAN HANDLE IT. CHEER UP.
8-9
© 1978 PAWS, INC. All Rights Reserved.
TAKE ME NOW, LORD!
JIM DAVIS

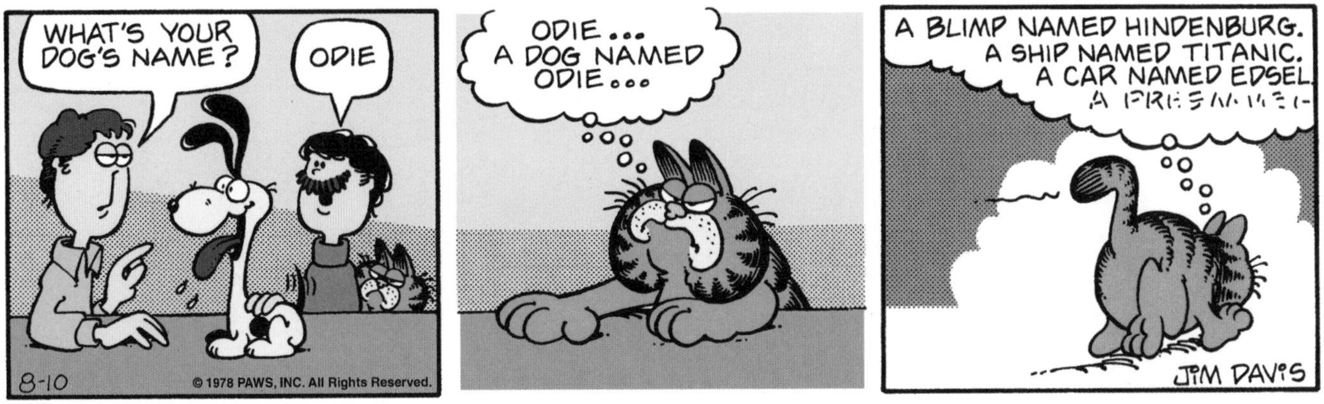
WHAT'S YOUR DOG'S NAME?
ODIE
8-10
© 1978 PAWS, INC. All Rights Reserved.
ODIE... A DOG NAMED ODIE...
A BLIMP NAMED HINDENBURG. A SHIP NAMED TITANIC. A CAR NAMED EDSEL.
JIM DAVIS

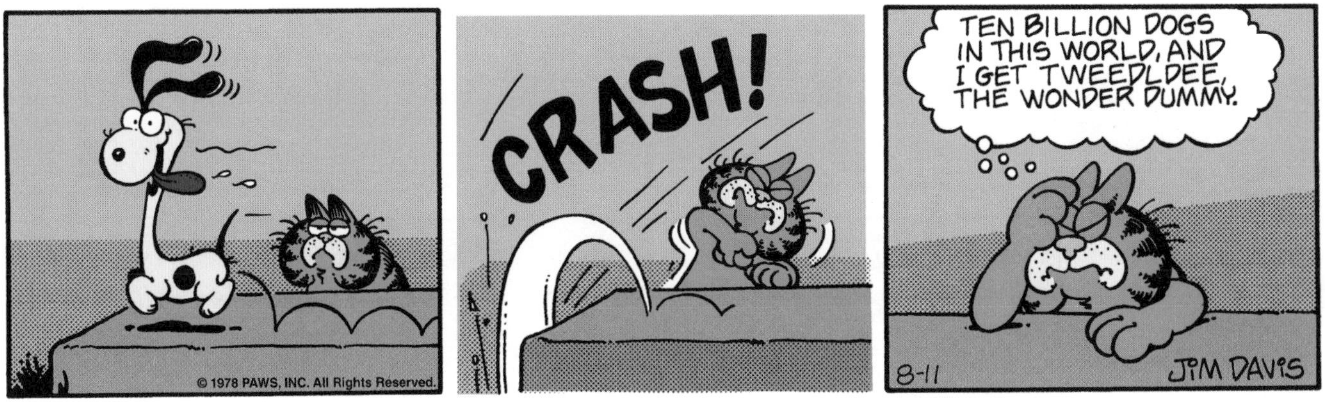
© 1978 PAWS, INC. All Rights Reserved.
CRASH!
TEN BILLION DOGS IN THIS WORLD, AND I GET TWEEDLDEE, THE WONDER DUMMY.
8-11
JIM DAVIS

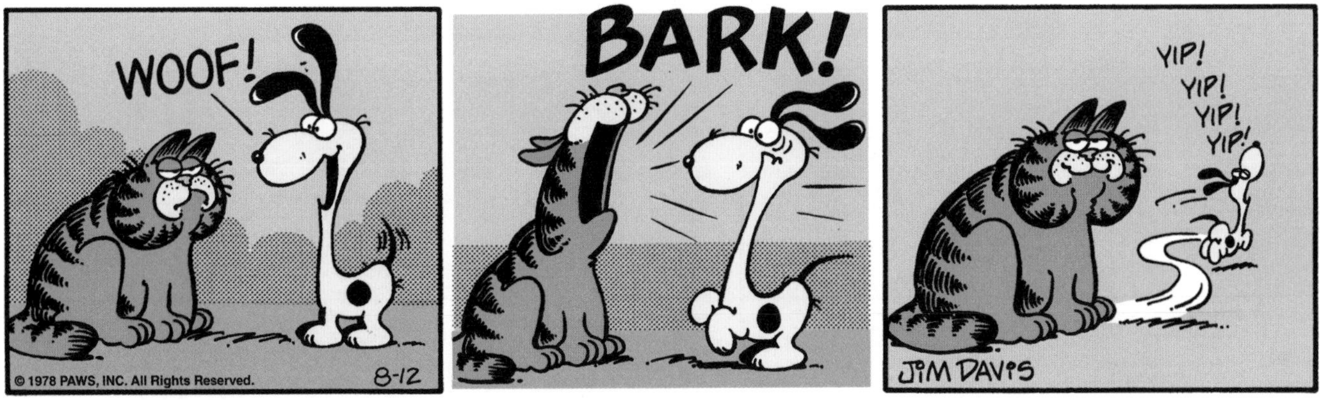
WOOF!
© 1978 PAWS, INC. All Rights Reserved.
8-12
BARK!
YIP!
YIP!
YIP!
YIP!
JIM DAVIS

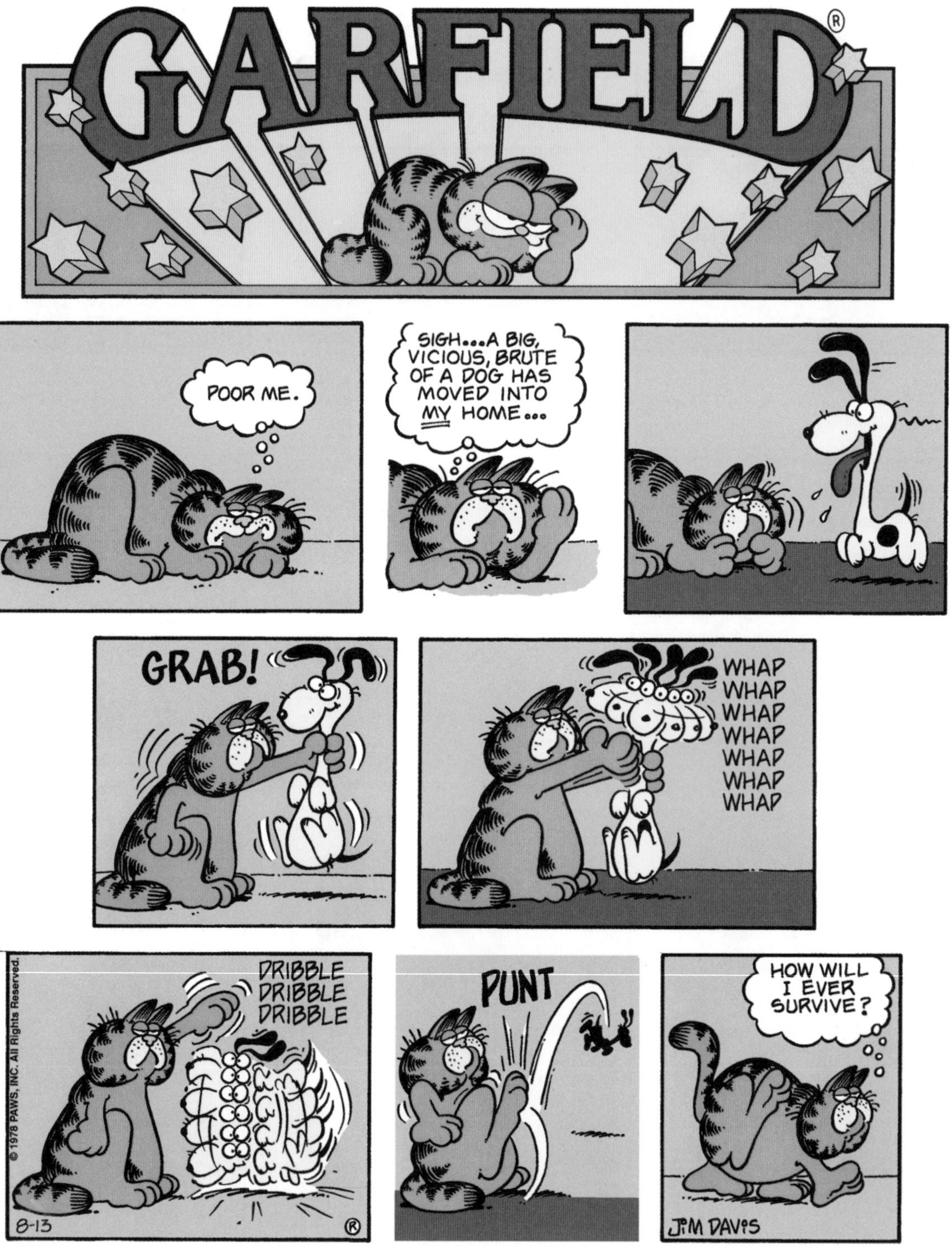
GARFIELD®
POOR ME.
SIGH...A BIG, VICIOUS, BRUTE OF A DOG HAS MOVED INTO MY HOME...
GRAB!
WHAP WHAP WHAP WHAP WHAP WHAP WHAP
DRIBBLE DRIBBLE DRIBBLE
8-13
PUNT
HOW WILL I EVER SURVIVE?
JIM DAVIS

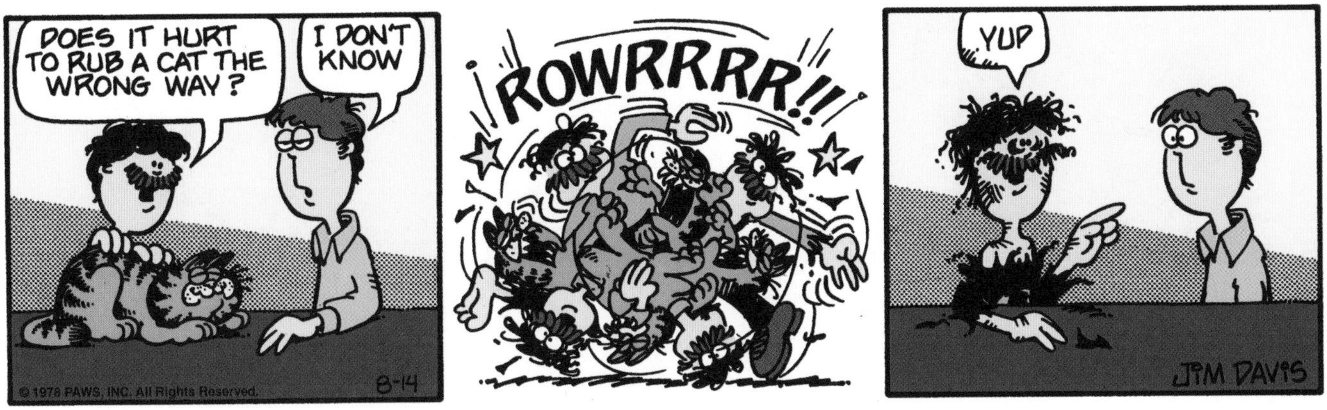
DOES IT HURT TO RUB A CAT THE WRONG WAY ?
I DON'T KNOW
© 1978 PAWS, INC. All Rights Reserved.
8-14
ROWRRRRR!!!
YUP
JIM DAVIS

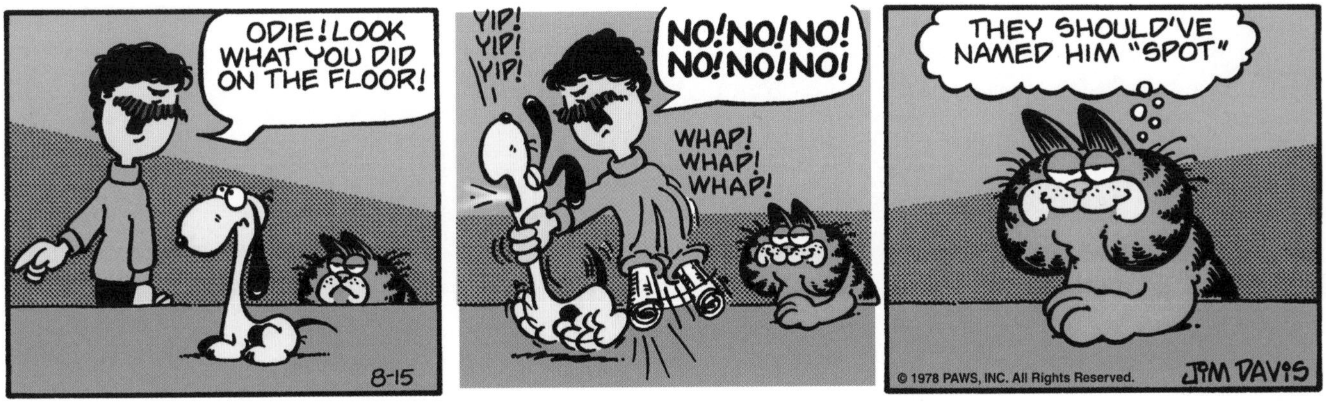
ODIE! LOOK WHAT YOU DID ON THE FLOOR!
8-15
YIP! YIP! YIP!
NO! NO! NO! NO! NO! NO!
WHAP! WHAP! WHAP!
THEY SHOULD'VE NAMED HIM "SPOT"
© 1978 PAWS, INC. All Rights Reserved.
JIM DAVIS

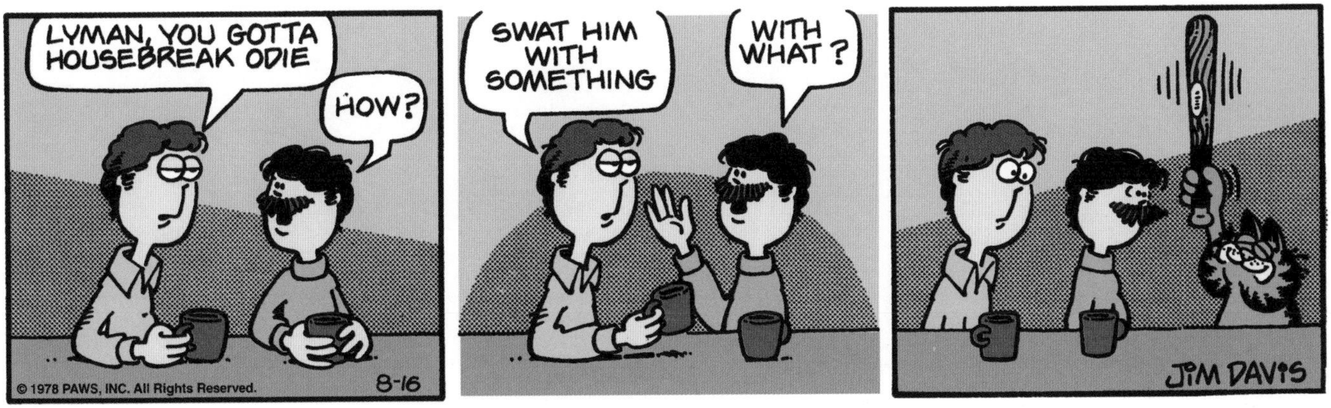
LYMAN, YOU GOTTA HOUSEBREAK ODIE
HOW?
© 1978 PAWS, INC. All Rights Reserved.
8-16
SWAT HIM WITH SOMETHING
WITH WHAT ?
JIM DAVIS

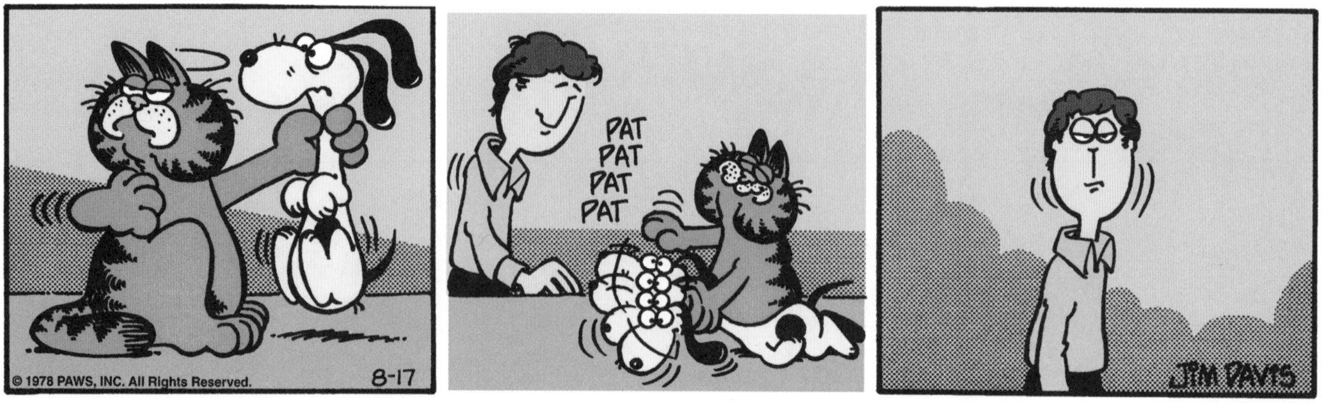
© 1978 PAWS, INC. All Rights Reserved.
8-17
PAT
PAT
PAT
PAT
JIM DAVIS

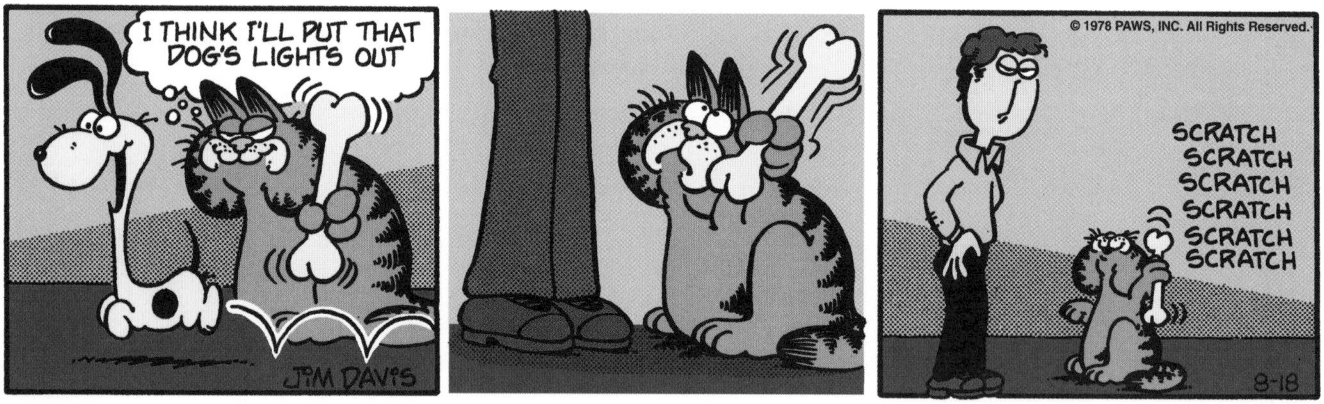
I THINK I'LL PUT THAT DOG'S LIGHTS OUT
JIM DAVIS
© 1978 PAWS, INC. All Rights Reserved.
SCRATCH
SCRATCH
SCRATCH
SCRATCH
SCRATCH
SCRATCH
8-18

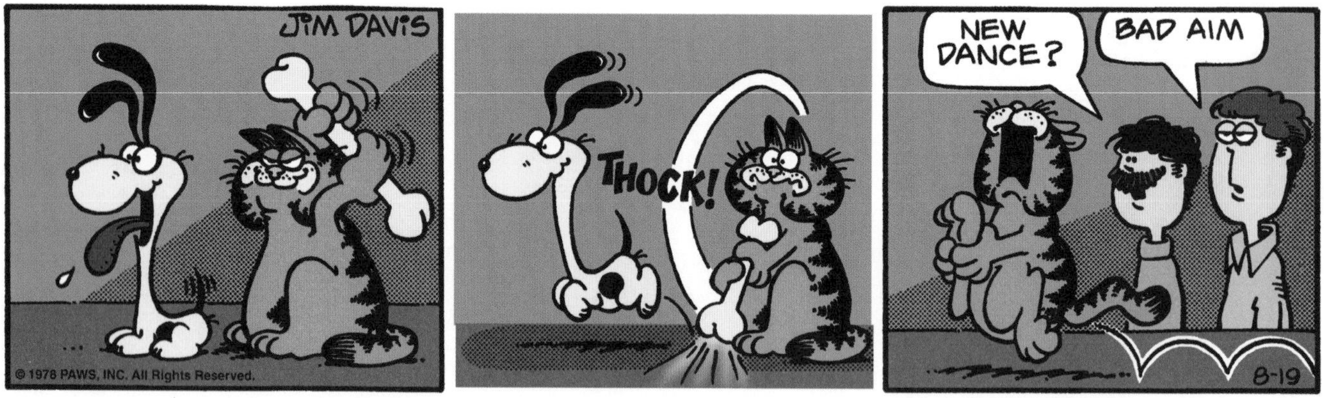
JIM DAVIS
© 1978 PAWS, INC. All Rights Reserved.
THOCK!
NEW DANCE?
BAD AIM
8-19

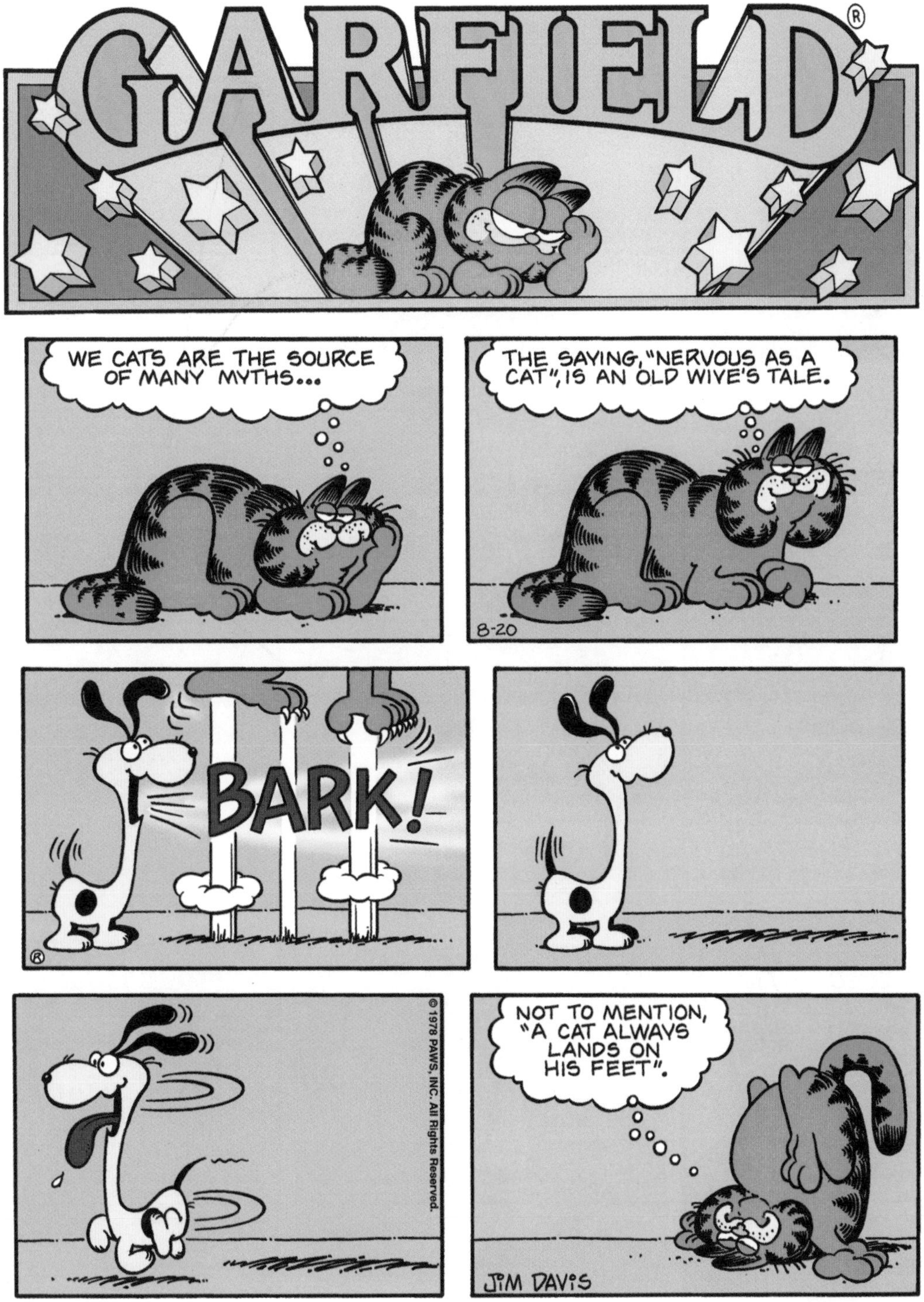
GARFIELD®
WE CATS ARE THE SOURCE OF MANY MYTHS...
THE SAYING, "NERVOUS AS A CAT", IS AN OLD WIVE'S TALE.
8-20
BARK!
© 1978 PAWS, INC. All Rights Reserved.
NOT TO MENTION, "A CAT ALWAYS LANDS ON HIS FEET".
JIM DAVIS

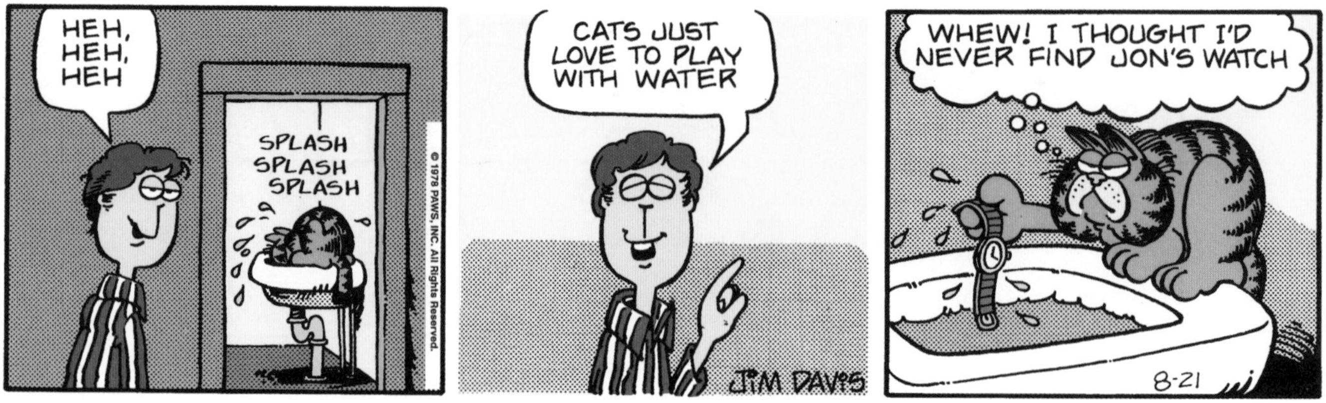
HEH, HEH, HEH
SPLASH SPLASH SPLASH
© 1978 PAWS, INC. All Rights Reserved.
CATS JUST LOVE TO PLAY WITH WATER
JIM DAVIS
WHEW! I THOUGHT I'D NEVER FIND JON'S WATCH
8-21

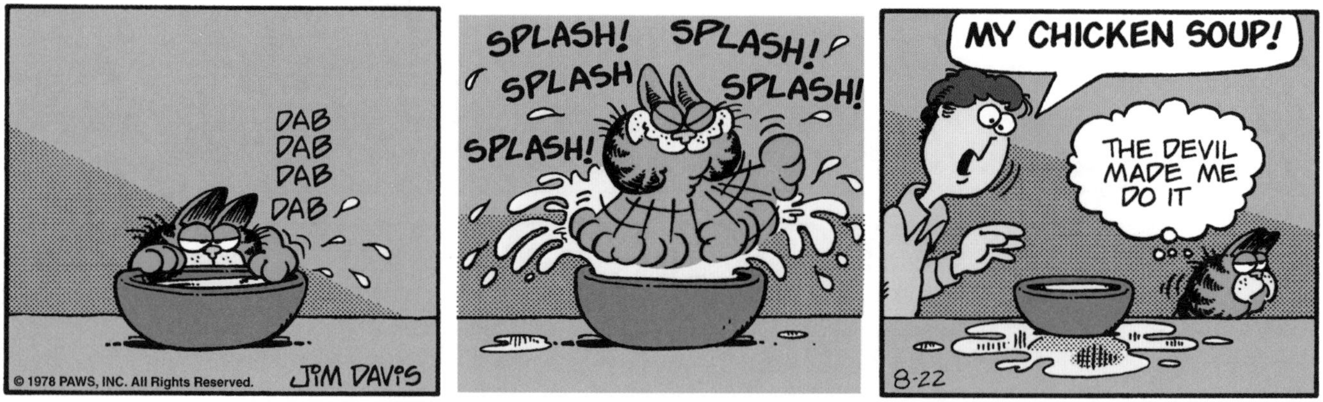
DAB DAB DAB DAB
© 1978 PAWS, INC. All Rights Reserved.
JIM DAVIS
SPLASH! SPLASH! SPLASH SPLASH! SPLASH!
MY CHICKEN SOUP!
THE DEVIL MADE ME DO IT
8-22

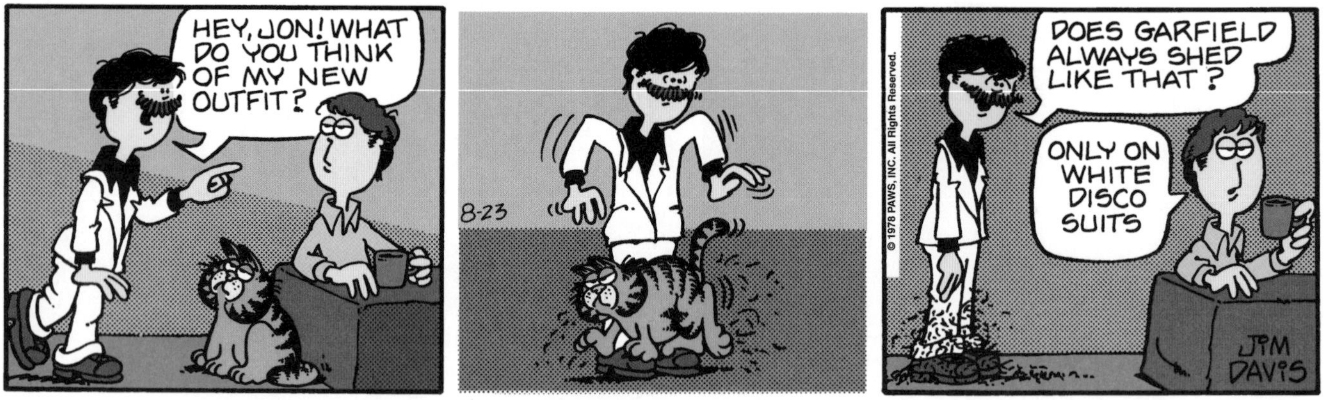
HEY, JON! WHAT DO YOU THINK OF MY NEW OUTFIT?
8-23
© 1978 PAWS, INC. All Rights Reserved.
DOES GARFIELD ALWAYS SHED LIKE THAT?
ONLY ON WHITE DISCO SUITS
JIM DAVIS

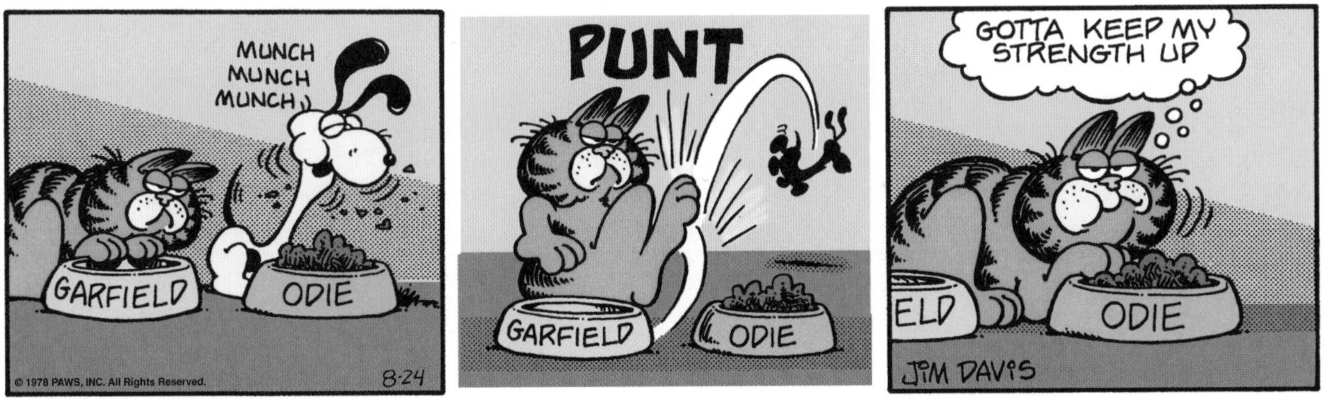
MUNCH
MUNCH
MUNCH
GARFIELD
ODIE
© 1978 PAWS, INC. All Rights Reserved.
8-24
PUNT
GARFIELD
ODIE
GOTTA KEEP MY STRENGTH UP
ELD
ODIE
JIM DAVIS

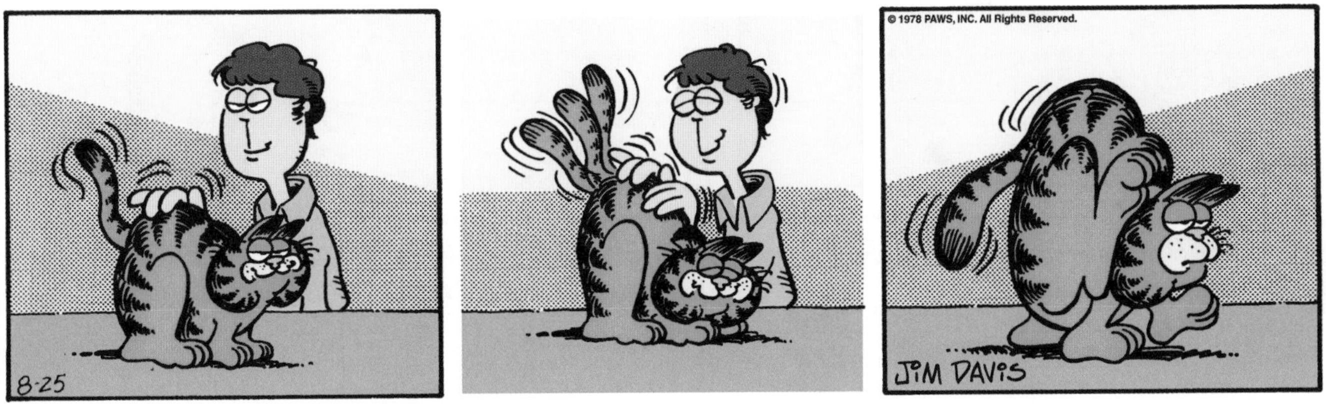
8-25
© 1978 PAWS, INC. All Rights Reserved.
JIM DAVIS

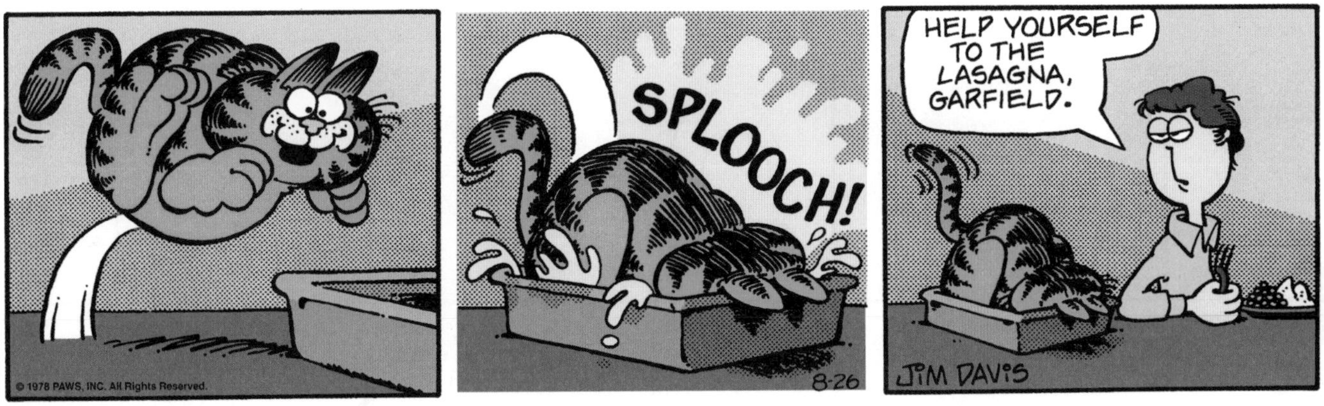
© 1978 PAWS, INC. All Rights Reserved.
SPLOOCH!
8-26
HELP YOURSELF TO THE LASAGNA, GARFIELD.
JIM DAVIS

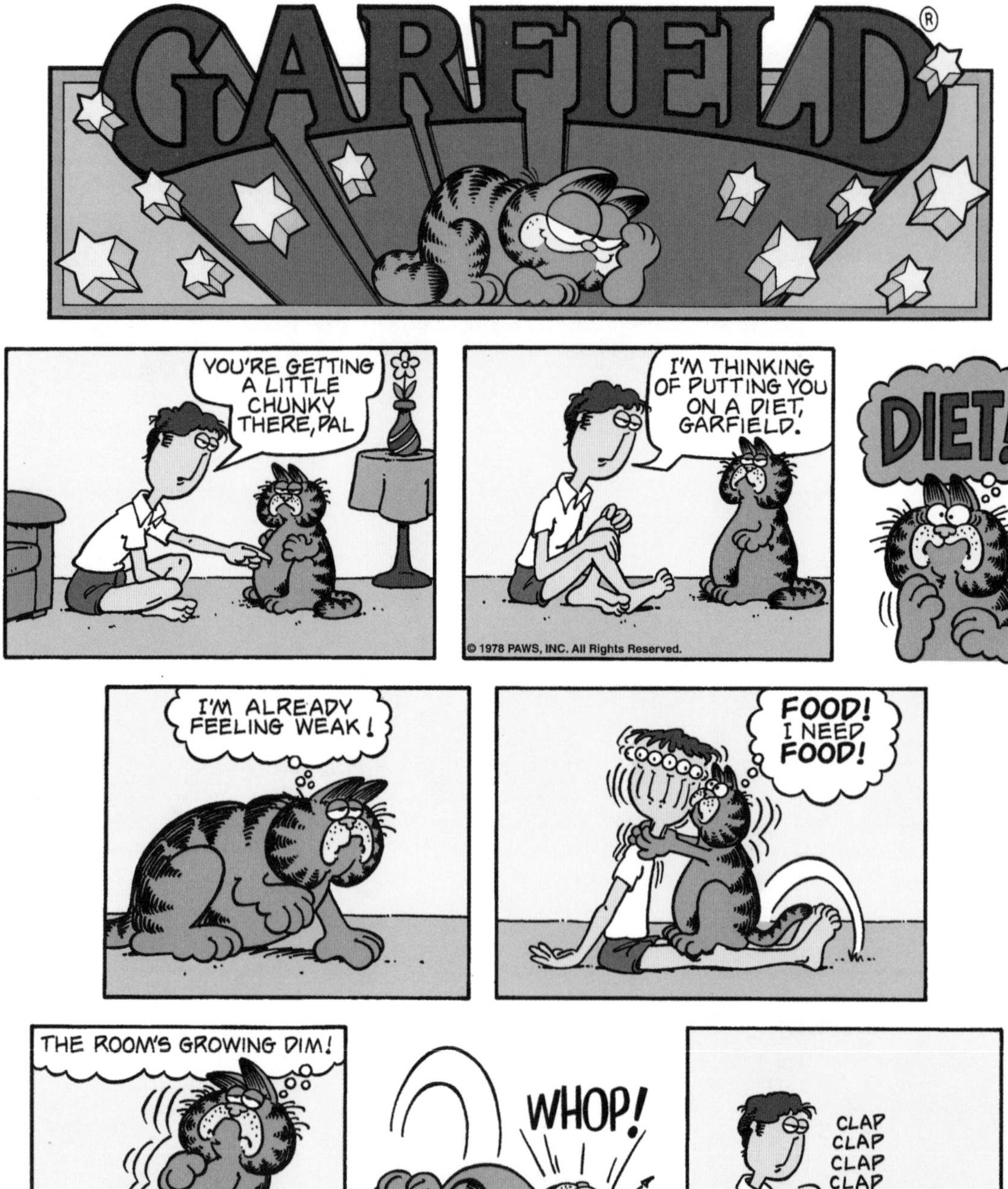
GARFIELD®
YOU'RE GETTING A LITTLE CHUNKY THERE, PAL
I'M THINKING OF PUTTING YOU ON A DIET, GARFIELD.
© 1978 PAWS, INC. All Rights Reserved.
DIET!
I'M ALREADY FEELING WEAK!
FOOD! I NEED FOOD!
THE ROOM'S GROWING DIM!
8-27 ®
WHOP!
CLAP CLAP CLAP CLAP CLAP CLAP
JIM DAVIS

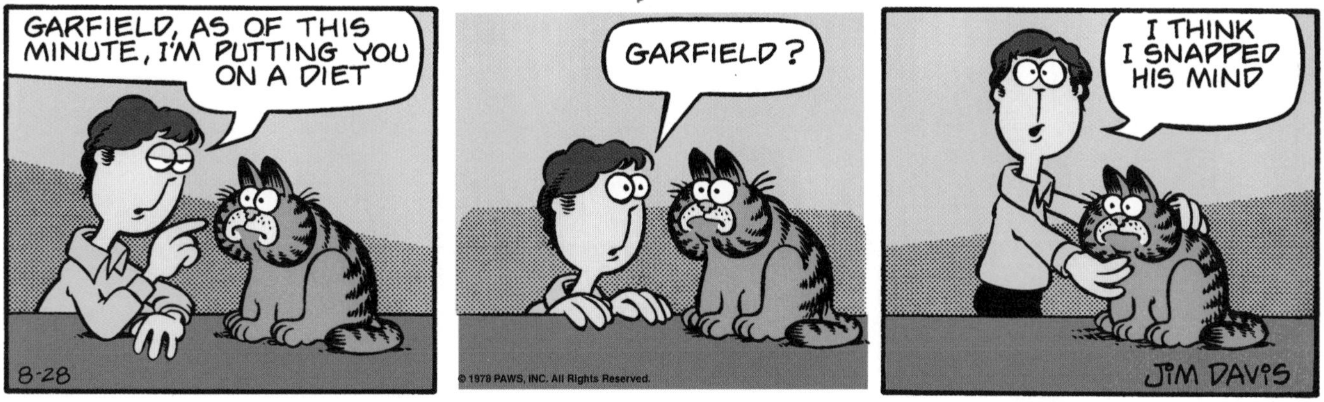
GARFIELD, AS OF THIS MINUTE, I'M PUTTING YOU ON A DIET
8-28
GARFIELD?
© 1978 PAWS, INC. All Rights Reserved.
I THINK I SNAPPED HIS MIND
JIM DAVIS

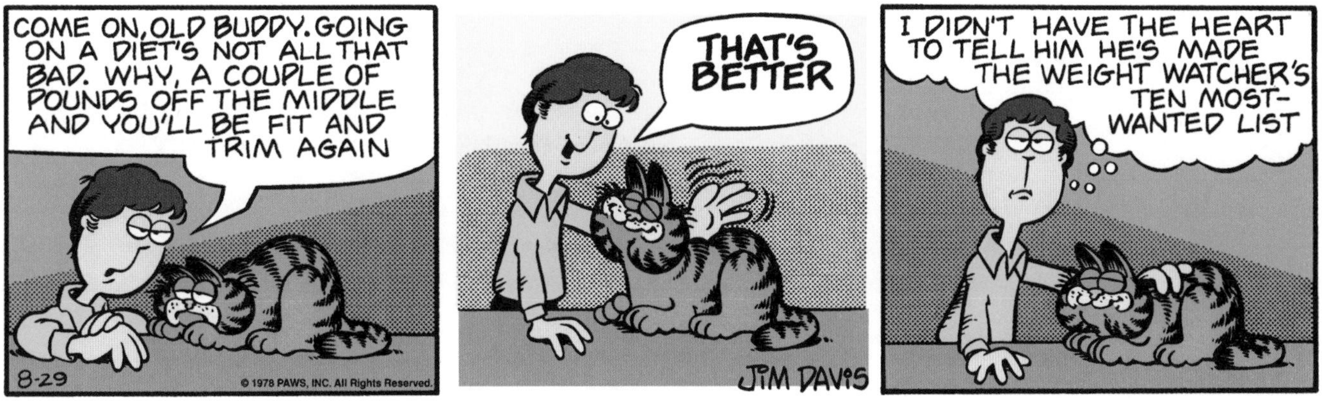
COME ON, OLD BUDDY. GOING ON A DIET'S NOT ALL THAT BAD. WHY, A COUPLE OF POUNDS OFF THE MIDDLE AND YOU'LL BE FIT AND TRIM AGAIN
8-29
© 1978 PAWS, INC. All Rights Reserved.
THAT'S BETTER
JIM DAVIS
I DIDN'T HAVE THE HEART TO TELL HIM HE'S MADE THE WEIGHT WATCHER'S TEN MOST-WANTED LIST

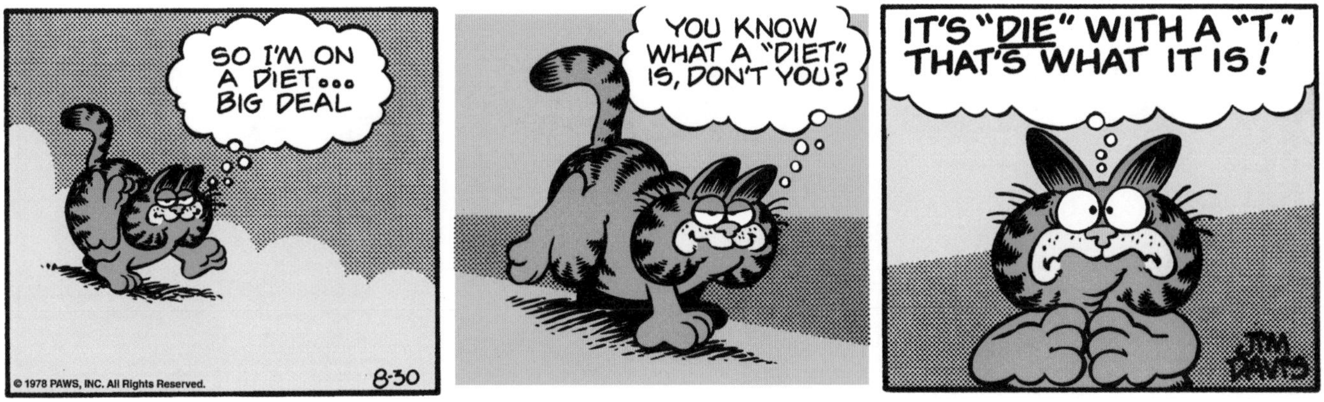
SO I'M ON A DIET... BIG DEAL
© 1978 PAWS, INC. All Rights Reserved.
8-30
YOU KNOW WHAT A "DIET" IS, DON'T YOU?
IT'S "DIE" WITH A "T," THAT'S WHAT IT IS!
JIM DAVIS

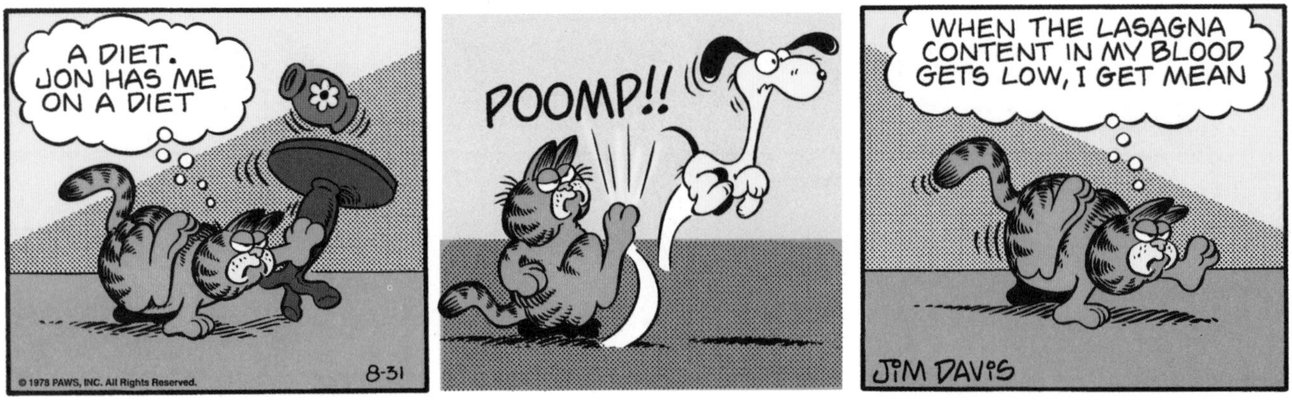
A DIET. JON HAS ME ON A DIET
© 1978 PAWS, INC. All Rights Reserved.
8-31
POOMP!!
WHEN THE LASAGNA CONTENT IN MY BLOOD GETS LOW, I GET MEAN
JIM DAVIS

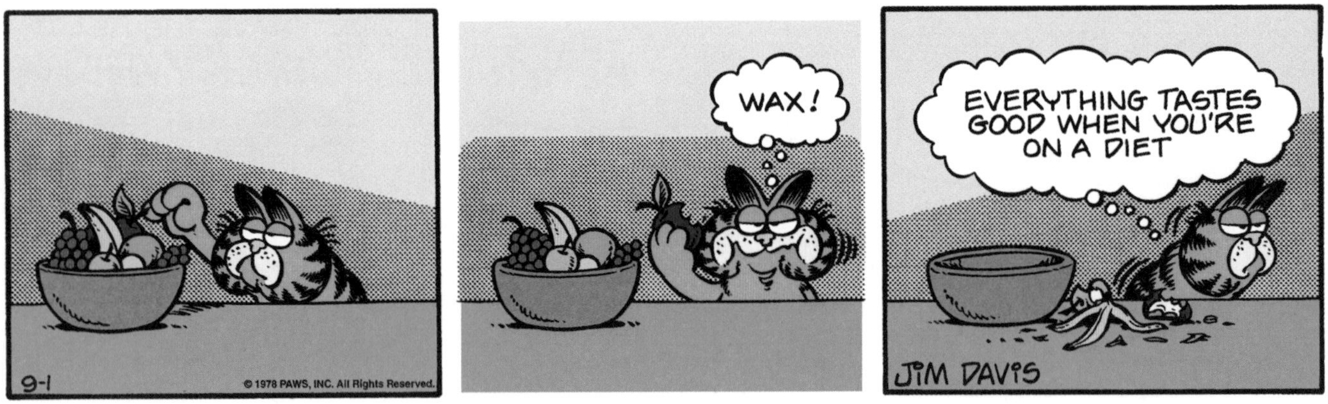
9-1
© 1978 PAWS, INC. All Rights Reserved.
WAX!
EVERYTHING TASTES GOOD WHEN YOU'RE ON A DIET
JIM DAVIS

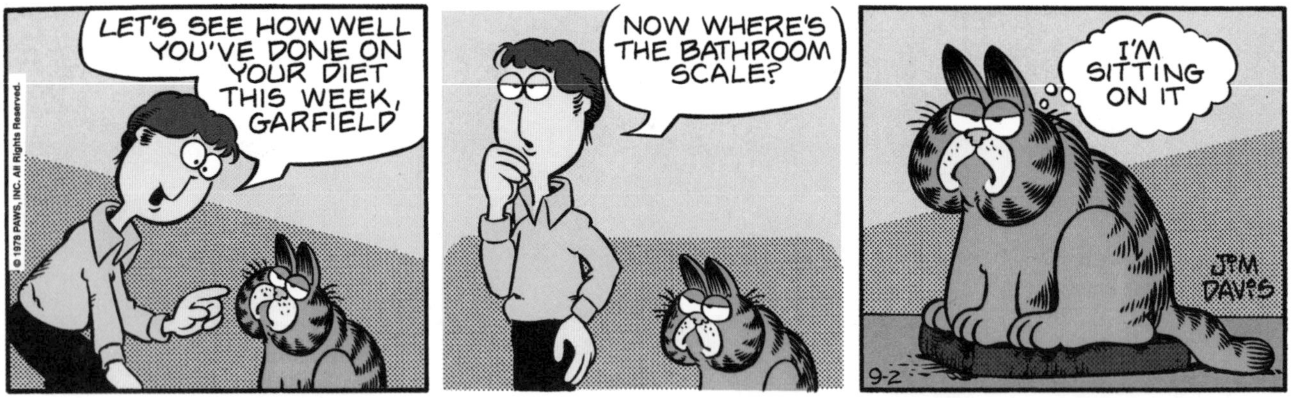
© 1978 PAWS, INC. All Rights Reserved.
LET'S SEE HOW WELL YOU'VE DONE ON YOUR DIET THIS WEEK, GARFIELD
NOW WHERE'S THE BATHROOM SCALE?
I'M SITTING ON IT
JIM DAVIS
9-2

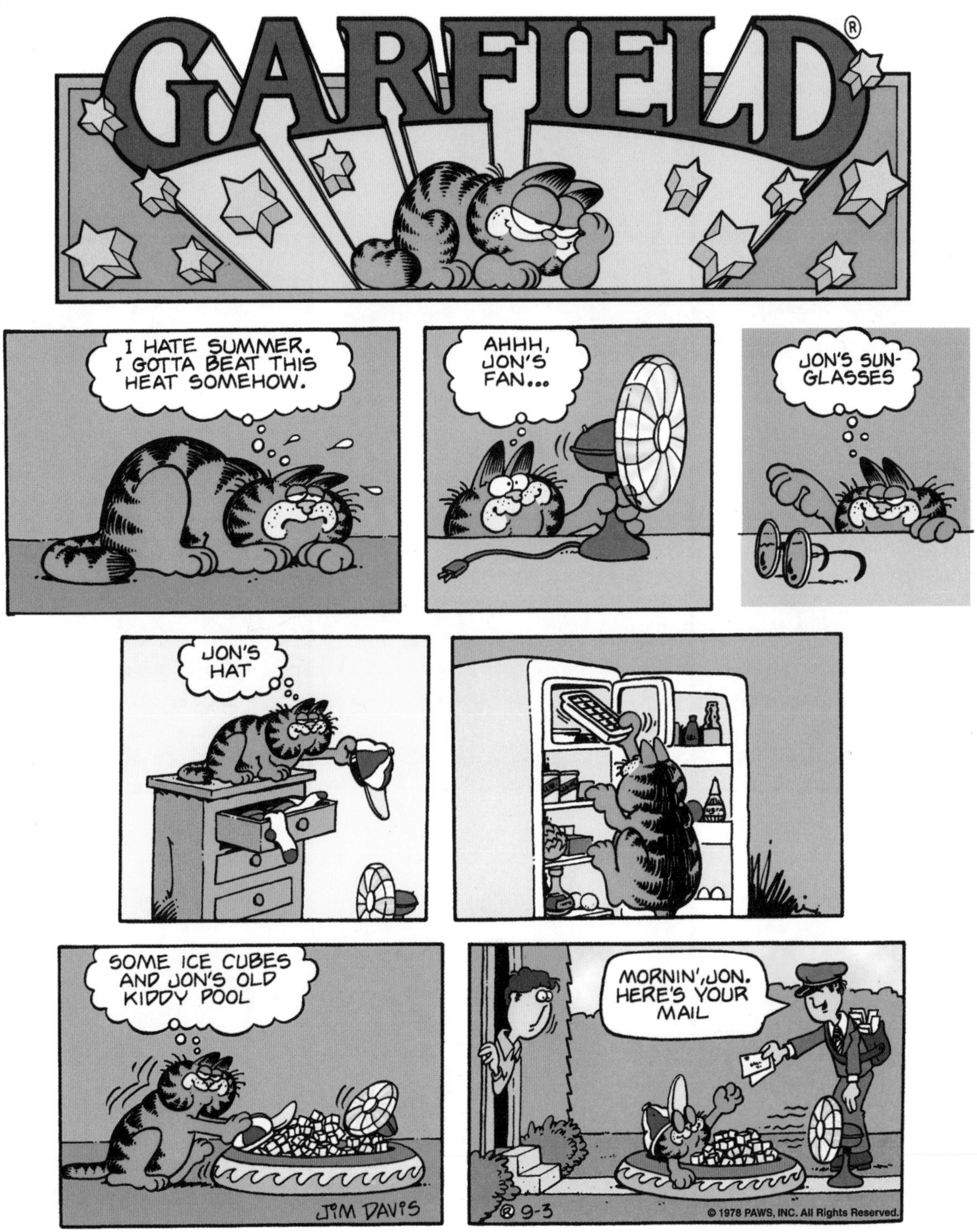
GARFIELD®
I HATE SUMMER. I GOTTA BEAT THIS HEAT SOMEHOW.
AHHH, JON'S FAN...
JON'S SUN-GLASSES
JON'S HAT
SOME ICE CUBES AND JON'S OLD KIDDY POOL
JIM DAVIS
MORNIN', JON. HERE'S YOUR MAIL
® 9-3
© 1978 PAWS, INC. All Rights Reserved.

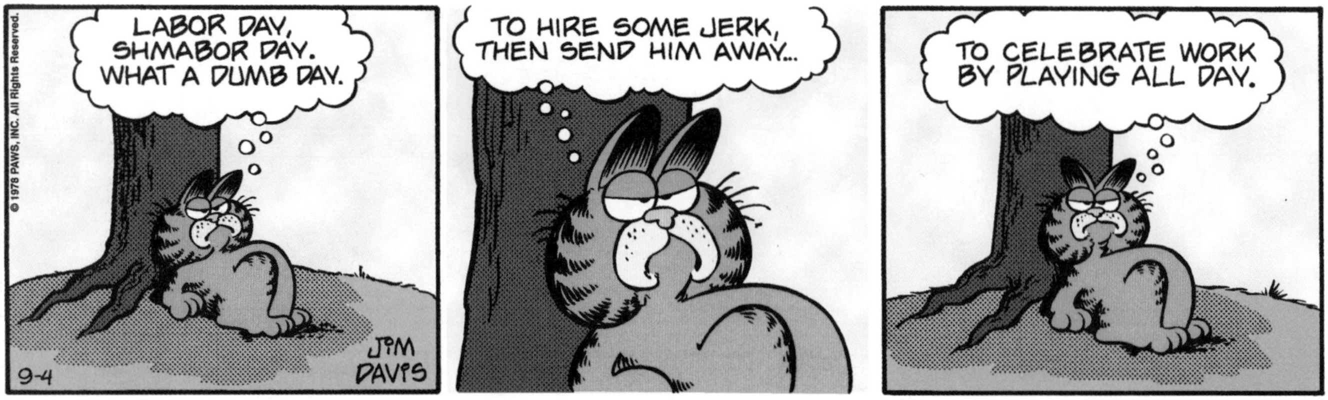
© 1978 PAWS, INC. All Rights Reserved.
LABOR DAY, SHMABOR DAY. WHAT A DUMB DAY.
9-4
JIM DAVIS
TO HIRE SOME JERK, THEN SEND HIM AWAY...
TO CELEBRATE WORK BY PLAYING ALL DAY.

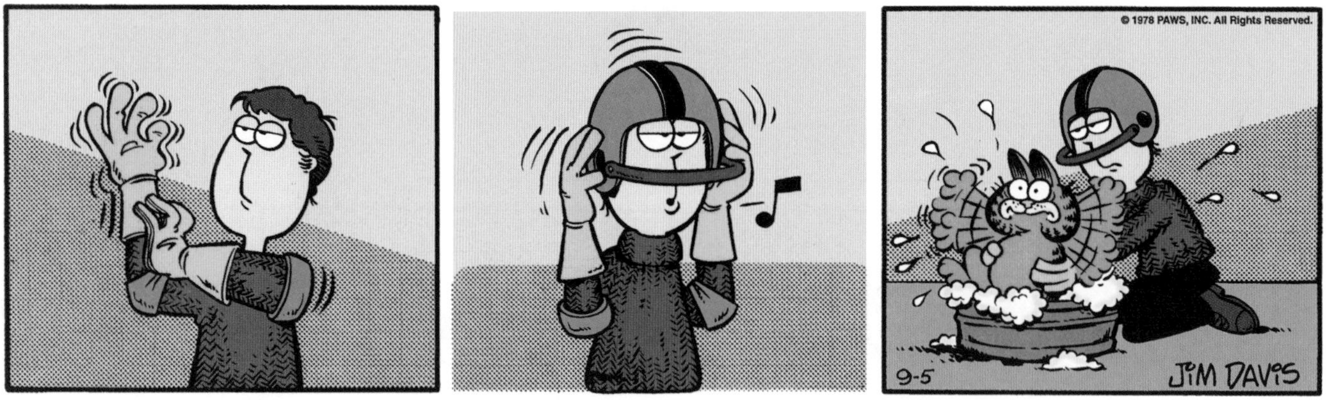
© 1978 PAWS, INC. All Rights Reserved.
9-5
JIM DAVIS

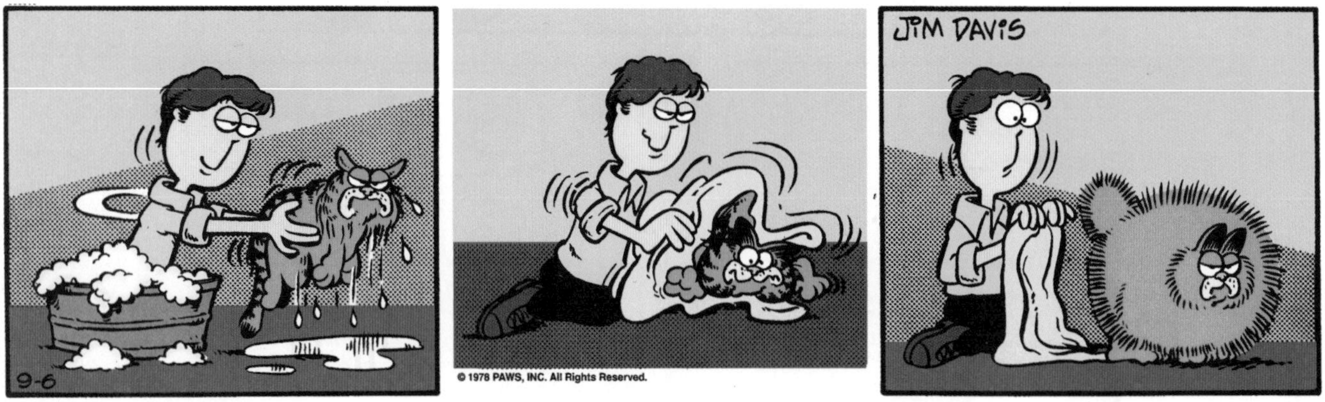
9-6
© 1978 PAWS, INC. All Rights Reserved.
JIM DAVIS

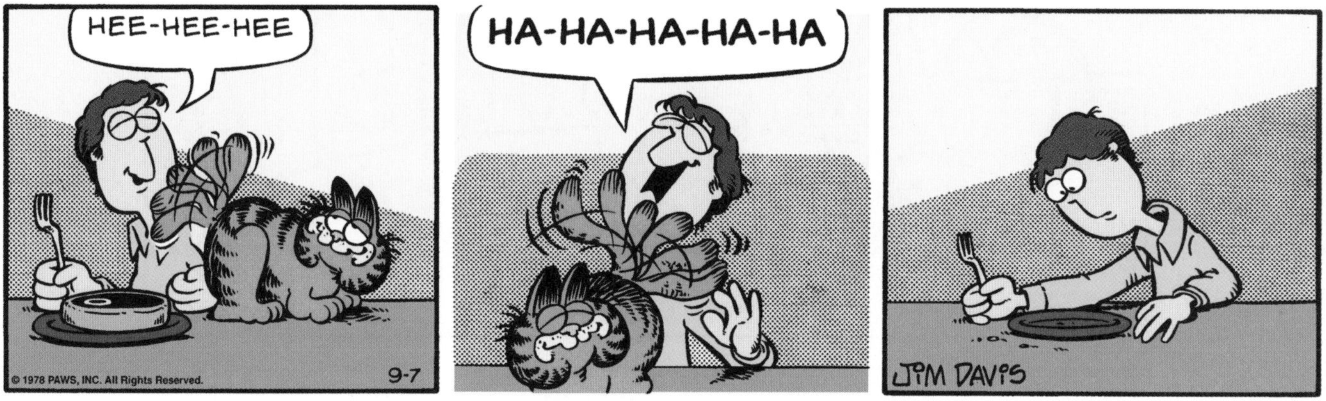
HEE-HEE-HEE
© 1978 PAWS, INC. All Rights Reserved.
9-7
HA-HA-HA-HA-HA
JIM DAVIS

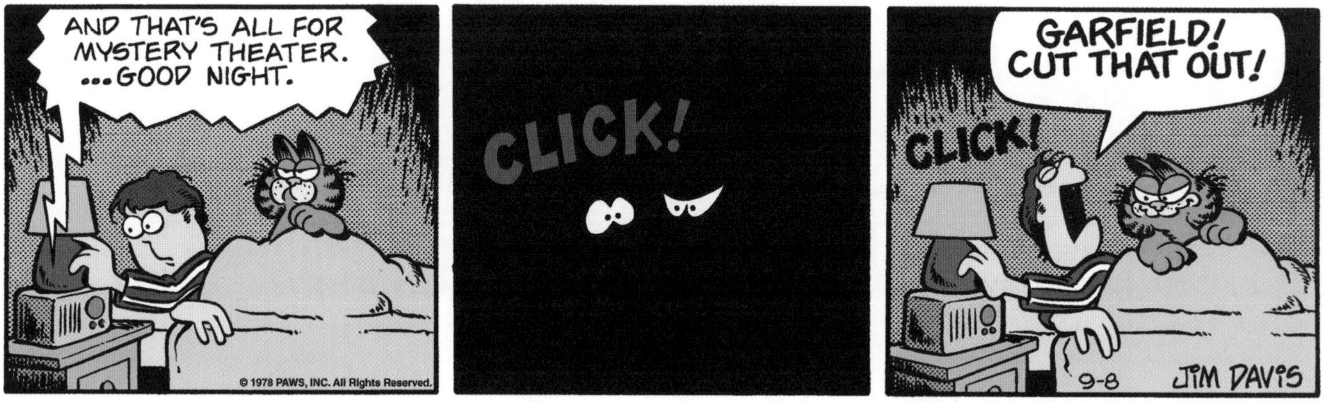
AND THAT'S ALL FOR MYSTERY THEATER. ...GOOD NIGHT.
© 1978 PAWS, INC. All Rights Reserved.
CLICK!
CLICK!
GARFIELD! CUT THAT OUT!
9-8
JIM DAVIS

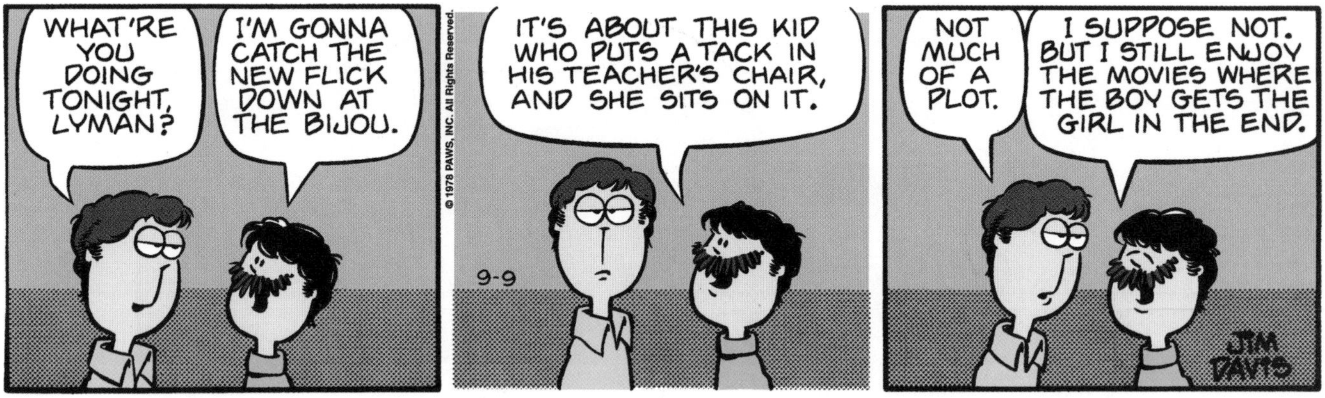
WHAT'RE YOU DOING TONIGHT, LYMAN?
I'M GONNA CATCH THE NEW FLICK DOWN AT THE BIJOU.
© 1978 PAWS, INC. All Rights Reserved.
IT'S ABOUT THIS KID WHO PUTS A TACK IN HIS TEACHER'S CHAIR, AND SHE SITS ON IT.
9-9
NOT MUCH OF A PLOT.
I SUPPOSE NOT. BUT I STILL ENJOY THE MOVIES WHERE THE BOY GETS THE GIRL IN THE END.
JIM DAVIS

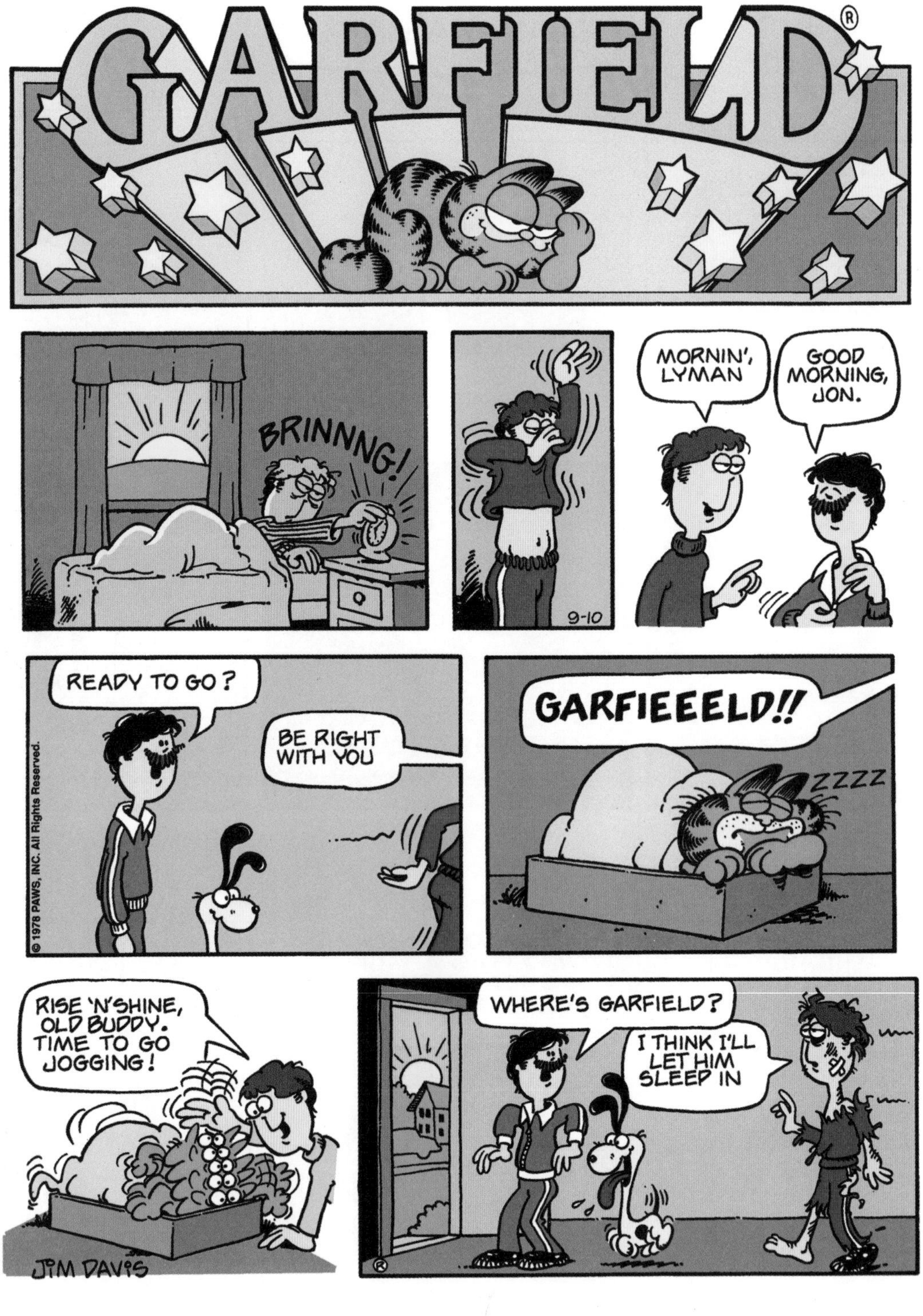
GARFIELD®
BRINNNG!
9-10
MORNIN', LYMAN
GOOD MORNING, JON.
READY TO GO?
BE RIGHT WITH YOU
© 1978 PAWS, INC. All Rights Reserved.
GARFIEEELD!!
ZZZZ
RISE 'N' SHINE, OLD BUDDY. TIME TO GO JOGGING!
JIM DAVIS
WHERE'S GARFIELD?
I THINK I'LL LET HIM SLEEP IN

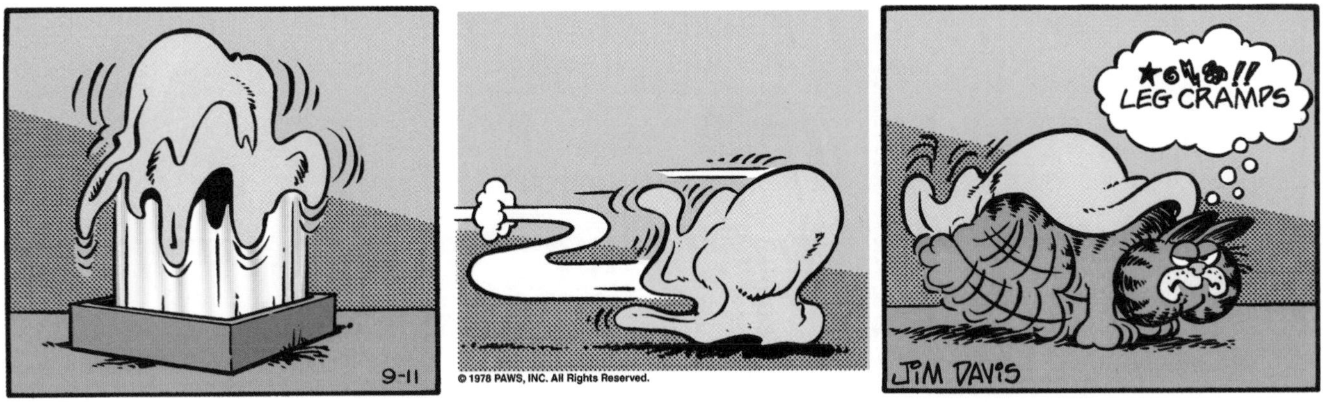
9-11
© 1978 PAWS, INC. All Rights Reserved.
LEG CRAMPS
JIM DAVIS

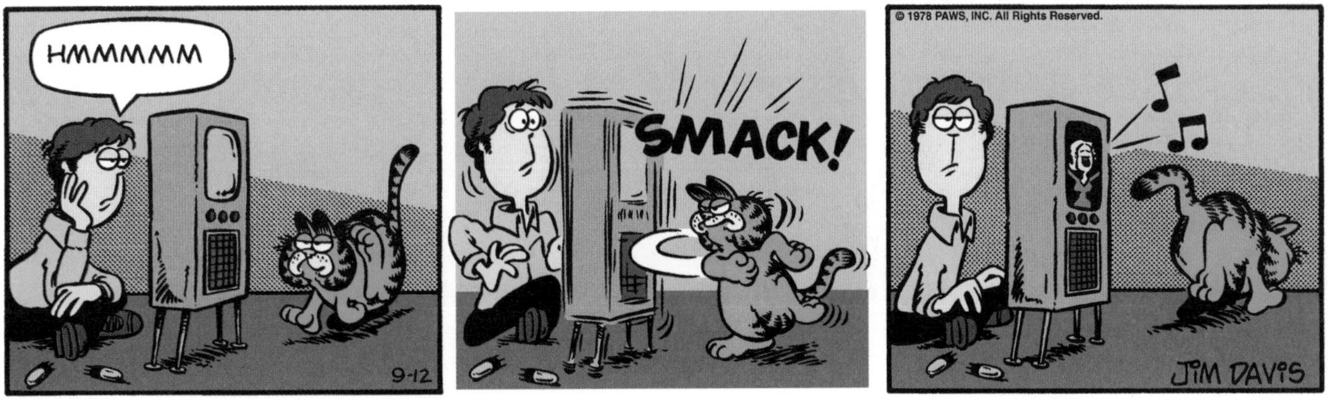
HMMMMM
9-12
SMACK!
© 1978 PAWS, INC. All Rights Reserved.
JIM DAVIS

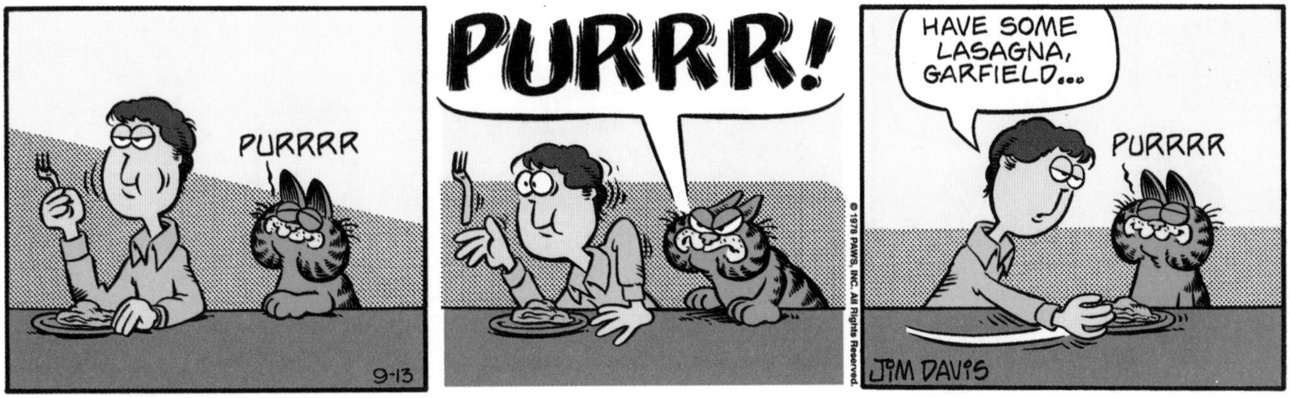
PURRRR
9-13
PURRR!
© 1978 PAWS, INC. All Rights Reserved.
HAVE SOME LASAGNA, GARFIELD...
PURRRR
JIM DAVIS

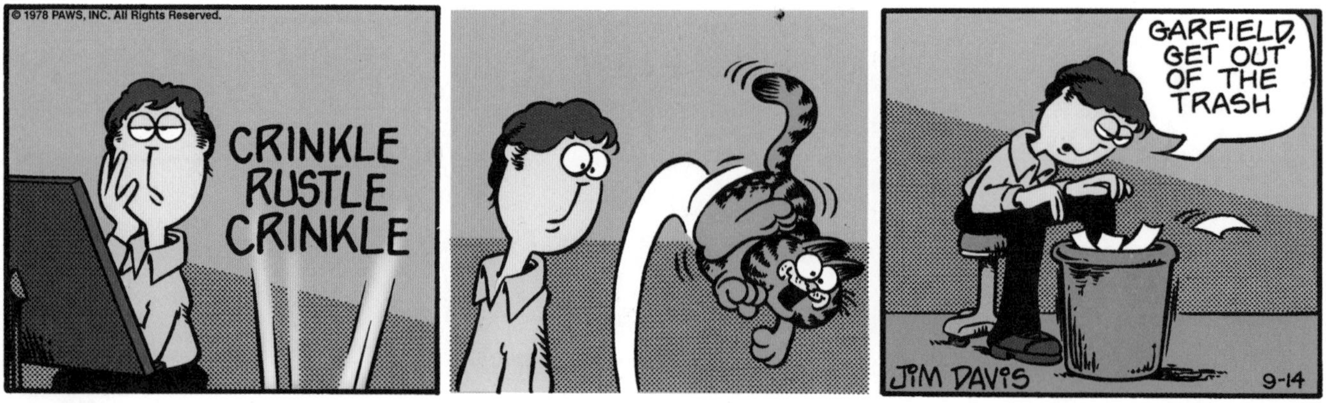
© 1978 PAWS, INC. All Rights Reserved.
CRINKLE RUSTLE CRINKLE
GARFIELD, GET OUT OF THE TRASH
JIM DAVIS
9-14

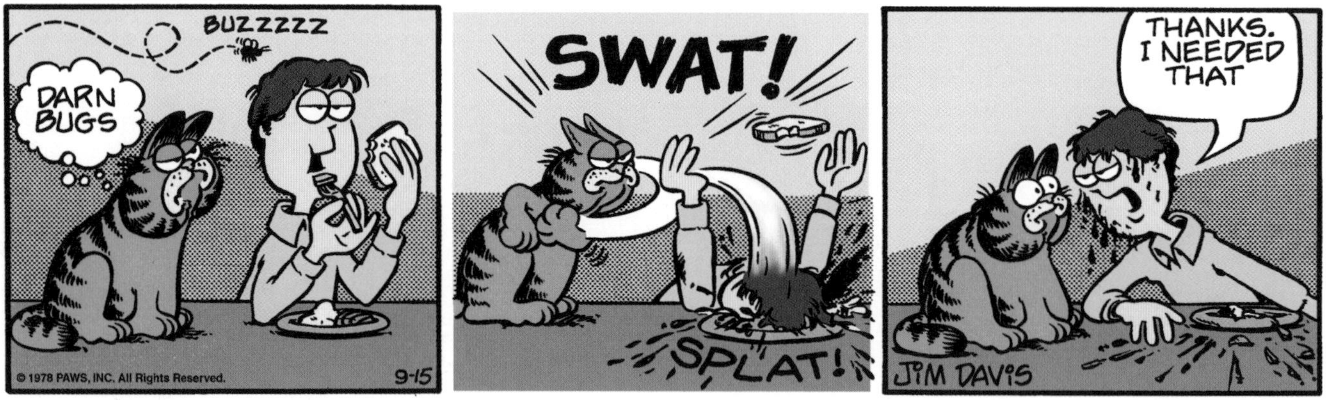
BUZZZZZ
DARN BUGS
© 1978 PAWS, INC. All Rights Reserved.
9-15
SWAT!
SPLAT!
THANKS. I NEEDED THAT
JIM DAVIS

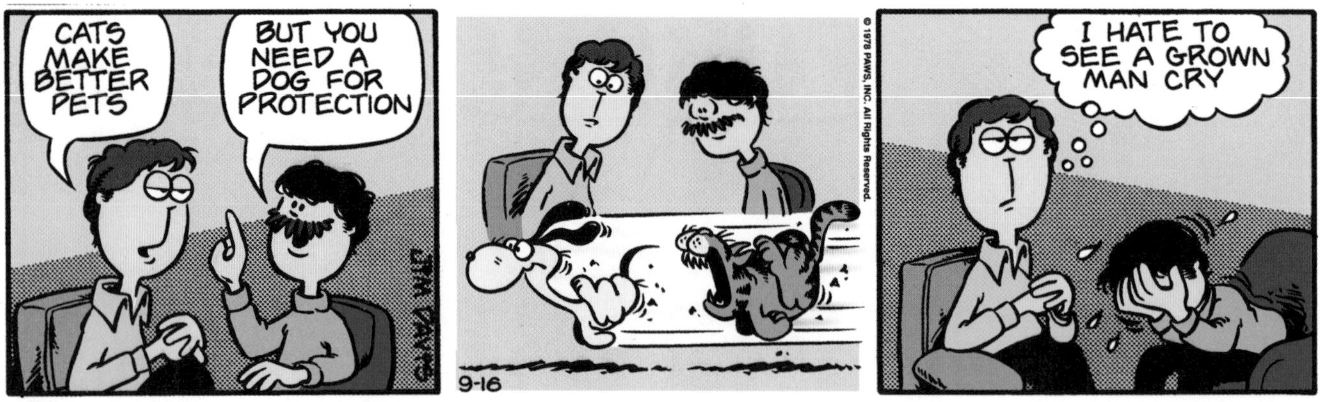
CATS MAKE BETTER PETS
BUT YOU NEED A DOG FOR PROTECTION
JIM DAVIS
9-16
© 1978 PAWS, INC. All Rights Reserved.
I HATE TO SEE A GROWN MAN CRY

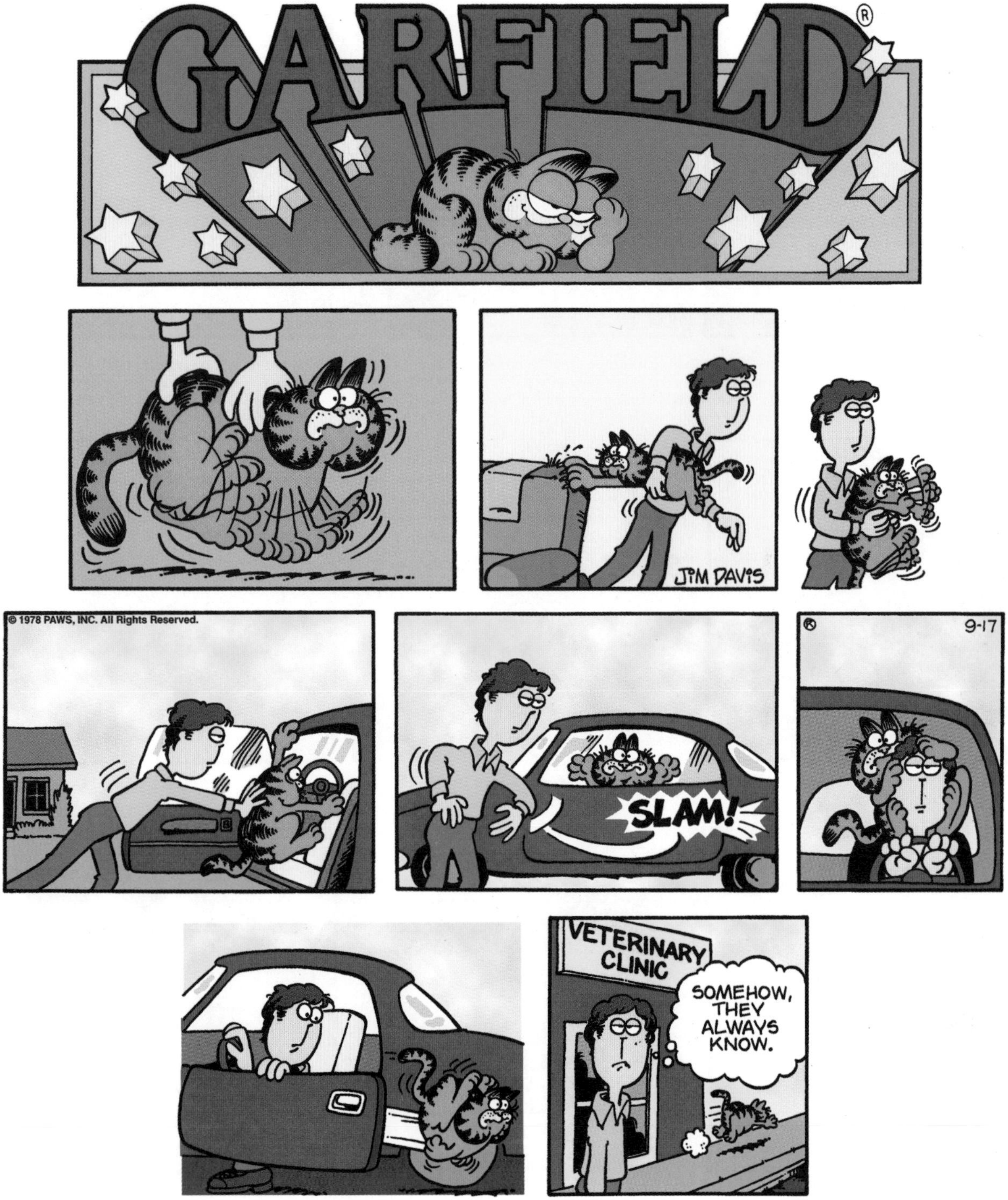
GARFIELD®
JIM DAVIS
© 1978 PAWS, INC. All Rights Reserved.
®
9-17
SLAM!
VETERINARY CLINIC
SOMEHOW, THEY ALWAYS KNOW.

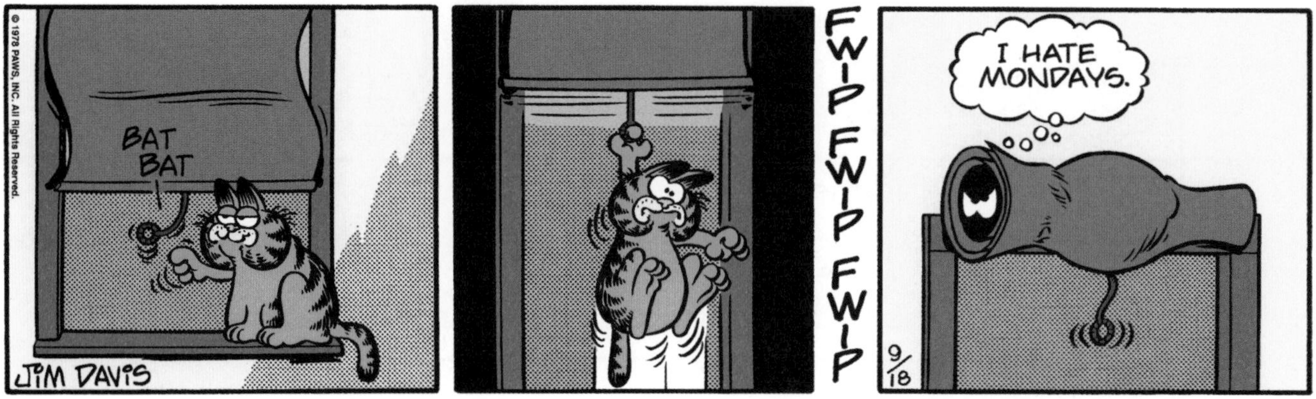
© 1978 PAWS, INC. All Rights Reserved.
BAT
BAT
JIM DAVIS
FWIP FWIP FWIP
I HATE MONDAYS.
9/18

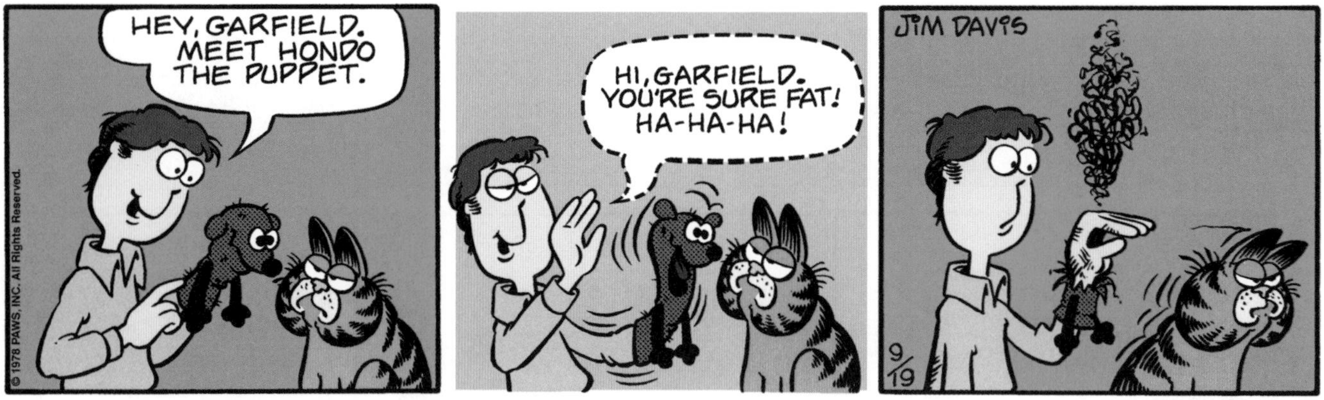
© 1978 PAWS, INC. All Rights Reserved.
HEY, GARFIELD. MEET HONDO THE PUPPET.
HI, GARFIELD. YOU'RE SURE FAT! HA-HA-HA!
JIM DAVIS
9/19

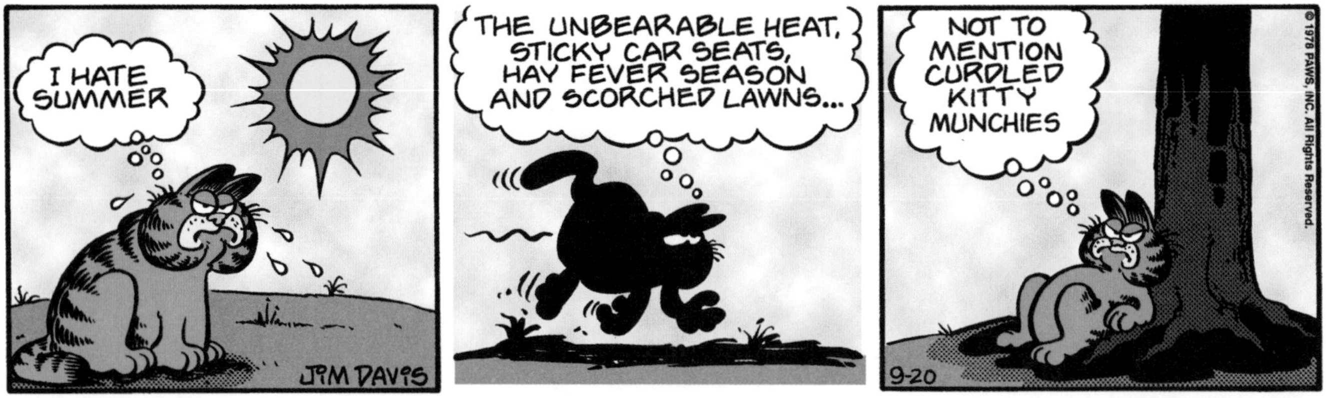
I HATE SUMMER
JIM DAVIS
THE UNBEARABLE HEAT, STICKY CAR SEATS, HAY FEVER SEASON AND SCORCHED LAWNS...
NOT TO MENTION CURDLED KITTY MUNCHIES
© 1978 PAWS, INC. All Rights Reserved.
9-20

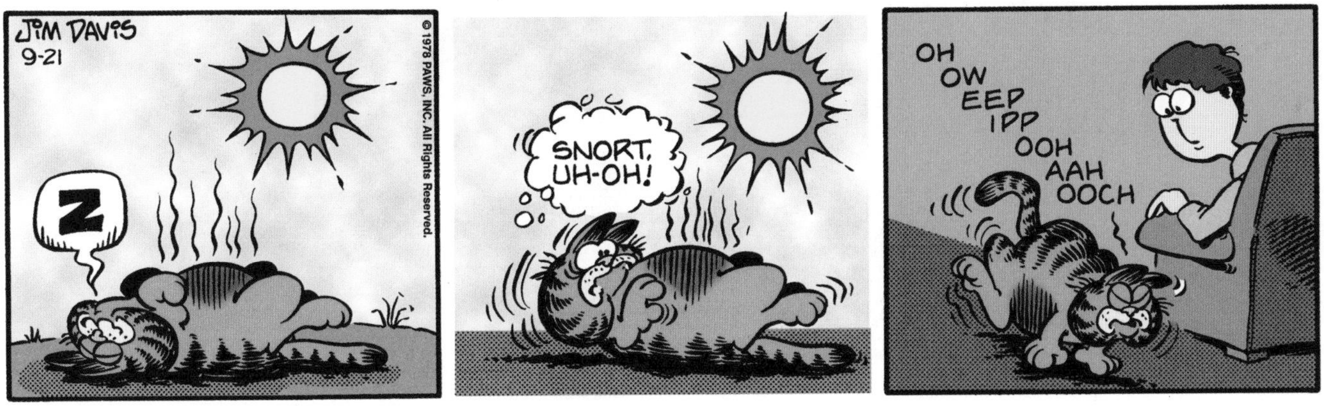
JIM DAVIS
9-21
© 1978 PAWS, INC. All Rights Reserved.
Z
SNORT, UH-OH!
OH
OW
EEP
IPP
OOH
AAH
OOCH

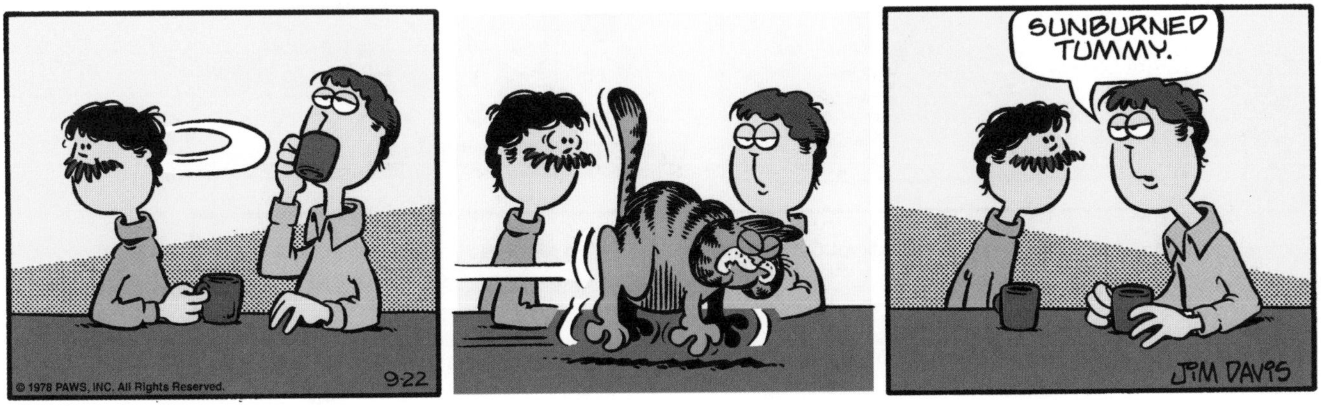
© 1978 PAWS, INC. All Rights Reserved.
9-22
SUNBURNED TUMMY.
JIM DAVIS

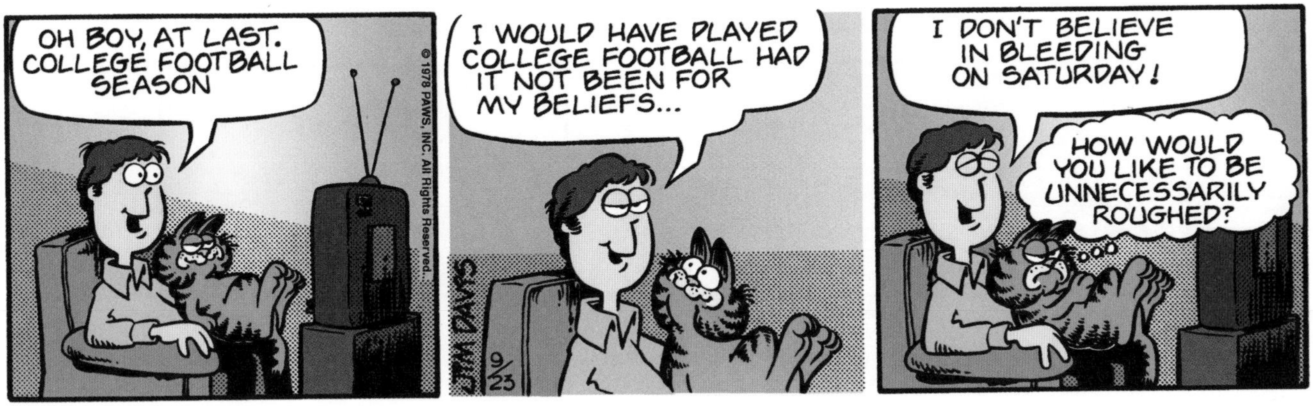
OH BOY, AT LAST. COLLEGE FOOTBALL SEASON
© 1978 PAWS, INC. All Rights Reserved.
I WOULD HAVE PLAYED COLLEGE FOOTBALL HAD IT NOT BEEN FOR MY BELIEFS...
JIM DAVIS
9/23
I DON'T BELIEVE IN BLEEDING ON SATURDAY!
HOW WOULD YOU LIKE TO BE UNNECESSARILY ROUGHED?

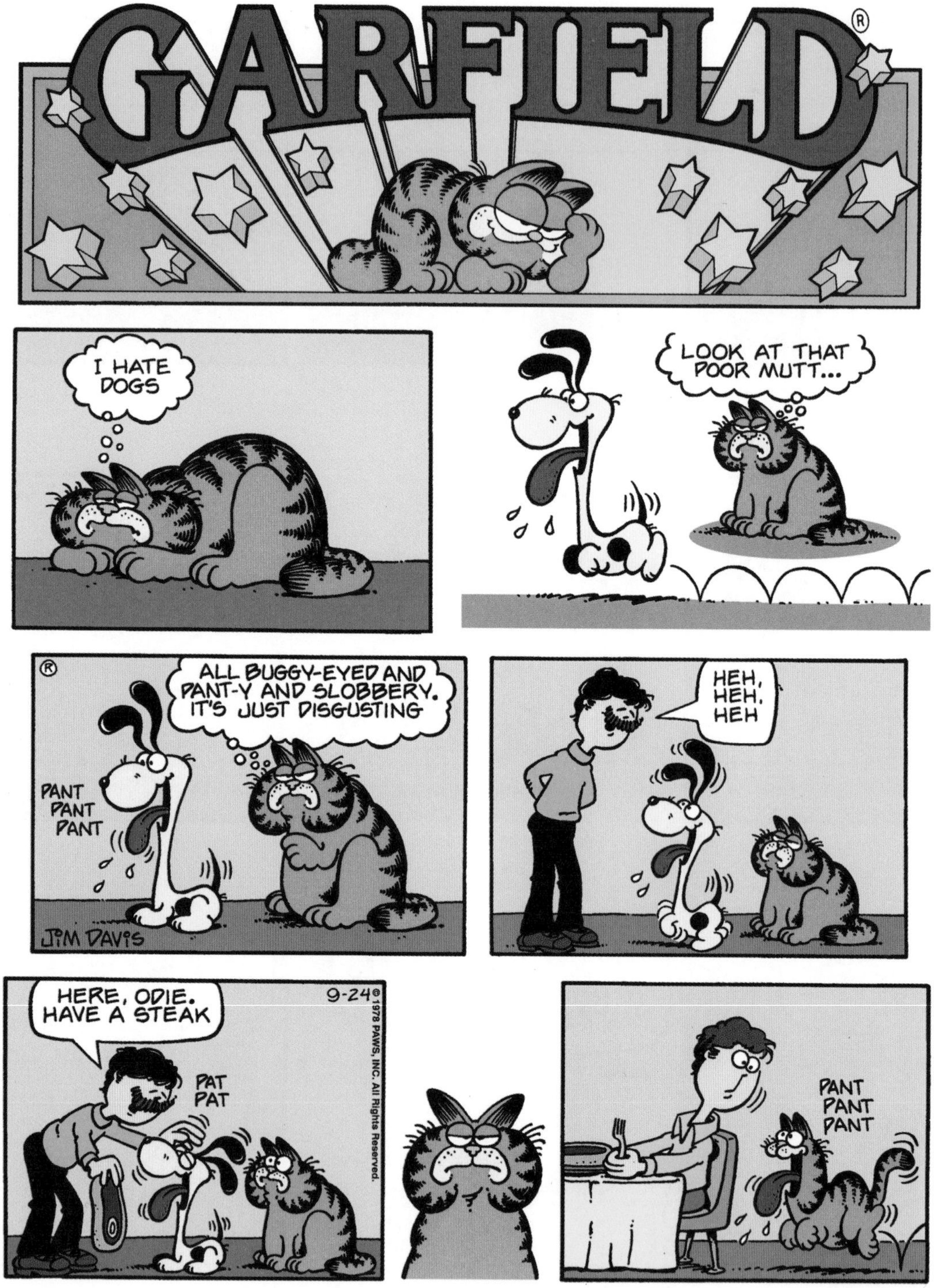
GARFIELD®
I HATE DOGS
LOOK AT THAT POOR MUTT...
®
ALL BUGGY-EYED AND PANT-Y AND SLOBBERY. IT'S JUST DISGUSTING
PANT PANT PANT
JIM DAVIS
HEH, HEH, HEH
HERE, ODIE. HAVE A STEAK
9-24 © 1978 PAWS, INC. All Rights Reserved.
PAT PAT
PANT PANT PANT

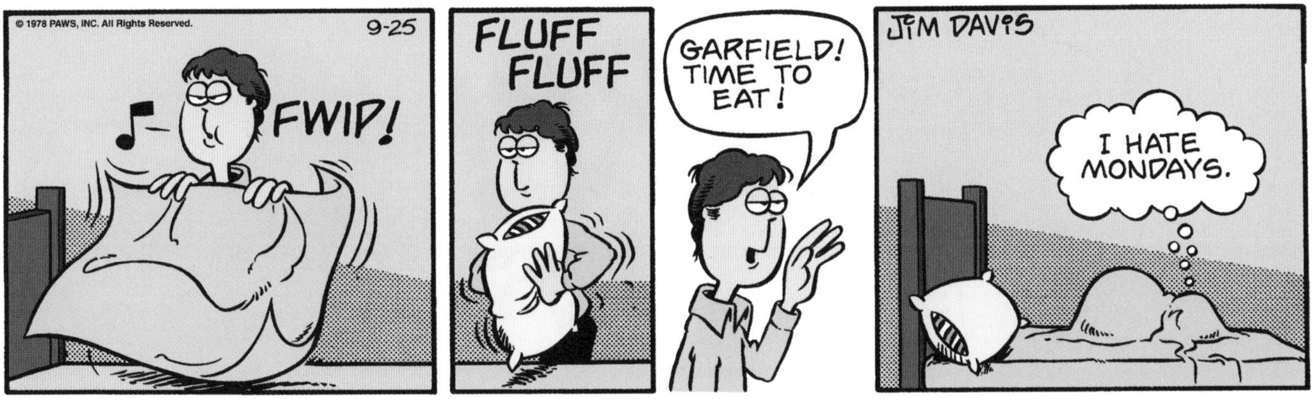
© 1978 PAWS, INC. All Rights Reserved.
9-25
FWIP!
FLUFF FLUFF
GARFIELD! TIME TO EAT!
JIM DAVIS
I HATE MONDAYS.

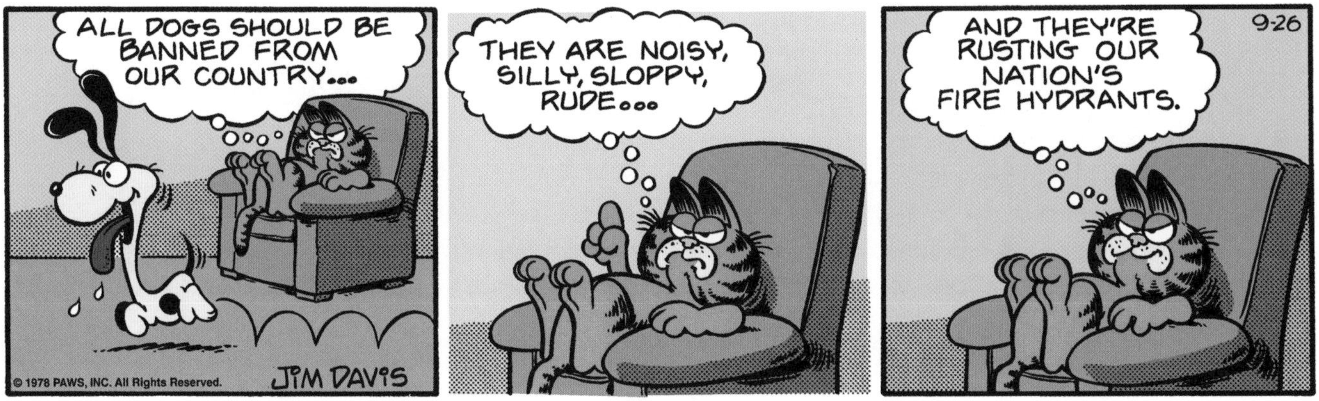
ALL DOGS SHOULD BE BANNED FROM OUR COUNTRY...
© 1978 PAWS, INC. All Rights Reserved.
JIM DAVIS
THEY ARE NOISY, SILLY, SLOPPY, RUDE...
9-26
AND THEY'RE RUSTING OUR NATION'S FIRE HYDRANTS.

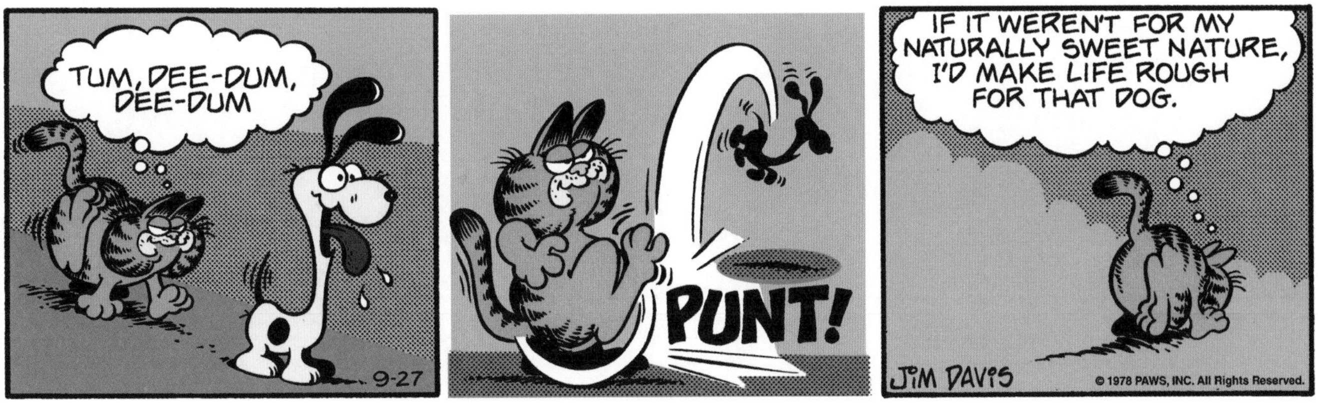
TUM, DEE-DUM, DEE-DUM
9-27
PUNT!
IF IT WEREN'T FOR MY NATURALLY SWEET NATURE, I'D MAKE LIFE ROUGH FOR THAT DOG.
JIM DAVIS
© 1978 PAWS, INC. All Rights Reserved.

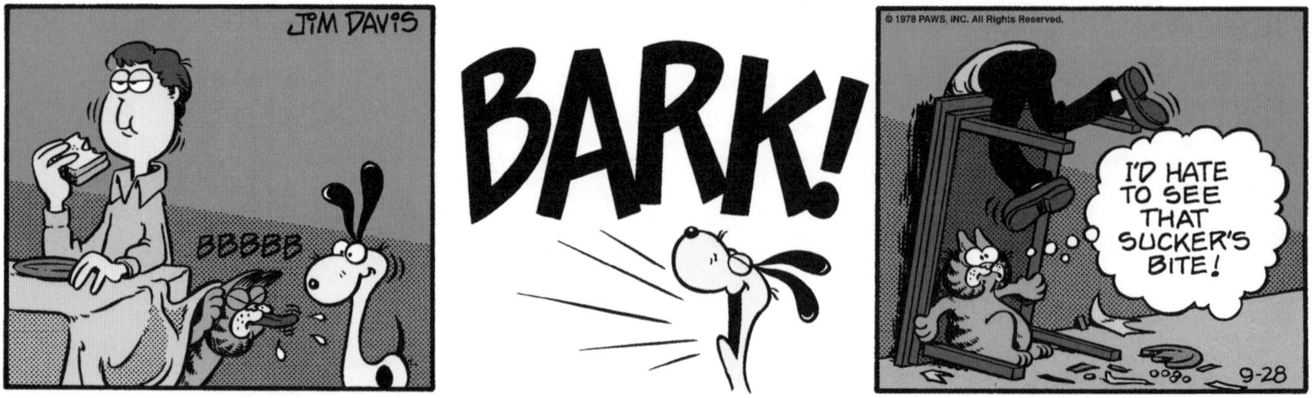
JIM DAVIS
BBBBB
BARK!
© 1978 PAWS, INC. All Rights Reserved.
I'D HATE TO SEE THAT SUCKER'S BITE!
9-28

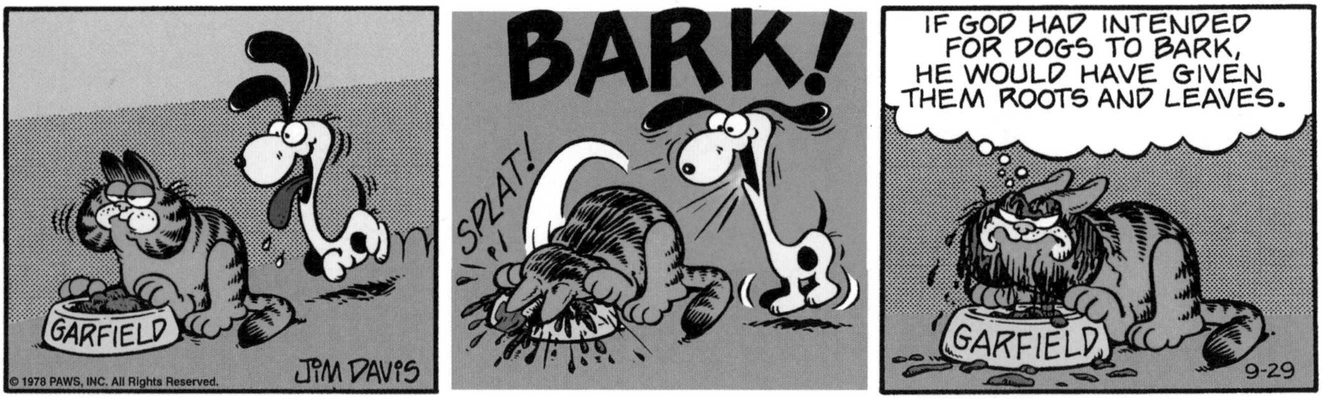
GARFIELD
© 1978 PAWS, INC. All Rights Reserved.
JIM DAVIS
BARK!
SPLAT!
IF GOD HAD INTENDED FOR DOGS TO BARK, HE WOULD HAVE GIVEN THEM ROOTS AND LEAVES.
GARFIELD
9-29

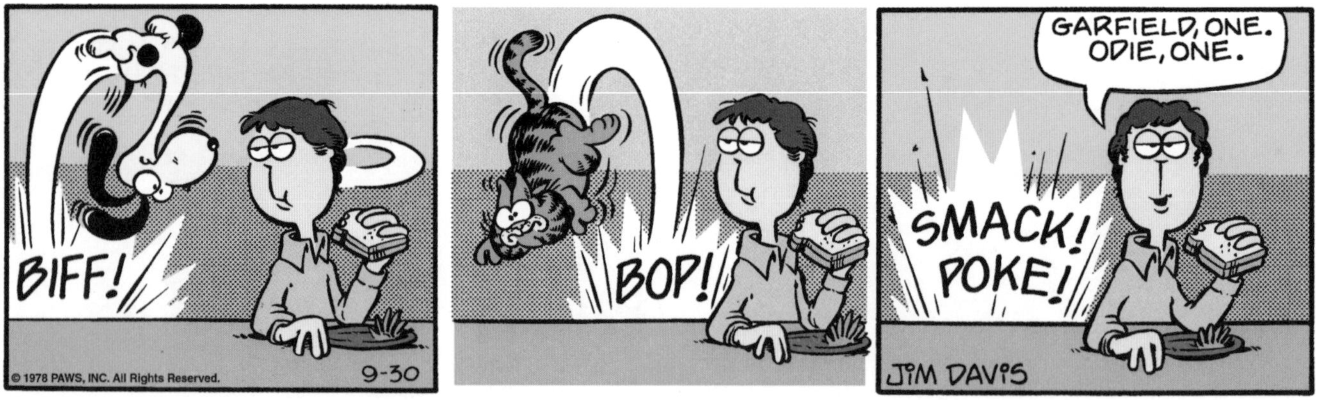
BIFF!
© 1978 PAWS, INC. All Rights Reserved.
9-30
BOP!
GARFIELD, ONE. ODIE, ONE.
SMACK! POKE!
JIM DAVIS

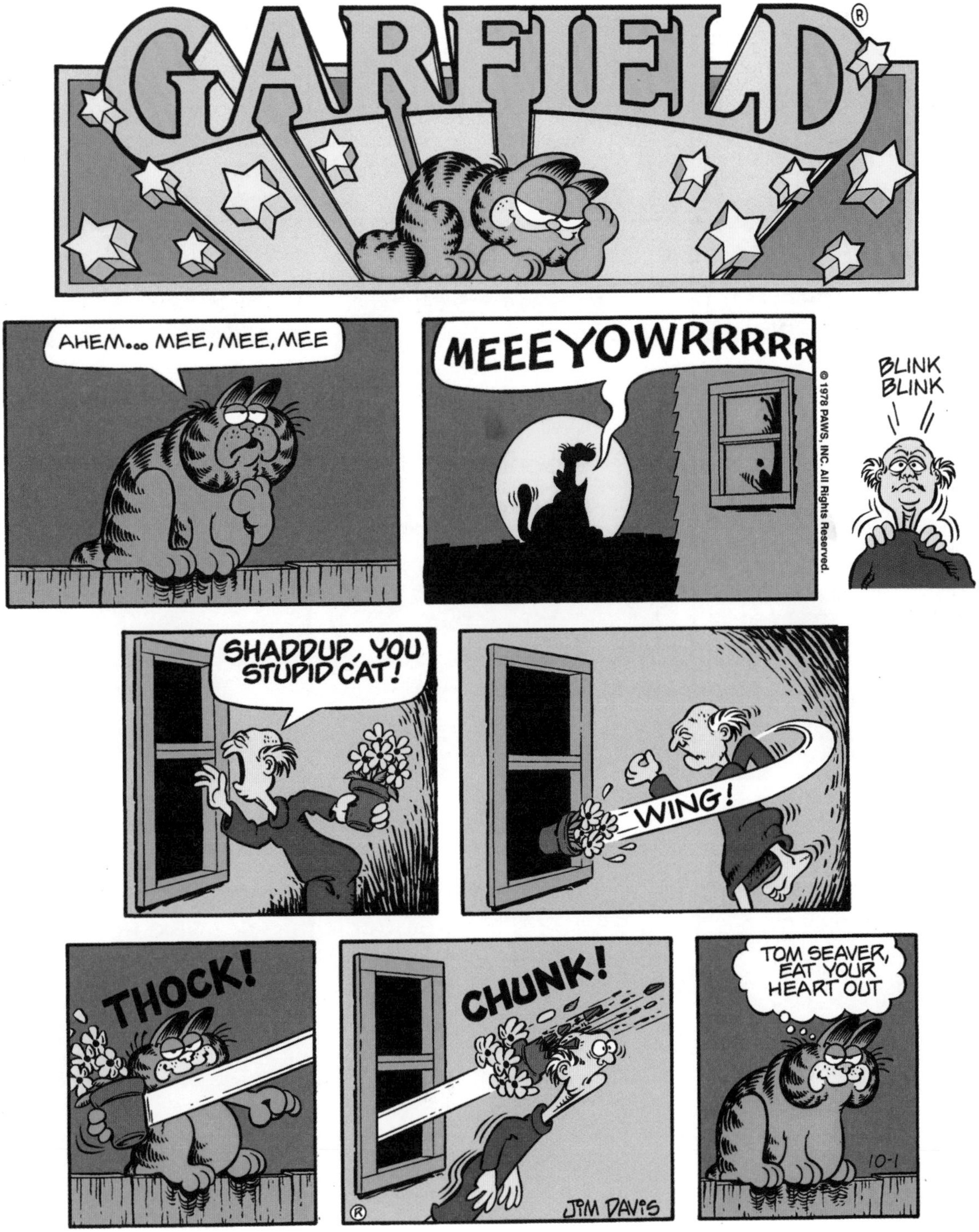
GARFIELD®
AHEM... MEE, MEE, MEE
MEEEYOWRRRRR
© 1978 PAWS, INC. All Rights Reserved.
BLINK BLINK
SHADDUP, YOU STUPID CAT!
WING!
THOCK!
CHUNK!
JIM DAVIS
TOM SEAVER, EAT YOUR HEART OUT
10-1

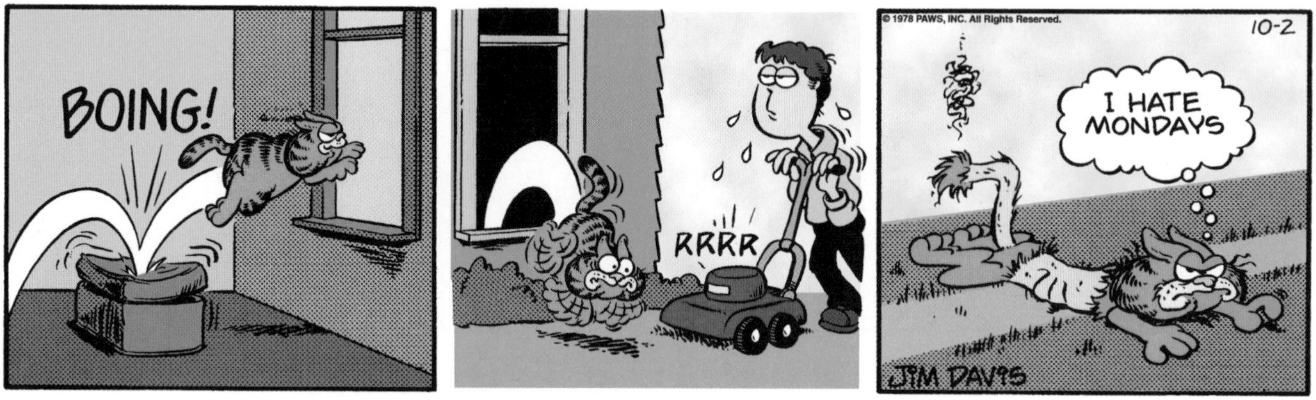
BOING!
RRRR
© 1978 PAWS, INC. All Rights Reserved.
10-2
I HATE MONDAYS
JIM DAVIS

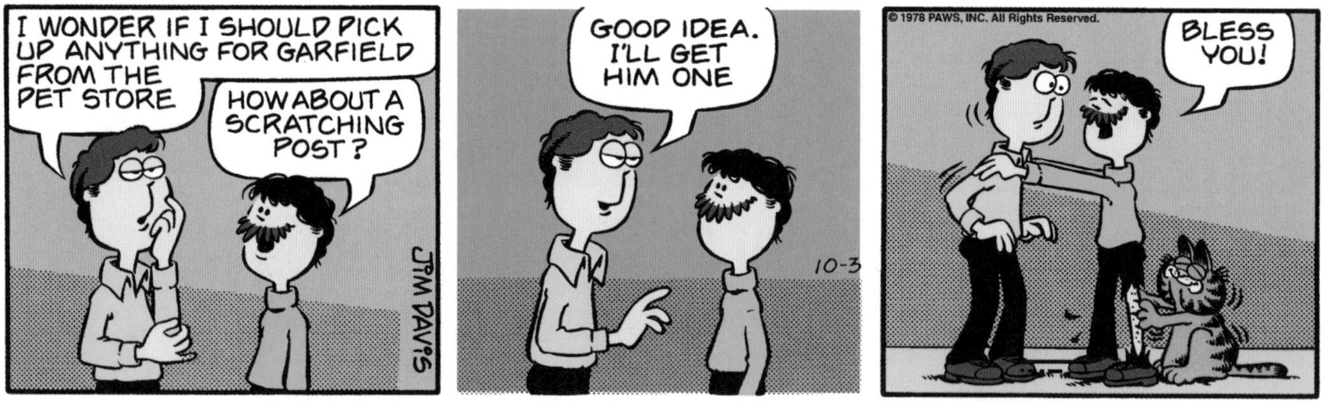
I WONDER IF I SHOULD PICK UP ANYTHING FOR GARFIELD FROM THE PET STORE
HOW ABOUT A SCRATCHING POST ?
JIM DAVIS
GOOD IDEA. I'LL GET HIM ONE
10-3
© 1978 PAWS, INC. All Rights Reserved.
BLESS YOU!

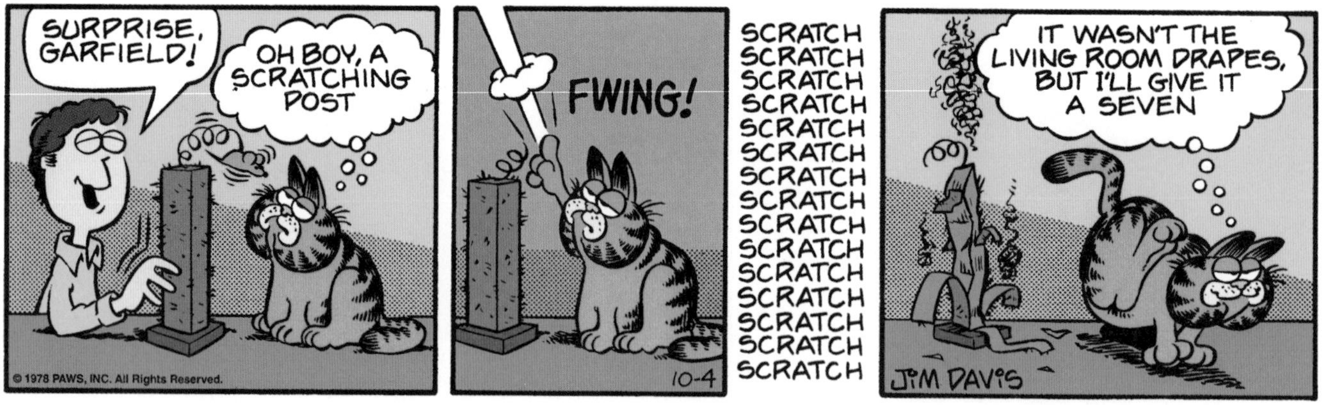
SURPRISE, GARFIELD!
OH BOY, A SCRATCHING POST
© 1978 PAWS, INC. All Rights Reserved.
FWING!
10-4
SCRATCH
SCRATCH
SCRATCH
SCRATCH
SCRATCH
SCRATCH
SCRATCH
SCRATCH
SCRATCH
SCRATCH
SCRATCH
SCRATCH
SCRATCH
SCRATCH
SCRATCH
IT WASN'T THE LIVING ROOM DRAPES, BUT I'LL GIVE IT A SEVEN
JIM DAVIS

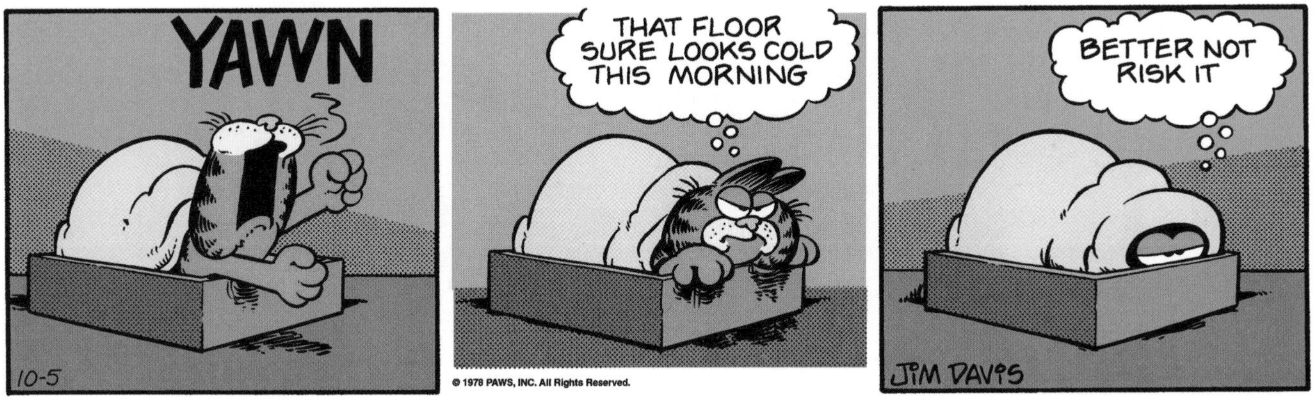
YAWN
10-5
THAT FLOOR SURE LOOKS COLD THIS MORNING
BETTER NOT RISK IT
JIM DAVIS

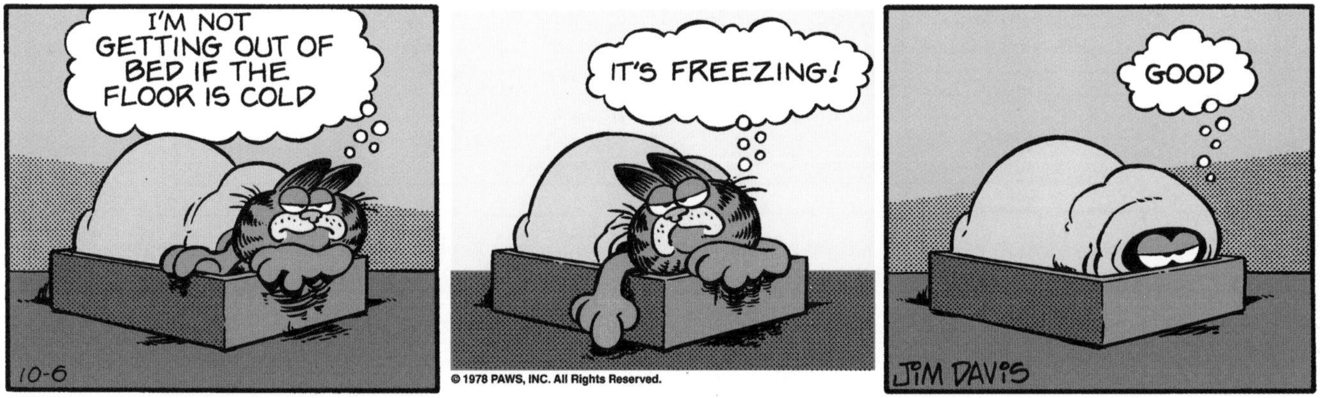
I'M NOT GETTING OUT OF BED IF THE FLOOR IS COLD
10-6
IT'S FREEZING!
GOOD
JIM DAVIS

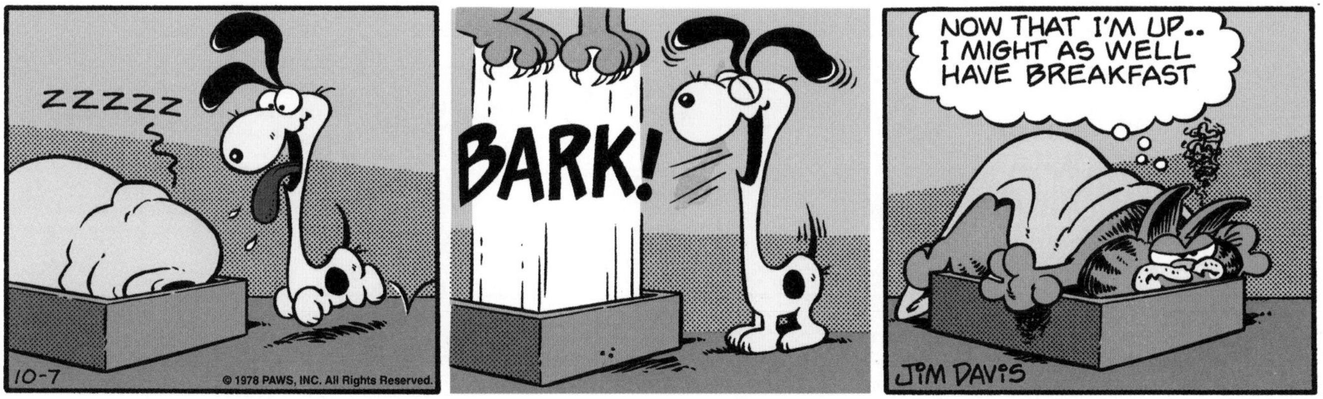
ZZZZZ
10-7
BARK!
NOW THAT I'M UP.. I MIGHT AS WELL HAVE BREAKFAST
JIM DAVIS

GARFIELD®
GOOD MORNING, GARFIELD
TODAY WE'RE GOING TO LEARN TO WALK ON A LEASH
JIM DAVIS
10-8
© 1978 PAWS, INC. All Rights Reserved.
KABONKA BONKA BONKA
ROWRR!
I TELL YOU, THELMA, THIS NEIGHBORHOOD IS GETTING WEIRDER BY THE MINUTE

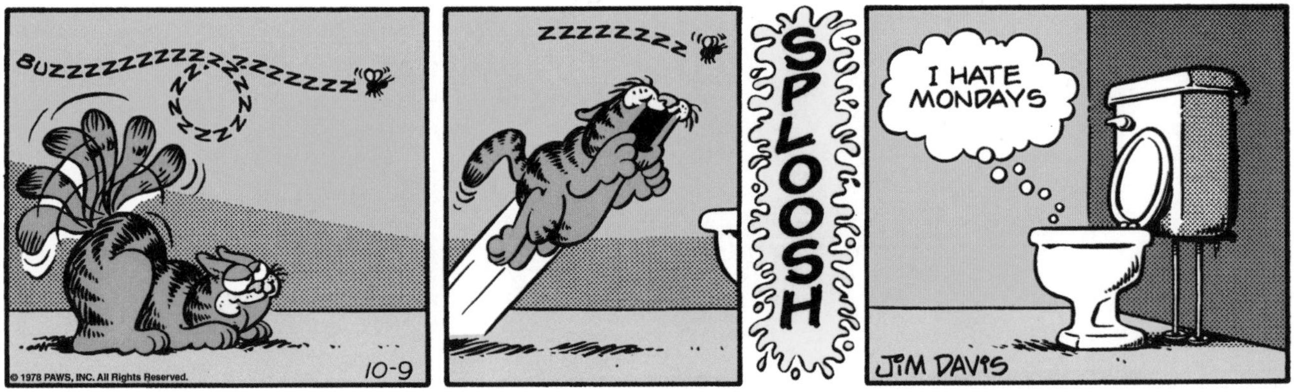
BUZZZZZZZZZZZZZZZZZZZ
ZZZZZZZZ
SPLOOSH
I HATE MONDAYS
© 1978 PAWS, INC. All Rights Reserved.
10-9
JIM DAVIS

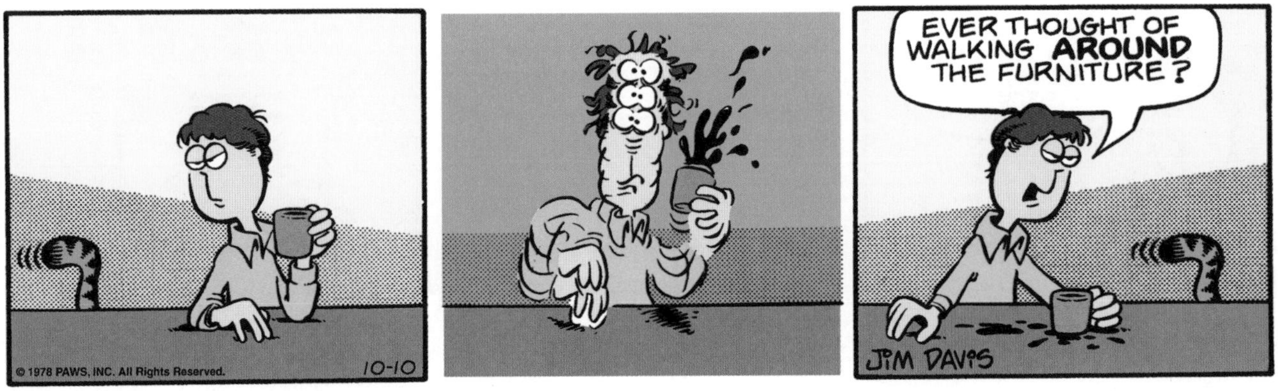
EVER THOUGHT OF WALKING **AROUND** THE FURNITURE?
© 1978 PAWS, INC. All Rights Reserved.
10-10
JIM DAVIS

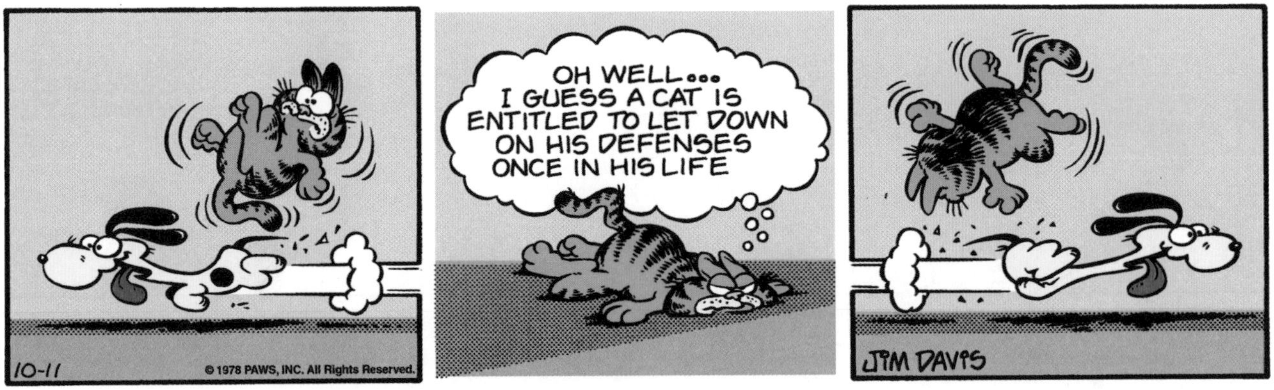
OH WELL... I GUESS A CAT IS ENTITLED TO LET DOWN ON HIS DEFENSES ONCE IN HIS LIFE
10-11
© 1978 PAWS, INC. All Rights Reserved.
JIM DAVIS

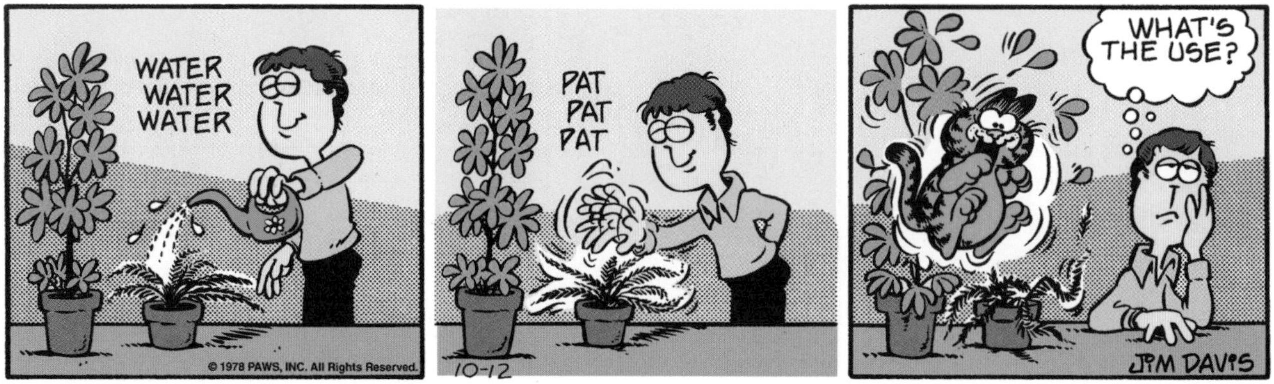
WATER WATER WATER
© 1978 PAWS, INC. All Rights Reserved.
PAT PAT PAT
10-12
WHAT'S THE USE?
JIM DAVIS

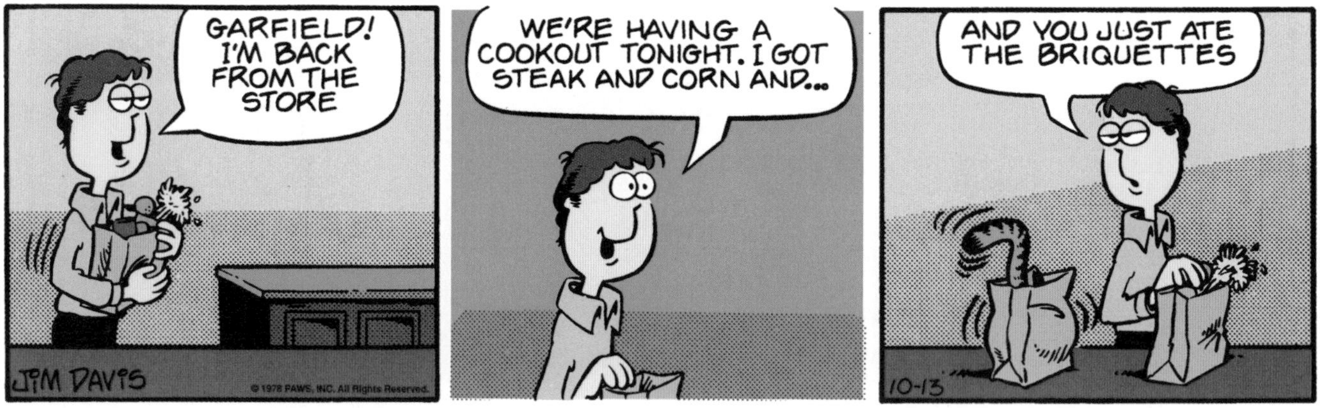
GARFIELD! I'M BACK FROM THE STORE
JIM DAVIS
© 1978 PAWS, INC. All Rights Reserved.
WE'RE HAVING A COOKOUT TONIGHT. I GOT STEAK AND CORN AND...
AND YOU JUST ATE THE BRIQUETTES
10-13

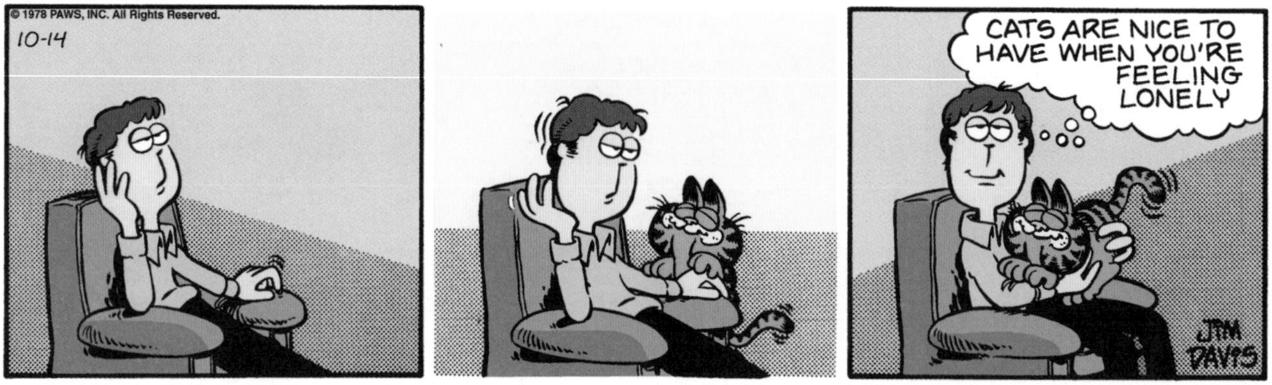
© 1978 PAWS, INC. All Rights Reserved.
10-14
CATS ARE NICE TO HAVE WHEN YOU'RE FEELING LONELY
JIM DAVIS

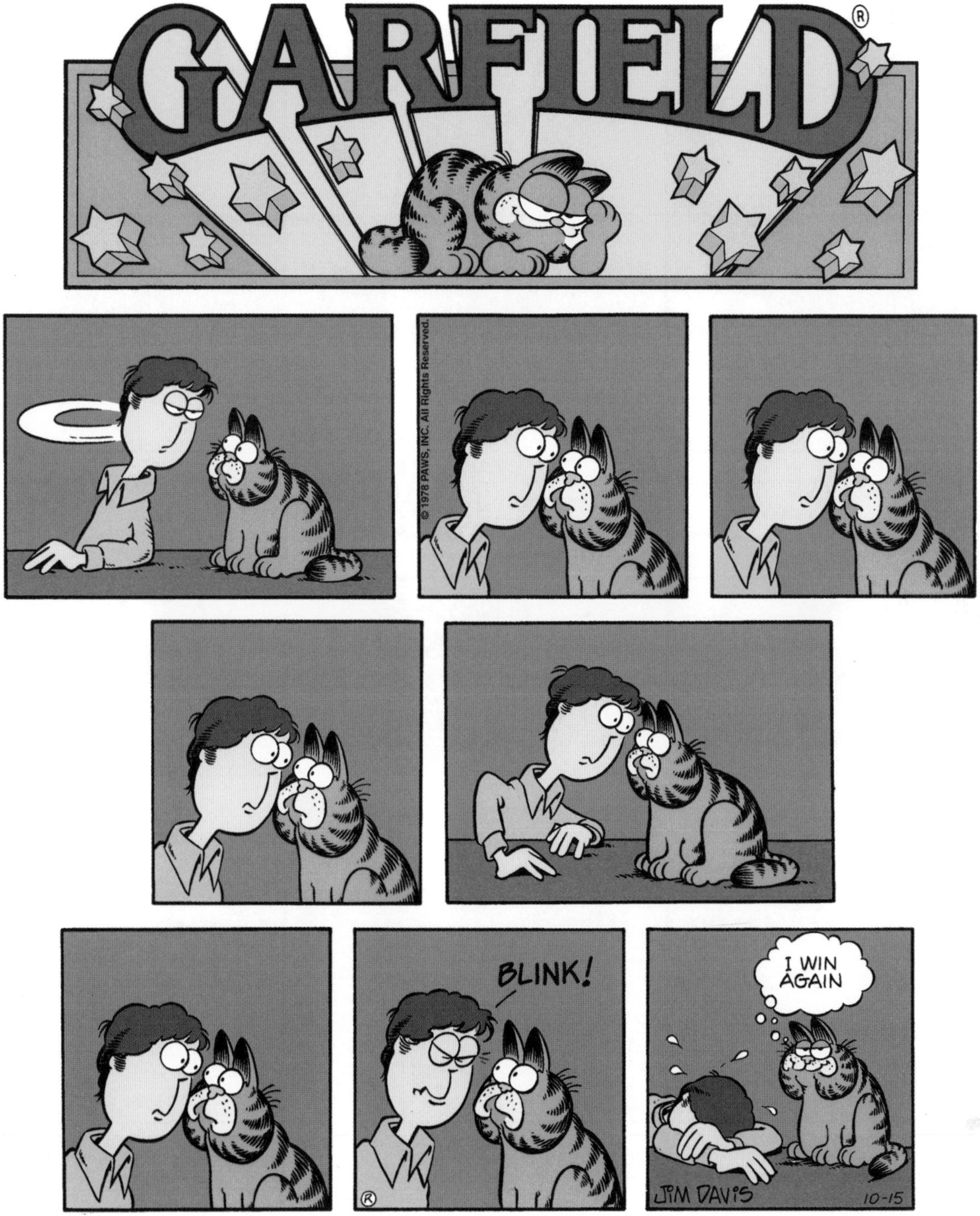
GARFIELD®
© 1978 PAWS, INC. All Rights Reserved.
BLINK!
I WIN AGAIN
JIM DAVIS
10-15

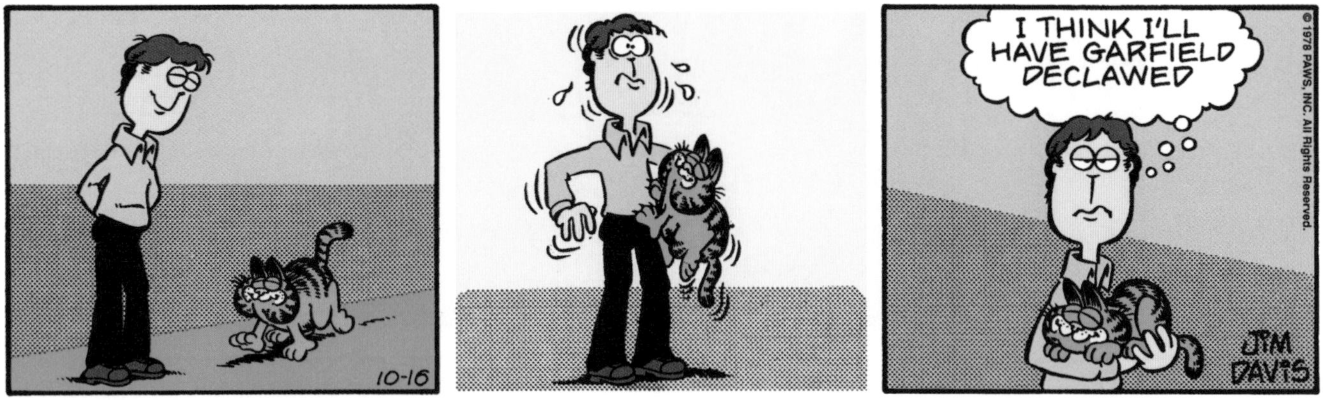
10-16
I THINK I'LL HAVE GARFIELD DECLAWED
© 1978 PAWS, INC. All Rights Reserved.
JIM DAVIS

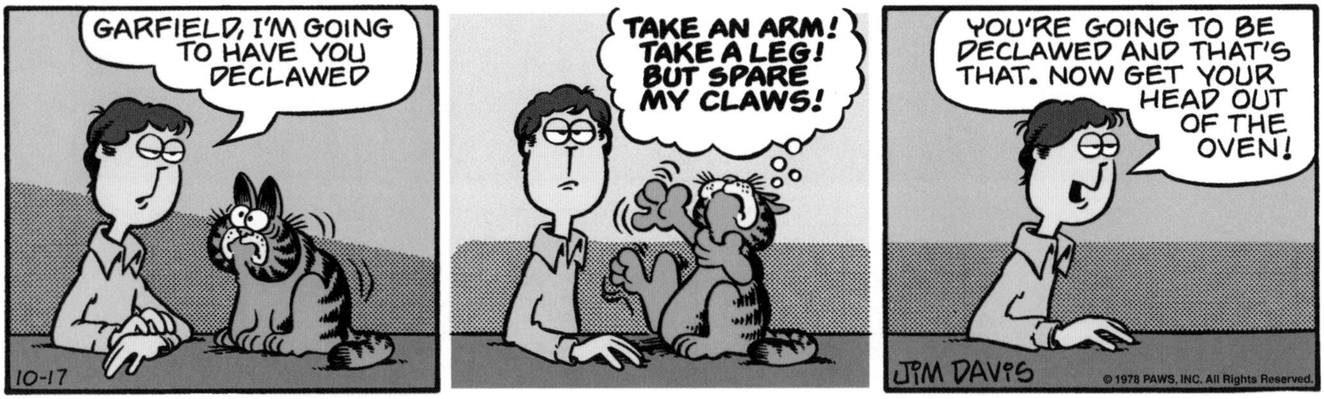
GARFIELD, I'M GOING TO HAVE YOU DECLAWED
10-17
TAKE AN ARM! TAKE A LEG! BUT SPARE MY CLAWS!
YOU'RE GOING TO BE DECLAWED AND THAT'S THAT. NOW GET YOUR HEAD OUT OF THE OVEN!
JIM DAVIS
© 1978 PAWS, INC. All Rights Reserved.

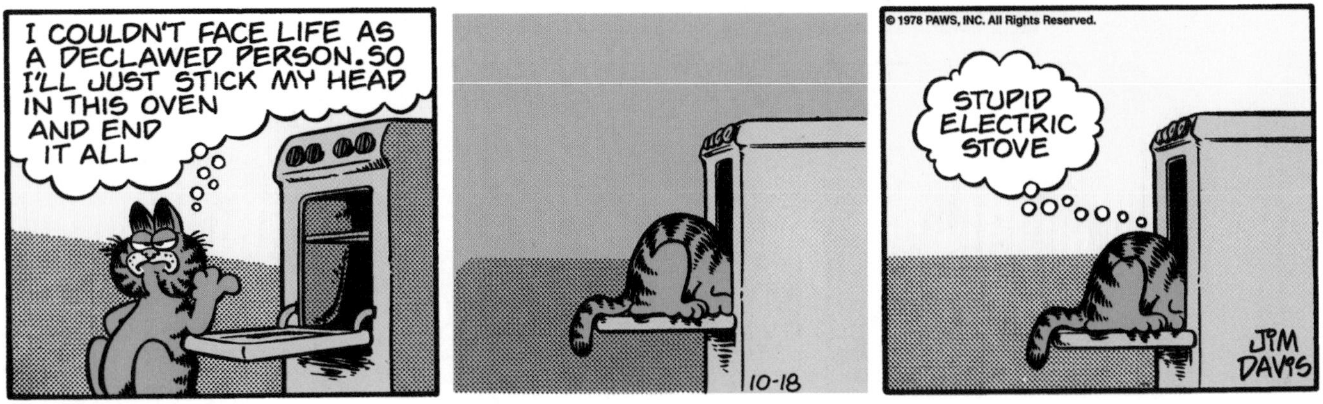
I COULDN'T FACE LIFE AS A DECLAWED PERSON. SO I'LL JUST STICK MY HEAD IN THIS OVEN AND END IT ALL
10-18
© 1978 PAWS, INC. All Rights Reserved.
STUPID ELECTRIC STOVE
JIM DAVIS

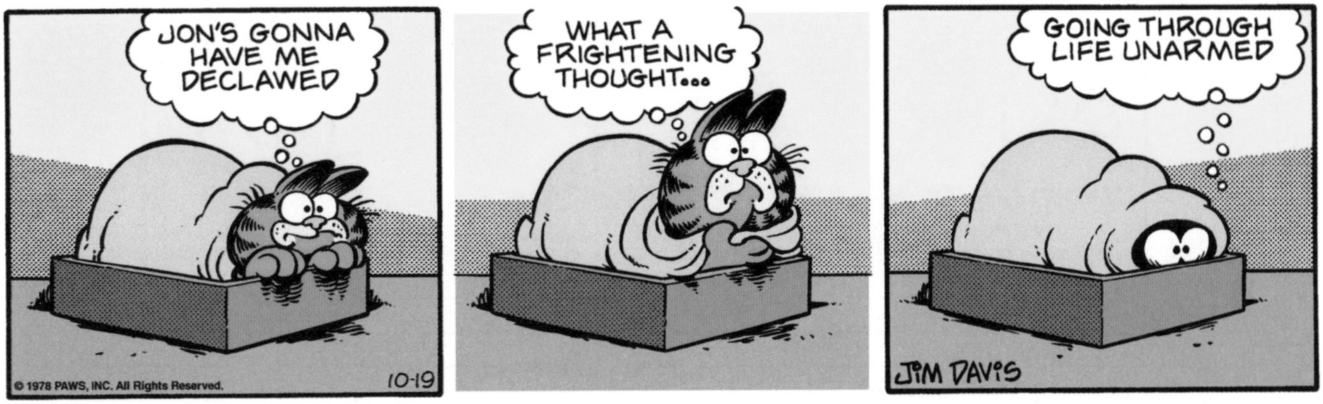
JON'S GONNA HAVE ME DECLAWED
WHAT A FRIGHTENING THOUGHT...
GOING THROUGH LIFE UNARMED
© 1978 PAWS, INC. All Rights Reserved.
10-19
JIM DAVIS

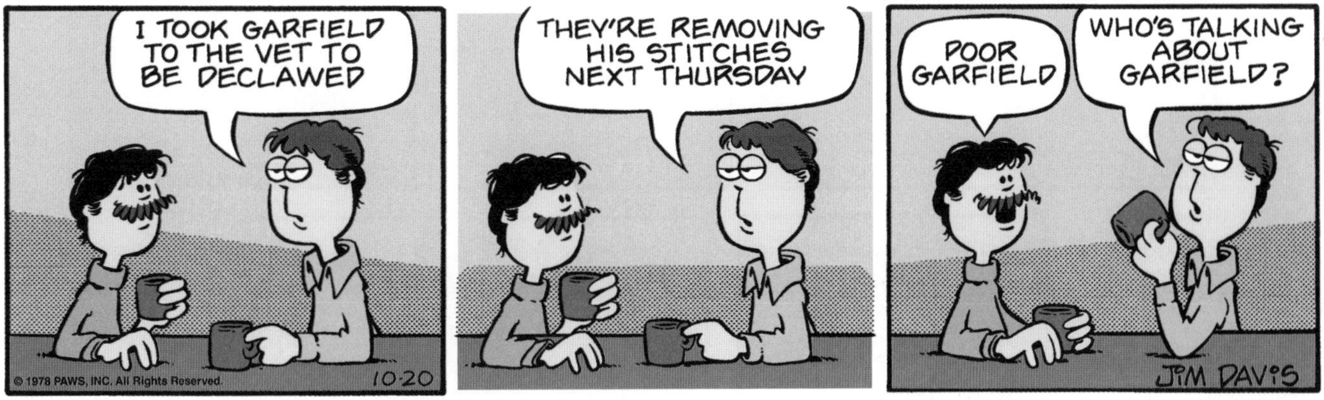
I TOOK GARFIELD TO THE VET TO BE DECLAWED
THEY'RE REMOVING HIS STITCHES NEXT THURSDAY
POOR GARFIELD
WHO'S TALKING ABOUT GARFIELD?
© 1978 PAWS, INC. All Rights Reserved.
10-20
JIM DAVIS

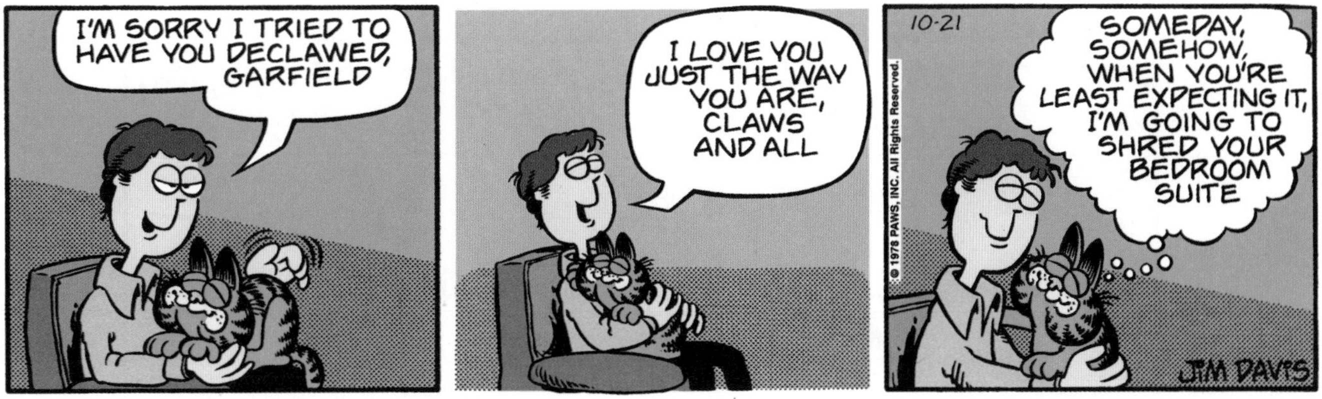
I'M SORRY I TRIED TO HAVE YOU DECLAWED, GARFIELD
I LOVE YOU JUST THE WAY YOU ARE, CLAWS AND ALL
SOMEDAY, SOMEHOW, WHEN YOU'RE LEAST EXPECTING IT, I'M GOING TO SHRED YOUR BEDROOM SUITE
10-21
© 1978 PAWS, INC. All Rights Reserved.
JIM DAVIS

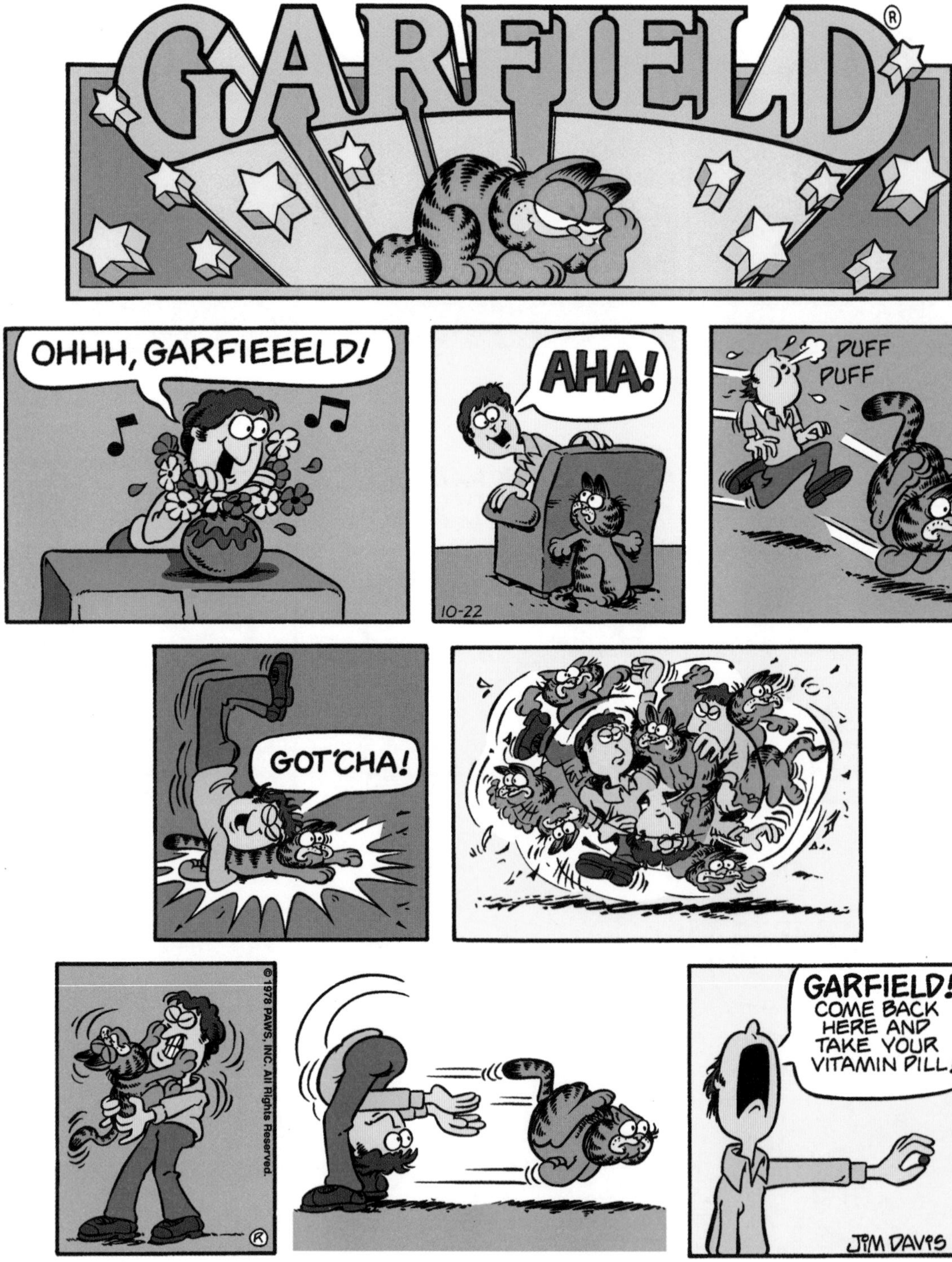
GARFIELD®
OHHH, GARFIEEELD!
AHA!
10-22
PUFF PUFF
GOT'CHA!
© 1978 PAWS, INC. All Rights Reserved.
GARFIELD! COME BACK HERE AND TAKE YOUR VITAMIN PILL!
JIM DAVIS

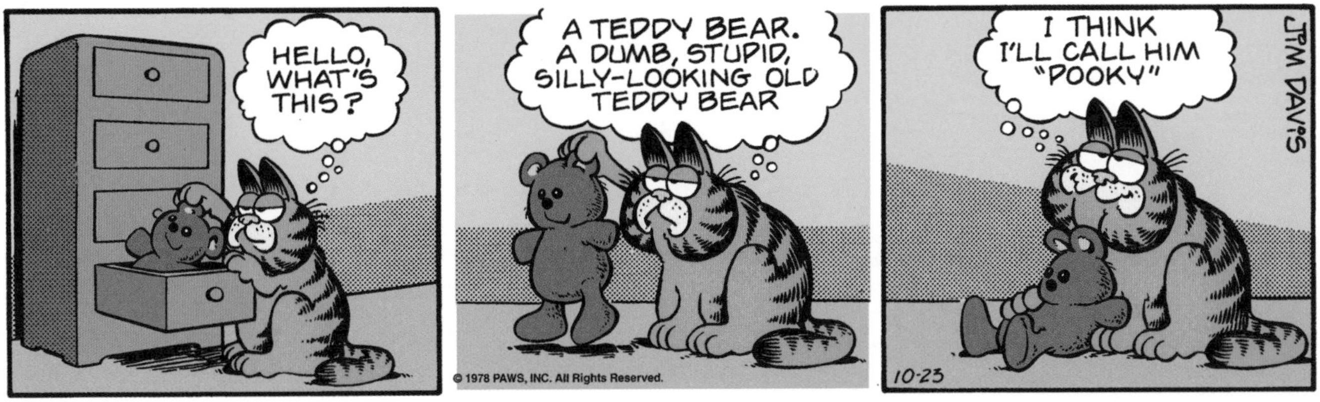
HELLO, WHAT'S THIS?
A TEDDY BEAR. A DUMB, STUPID, SILLY-LOOKING OLD TEDDY BEAR
I THINK I'LL CALL HIM "POOKY"
JIM DAVIS
© 1978 PAWS, INC. All Rights Reserved.
10-23

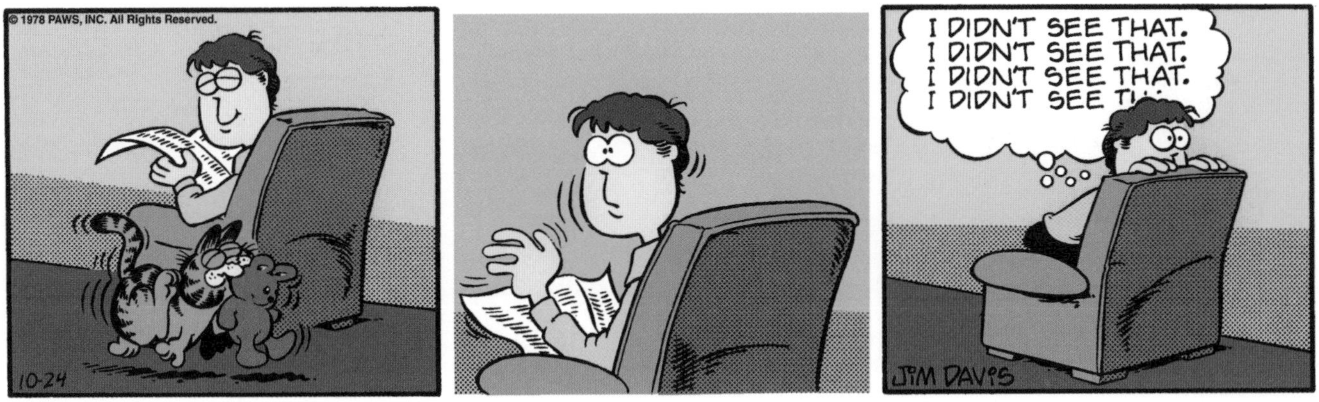
© 1978 PAWS, INC. All Rights Reserved.
10-24
I DIDN'T SEE THAT.
I DIDN'T SEE THAT.
I DIDN'T SEE THAT.
I DIDN'T SEE
JIM DAVIS

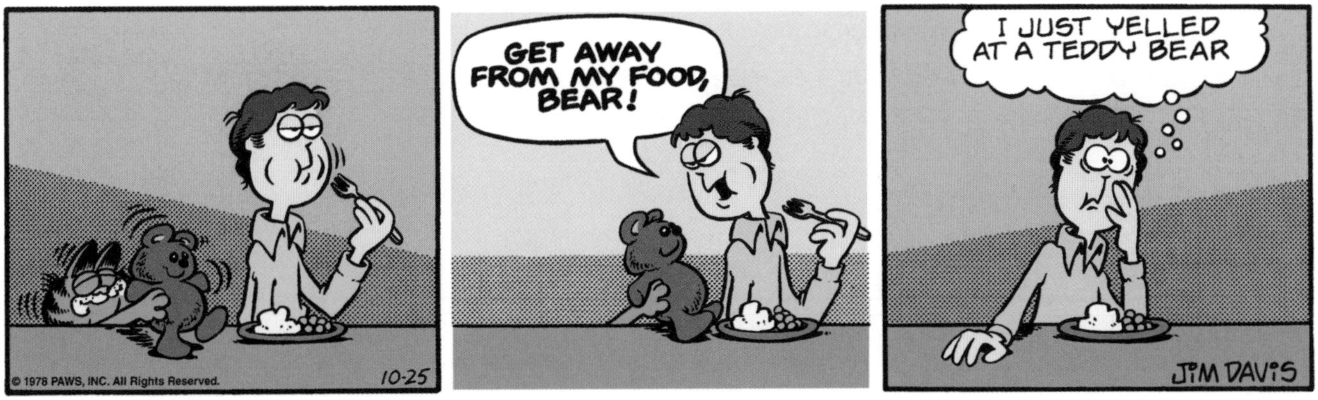
© 1978 PAWS, INC. All Rights Reserved.
10-25
GET AWAY FROM MY FOOD, BEAR!
I JUST YELLED AT A TEDDY BEAR
JIM DAVIS

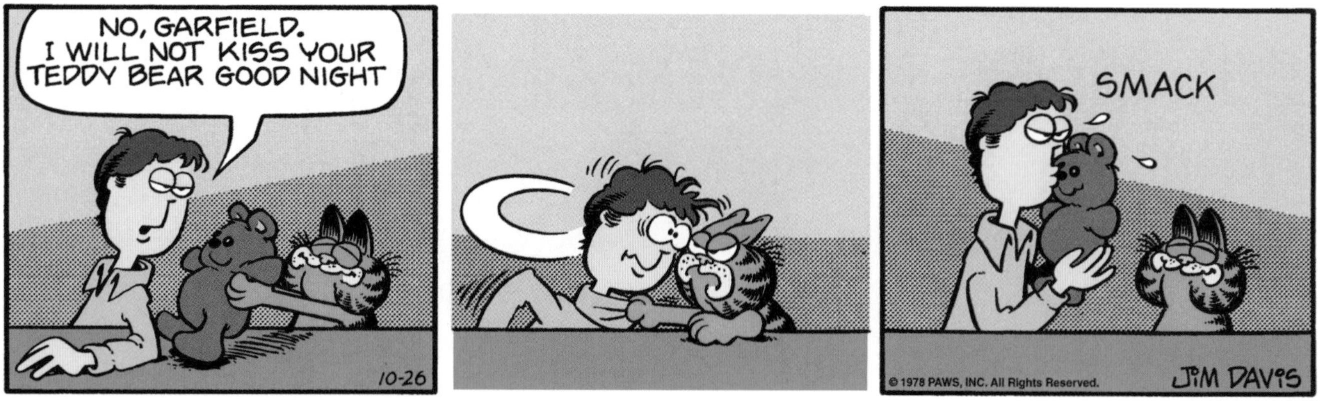
NO, GARFIELD. I WILL NOT KISS YOUR TEDDY BEAR GOOD NIGHT
10-26
SMACK
© 1978 PAWS, INC. All Rights Reserved.
JIM DAVIS

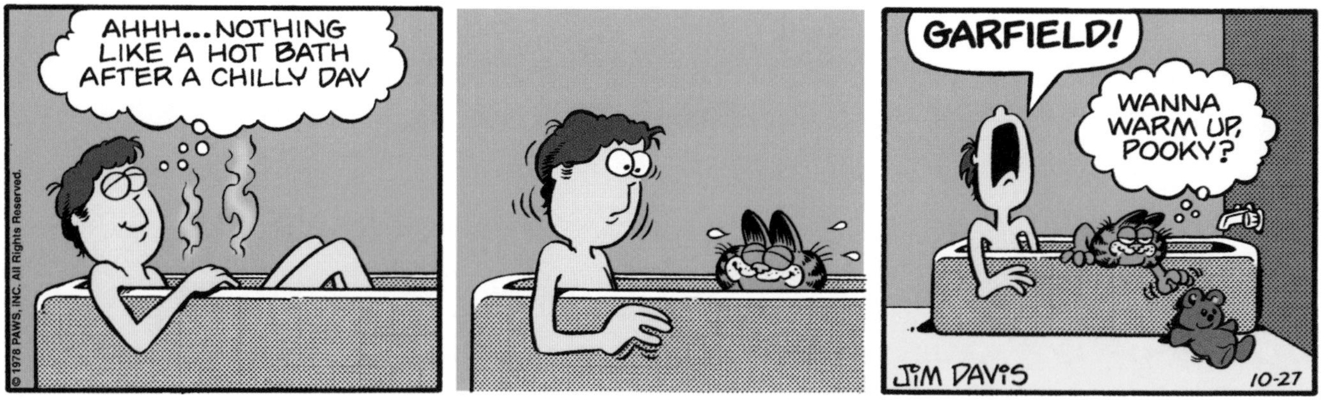
AHHH...NOTHING LIKE A HOT BATH AFTER A CHILLY DAY
© 1978 PAWS, INC. All Rights Reserved.
GARFIELD!
WANNA WARM UP, POOKY?
JIM DAVIS
10-27

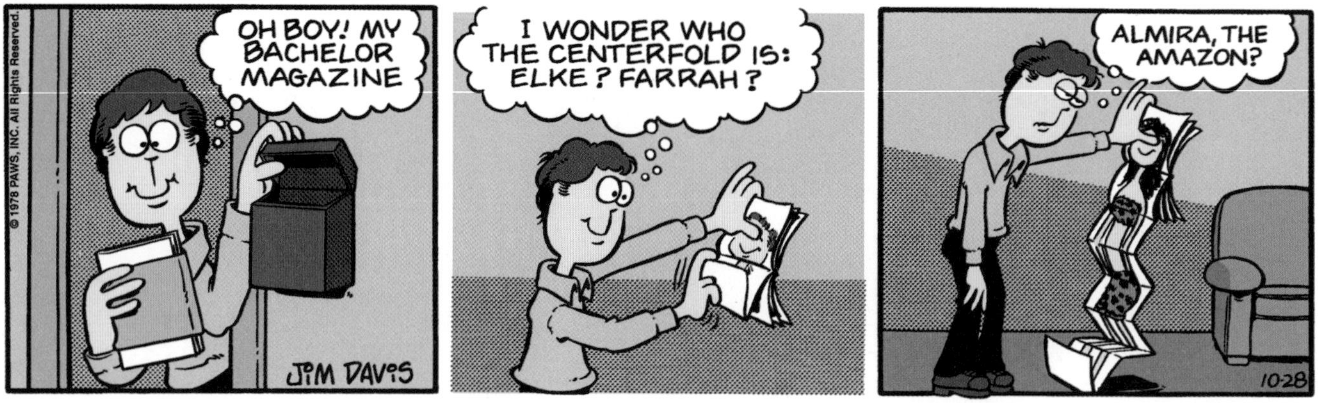
© 1978 PAWS, INC. All Rights Reserved.
OH BOY! MY BACHELOR MAGAZINE
JIM DAVIS
I WONDER WHO THE CENTERFOLD IS: ELKE? FARRAH?
ALMIRA, THE AMAZON?
10-28

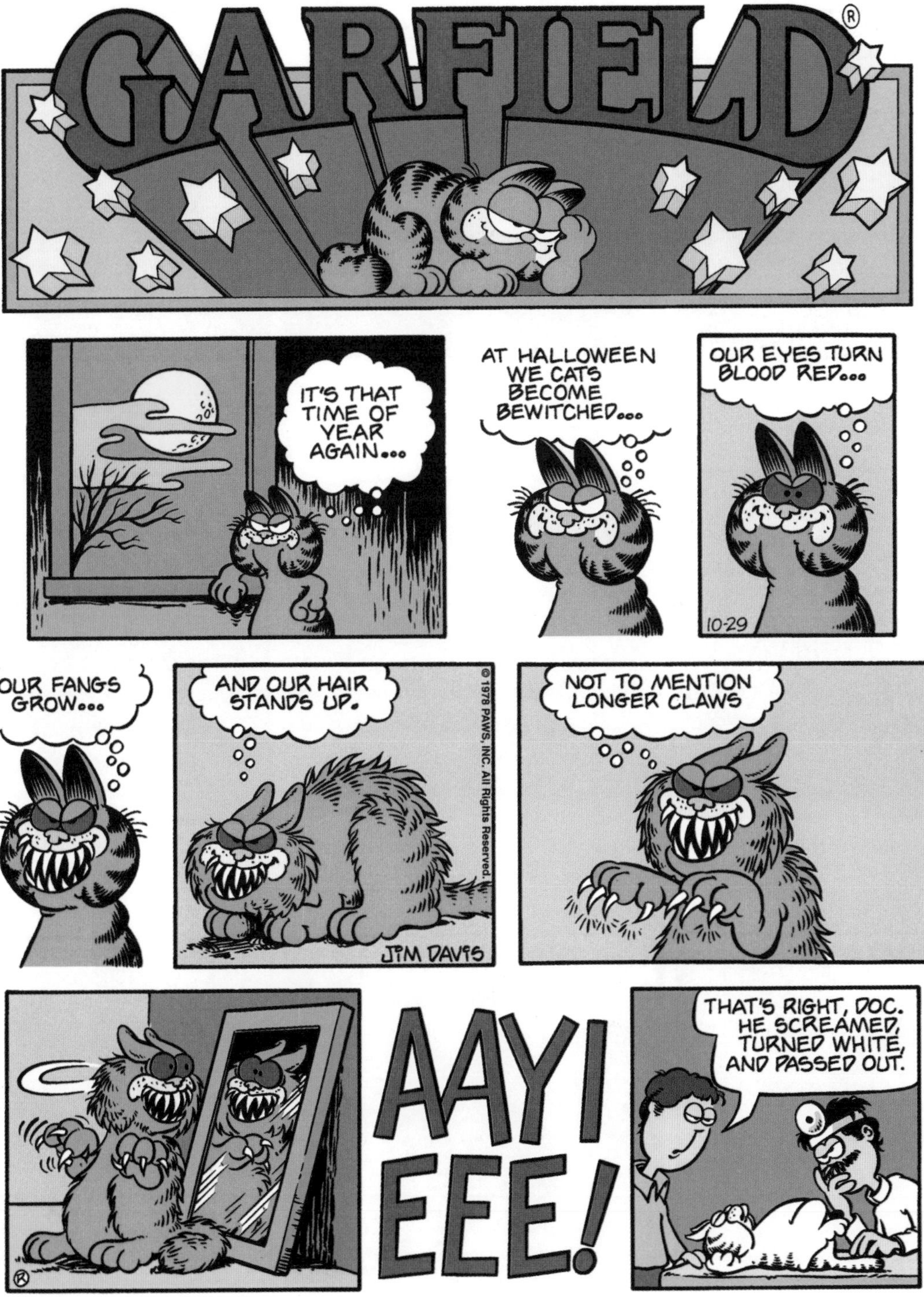
GARFIELD®
IT'S THAT TIME OF YEAR AGAIN...
AT HALLOWEEN WE CATS BECOME BEWITCHED...
OUR EYES TURN BLOOD RED...
10-29
OUR FANGS GROW...
AND OUR HAIR STANDS UP.
© 1978 PAWS, INC. All Rights Reserved.
JIM DAVIS
NOT TO MENTION LONGER CLAWS
AAYIEEE!
THAT'S RIGHT, DOC. HE SCREAMED, TURNED WHITE, AND PASSED OUT.

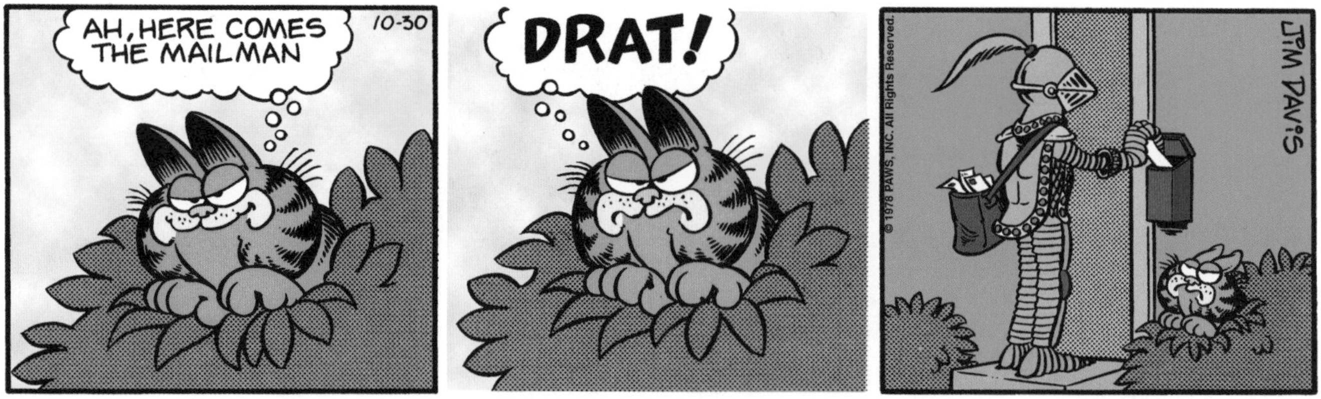
AH, HERE COMES THE MAILMAN
10-30
DRAT!
© 1978 PAWS, INC. All Rights Reserved.
JIM DAVIS

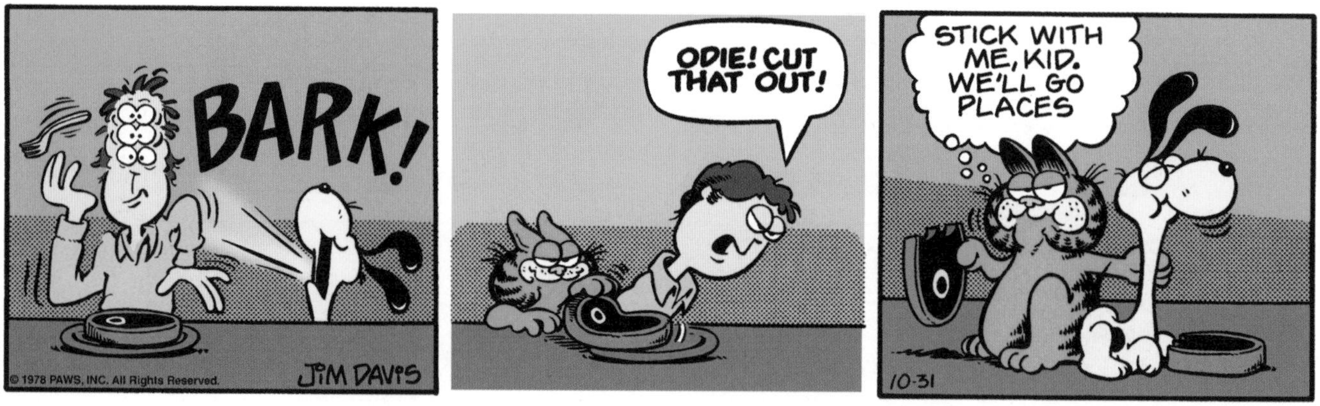
BARK!
© 1978 PAWS, INC. All Rights Reserved.
JIM DAVIS
ODIE! CUT THAT OUT!
STICK WITH ME, KID. WE'LL GO PLACES
10-31

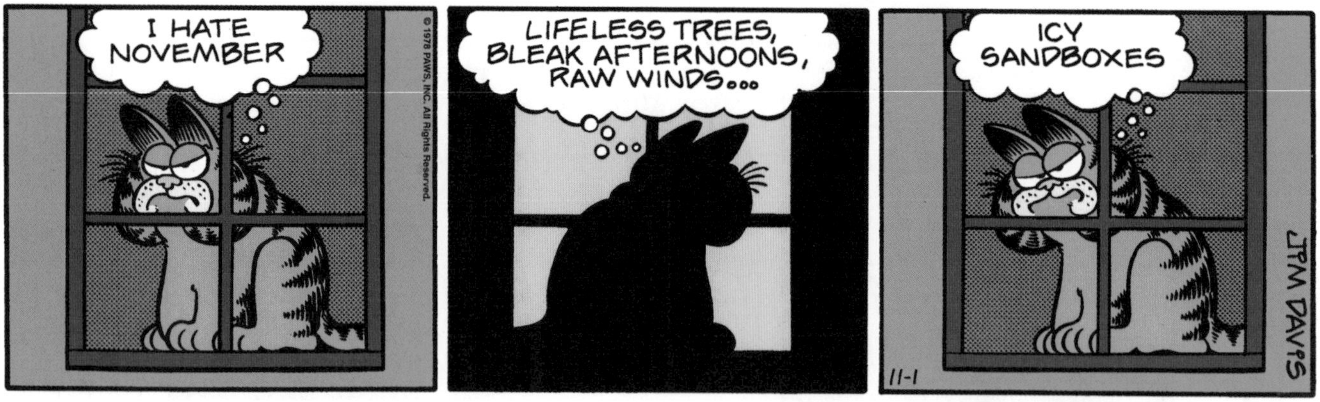
I HATE NOVEMBER
© 1978 PAWS, INC. All Rights Reserved.
LIFELESS TREES, BLEAK AFTERNOONS, RAW WINDS...
ICY SANDBOXES
11-1
JIM DAVIS

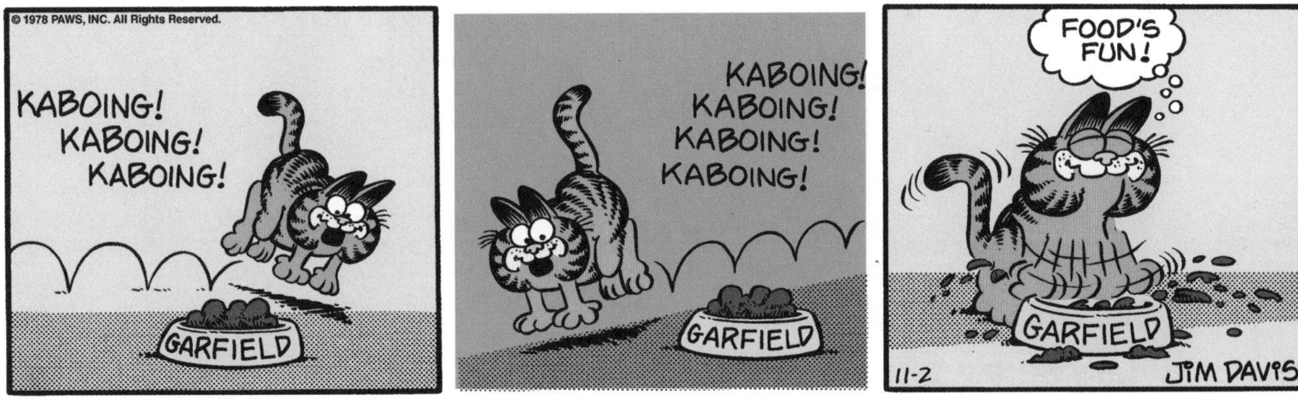
© 1978 PAWS, INC. All Rights Reserved.
KABOING! KABOING! KABOING!
GARFIELD
KABOING! KABOING! KABOING! KABOING!
GARFIELD
FOOD'S FUN!
GARFIELD
11-2
JIM DAVIS

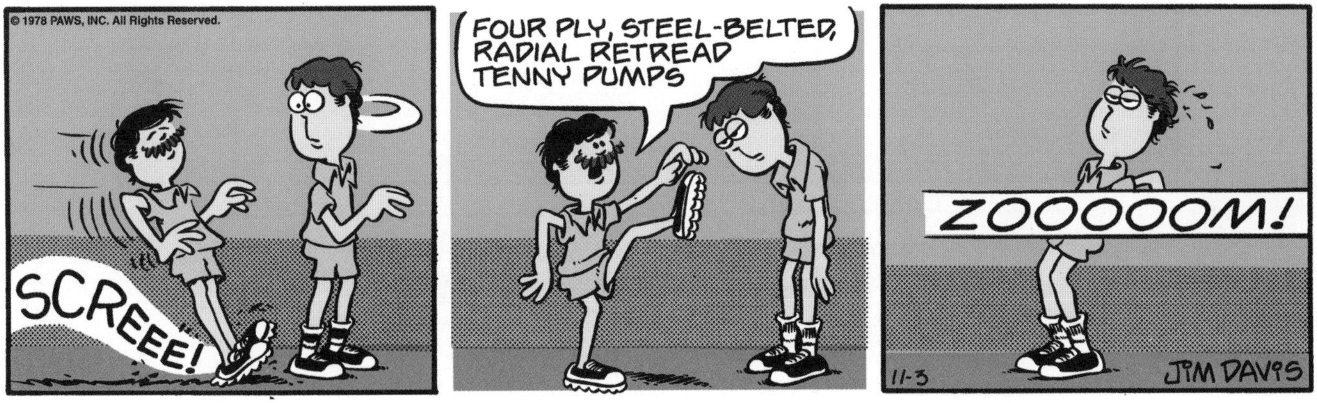
© 1978 PAWS, INC. All Rights Reserved.
SCREEEE!
FOUR PLY, STEEL-BELTED, RADIAL RETREAD TENNY PUMPS
ZOOOOOM!
11-3
JIM DAVIS

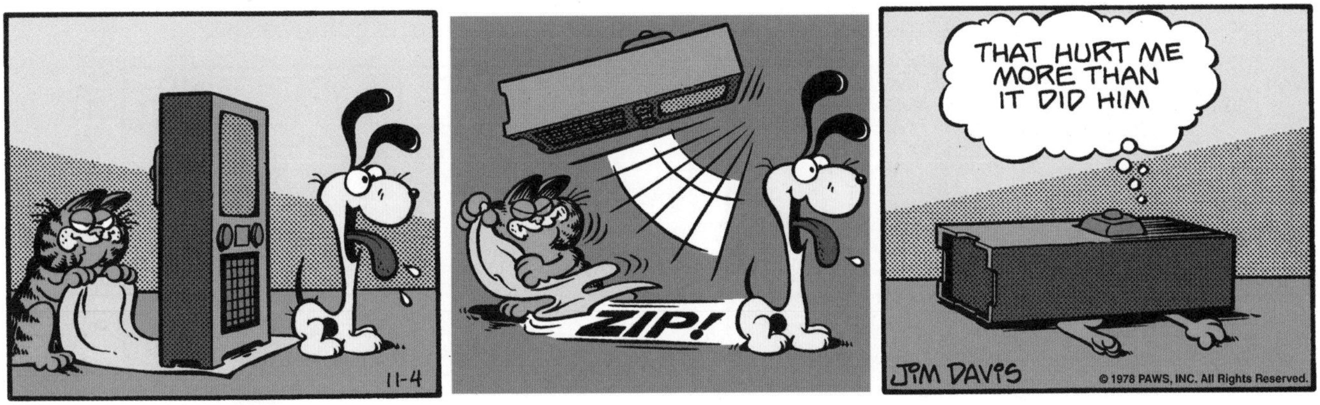
11-4
ZIP!
THAT HURT ME MORE THAN IT DID HIM
JIM DAVIS
© 1978 PAWS, INC. All Rights Reserved.

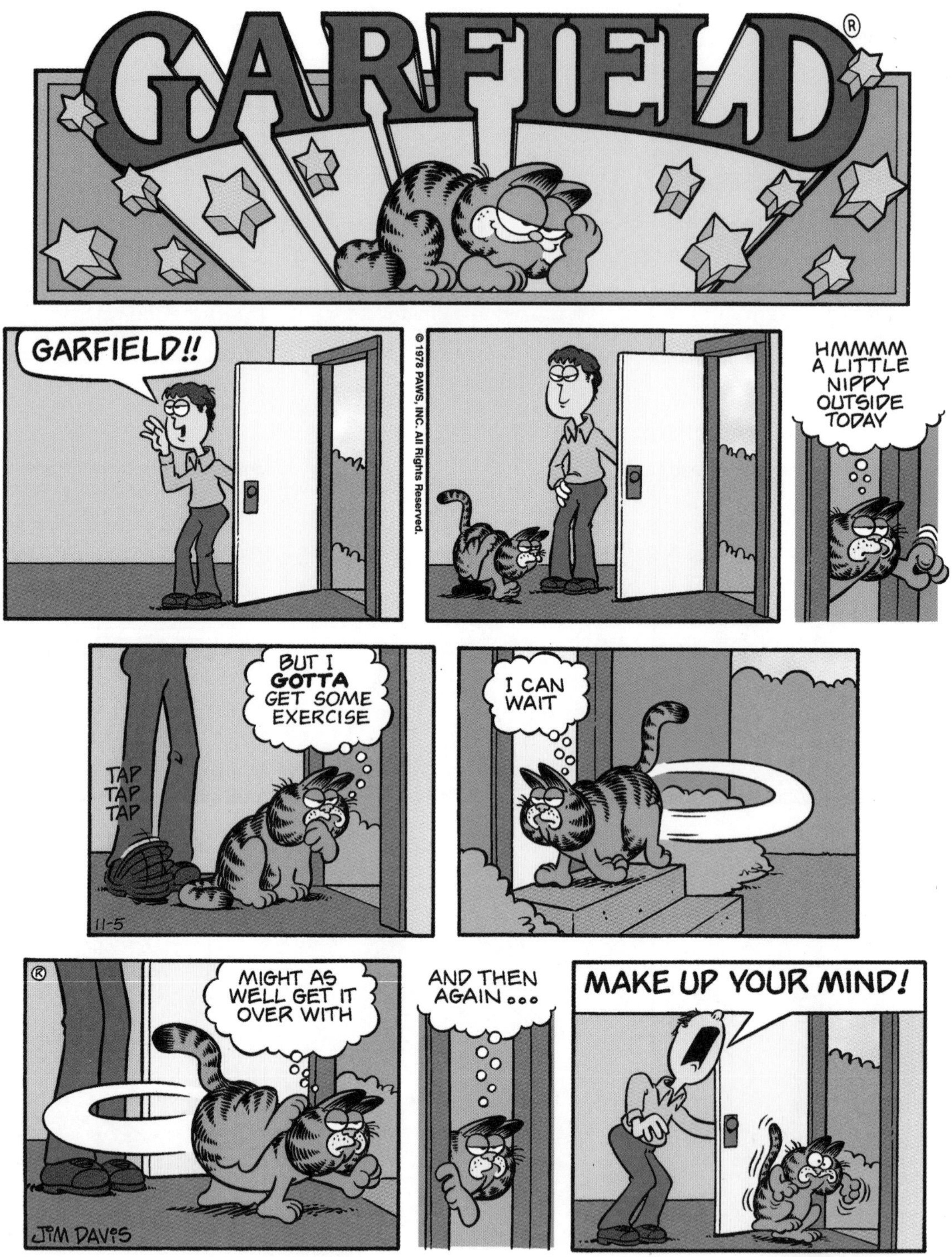
GARFIELD®
GARFIELD!!
© 1978 PAWS, INC. All Rights Reserved.
HMMMM A LITTLE NIPPY OUTSIDE TODAY
TAP TAP TAP
BUT I GOTTA GET SOME EXERCISE
11-5
I CAN WAIT
®
MIGHT AS WELL GET IT OVER WITH
JIM DAVIS
AND THEN AGAIN...
MAKE UP YOUR MIND!

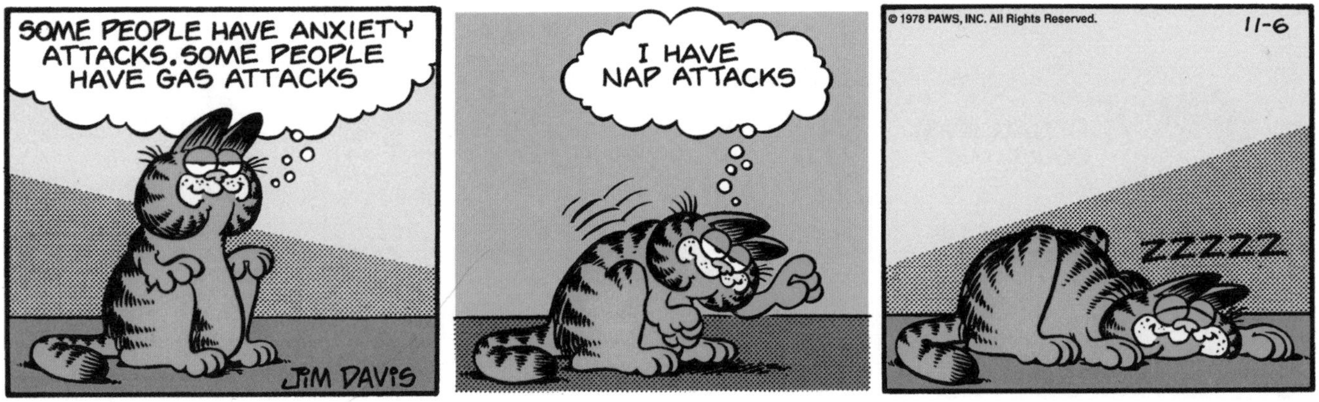
SOME PEOPLE HAVE ANXIETY ATTACKS. SOME PEOPLE HAVE GAS ATTACKS
JIM DAVIS
I HAVE NAP ATTACKS
© 1978 PAWS, INC. All Rights Reserved.
11-6
ZZZZZ

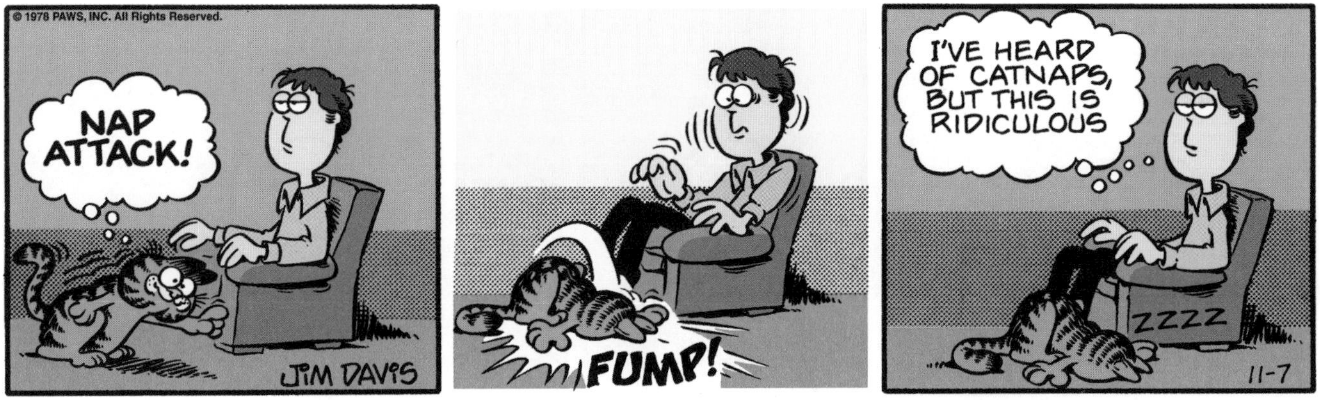
© 1978 PAWS, INC. All Rights Reserved.
NAP ATTACK!
JIM DAVIS
FUMP!
I'VE HEARD OF CATNAPS, BUT THIS IS RIDICULOUS
ZZZZ
11-7

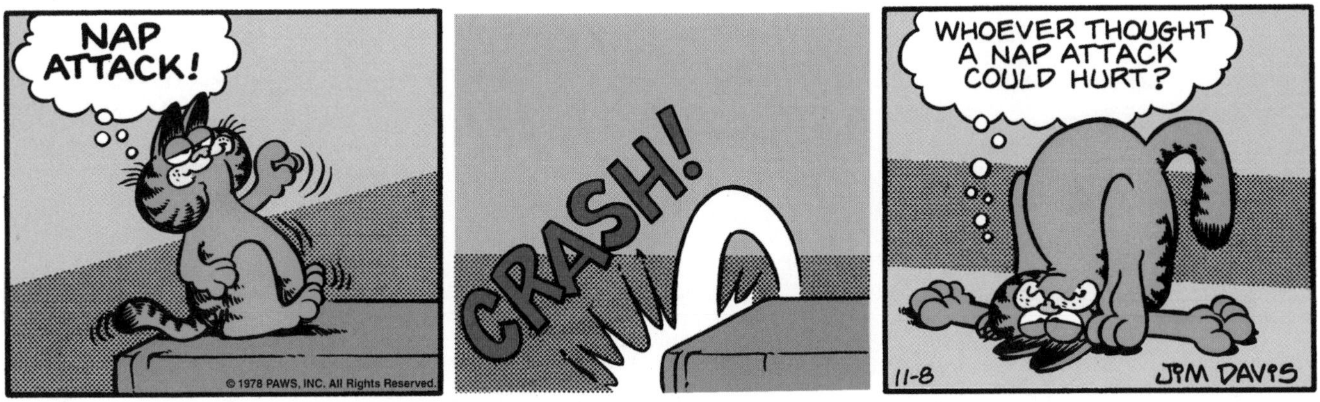
NAP ATTACK!
© 1978 PAWS, INC. All Rights Reserved.
CRASH!
WHOEVER THOUGHT A NAP ATTACK COULD HURT?
11-8
JIM DAVIS

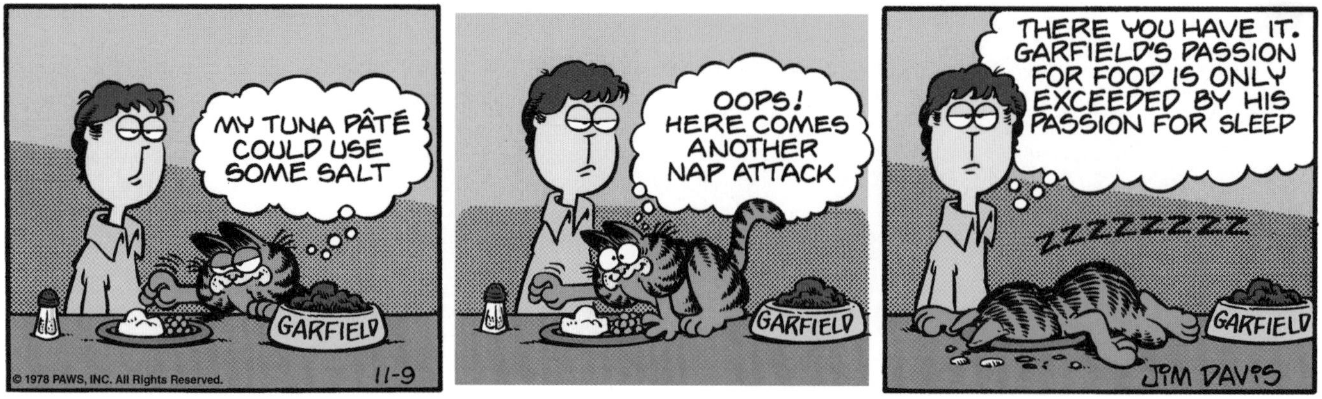
MY TUNA PÂTÉ COULD USE SOME SALT
GARFIELD
© 1978 PAWS, INC. All Rights Reserved.
11-9
OOPS! HERE COMES ANOTHER NAP ATTACK
GARFIELD
THERE YOU HAVE IT. GARFIELD'S PASSION FOR FOOD IS ONLY EXCEEDED BY HIS PASSION FOR SLEEP
ZZZZZZZZ
GARFIELD
JIM DAVIS

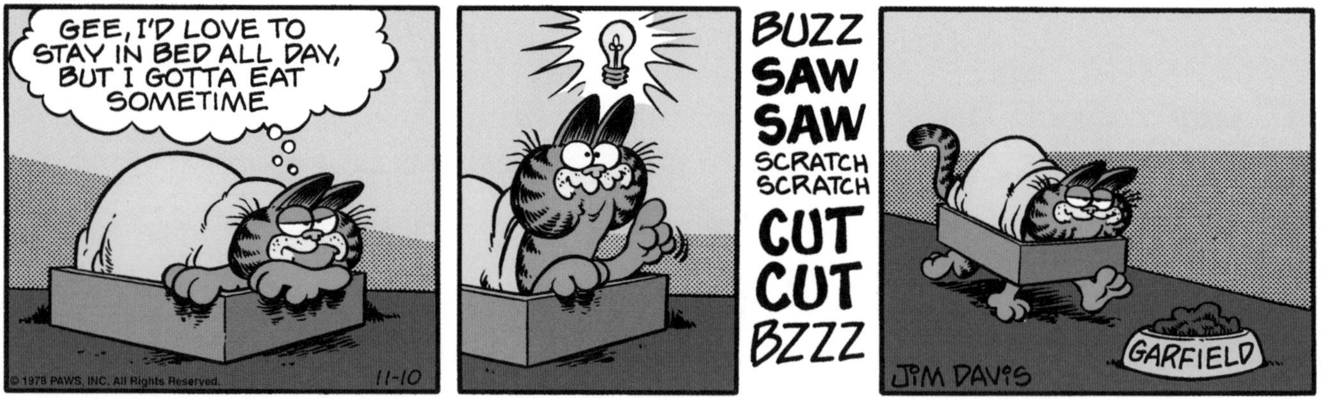
GEE, I'D LOVE TO STAY IN BED ALL DAY, BUT I GOTTA EAT SOMETIME
© 1978 PAWS, INC. All Rights Reserved.
11-10
BUZZ
SAW
SAW
SCRATCH
SCRATCH
CUT
CUT
BZZZ
GARFIELD
JIM DAVIS

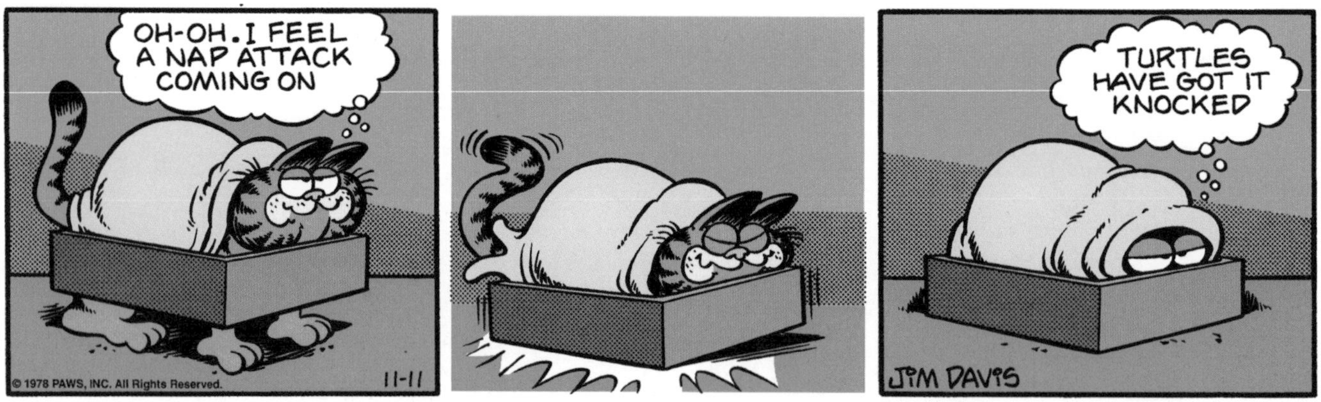
OH-OH. I FEEL A NAP ATTACK COMING ON
© 1978 PAWS, INC. All Rights Reserved.
11-11
TURTLES HAVE GOT IT KNOCKED
JIM DAVIS

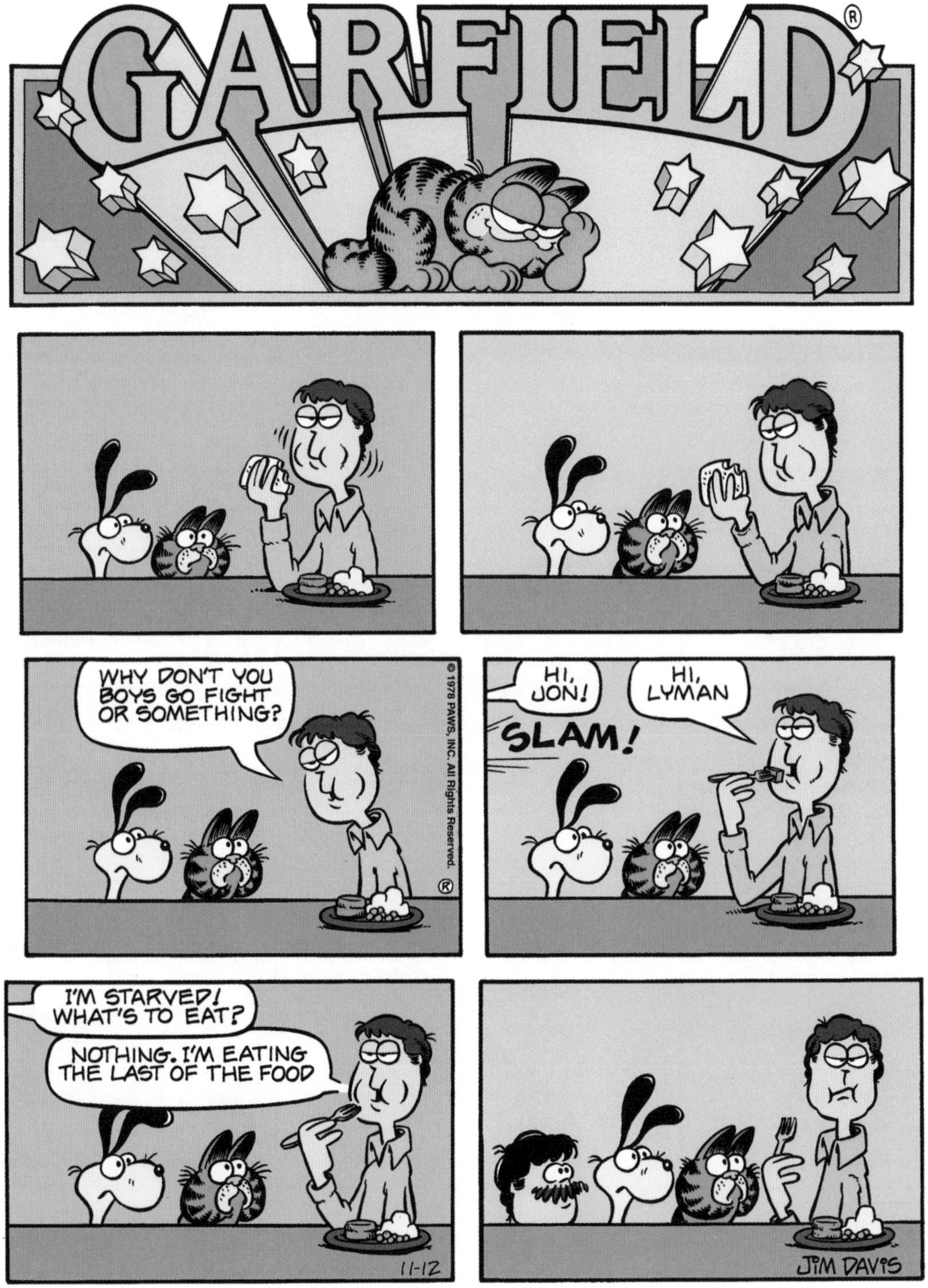
GARFIELD®
WHY DON'T YOU BOYS GO FIGHT OR SOMETHING?
© 1978 PAWS, INC. All Rights Reserved.
HI, JON!
HI, LYMAN
SLAM!
I'M STARVED! WHAT'S TO EAT?
NOTHING. I'M EATING THE LAST OF THE FOOD
11-12
JIM DAVIS

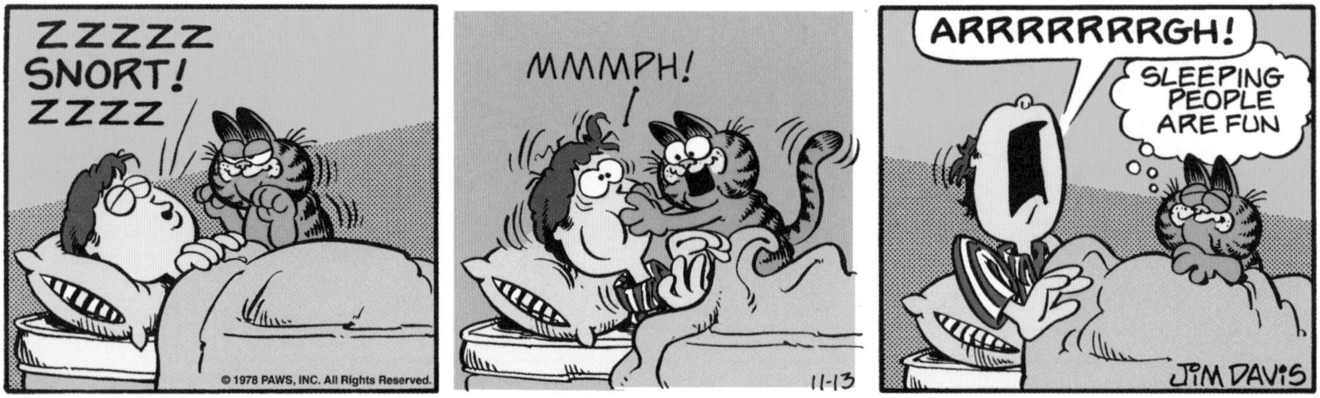
ZZZZZ
SNORT!
ZZZZ
© 1978 PAWS, INC. All Rights Reserved.
MMMPH!
11-13
ARRRRRRRGH!
SLEEPING PEOPLE ARE FUN
JIM DAVIS

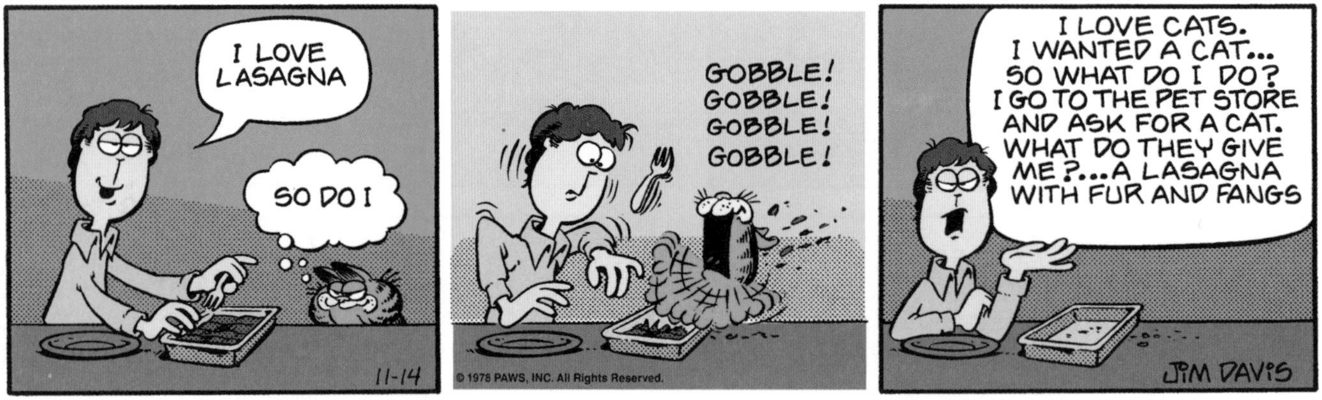
I LOVE LASAGNA
SO DO I
11-14
GOBBLE! GOBBLE! GOBBLE! GOBBLE!
© 1978 PAWS, INC. All Rights Reserved.
I LOVE CATS. I WANTED A CAT... SO WHAT DO I DO? I GO TO THE PET STORE AND ASK FOR A CAT. WHAT DO THEY GIVE ME?...A LASAGNA WITH FUR AND FANGS
JIM DAVIS

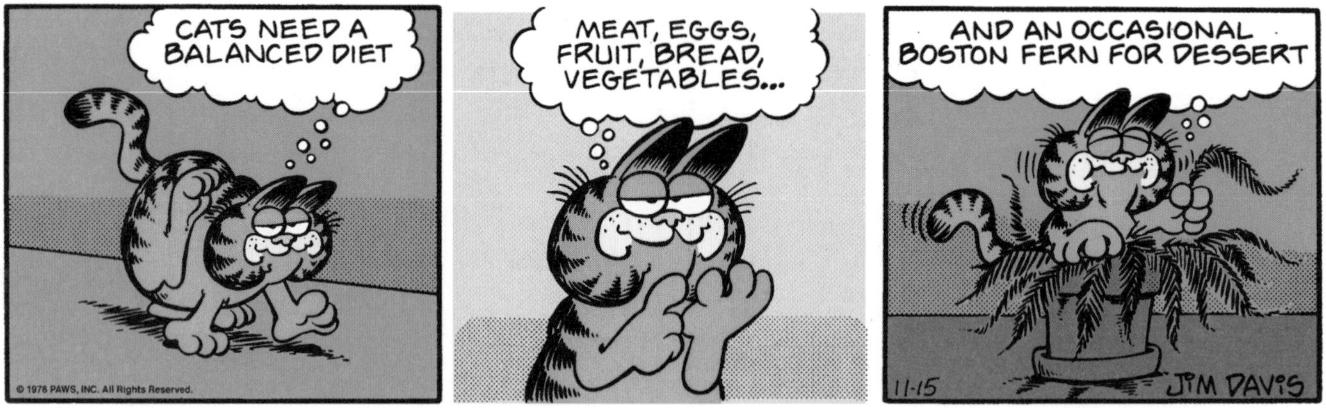
CATS NEED A BALANCED DIET
© 1978 PAWS, INC. All Rights Reserved.
MEAT, EGGS, FRUIT, BREAD, VEGETABLES...
AND AN OCCASIONAL BOSTON FERN FOR DESSERT
11-15
JIM DAVIS

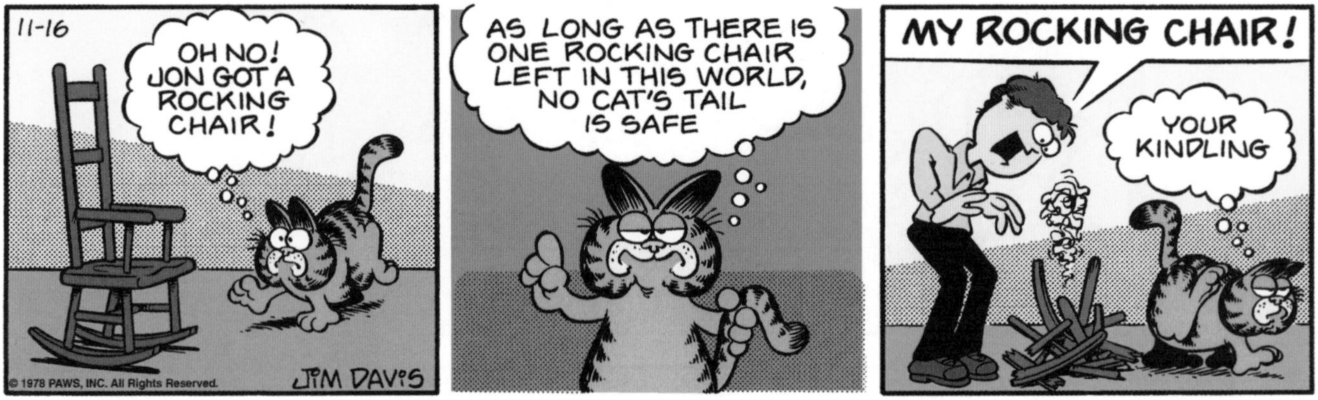
11-16
OH NO! JON GOT A ROCKING CHAIR!
© 1978 PAWS, INC. All Rights Reserved.
JIM DAVIS
AS LONG AS THERE IS ONE ROCKING CHAIR LEFT IN THIS WORLD, NO CAT'S TAIL IS SAFE
MY ROCKING CHAIR!
YOUR KINDLING

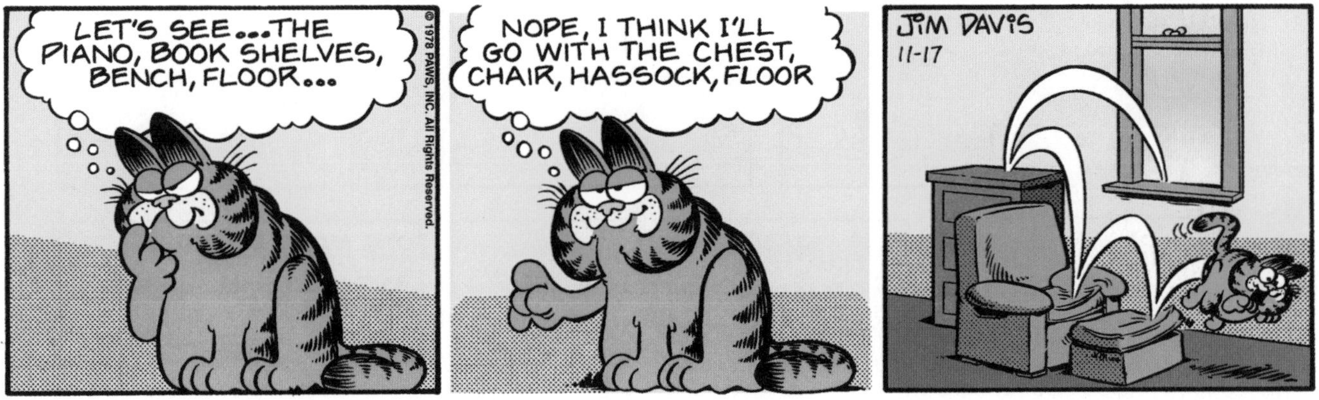
LET'S SEE...THE PIANO, BOOK SHELVES, BENCH, FLOOR...
© 1978 PAWS, INC. All Rights Reserved.
NOPE, I THINK I'LL GO WITH THE CHEST, CHAIR, HASSOCK, FLOOR
JIM DAVIS
11-17

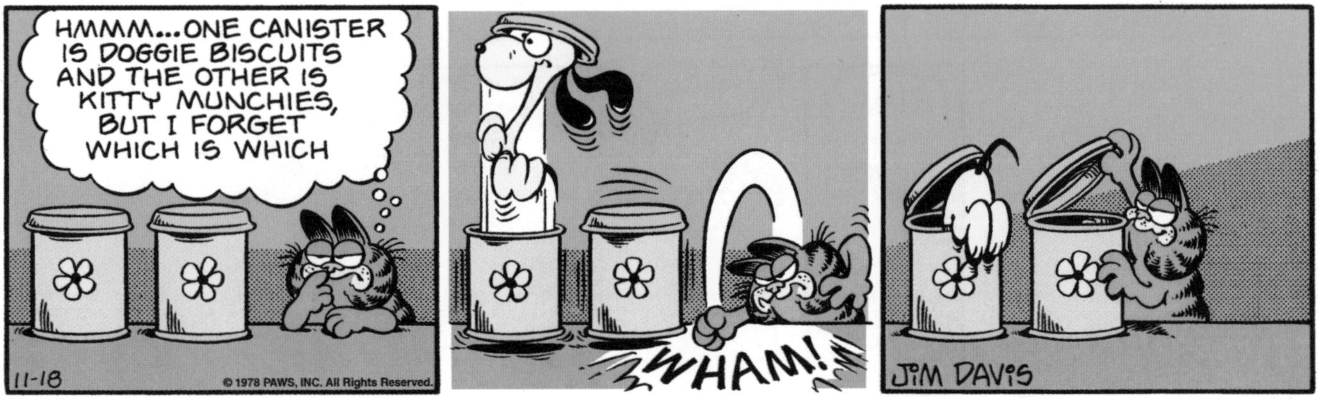
HMMM...ONE CANISTER IS DOGGIE BISCUITS AND THE OTHER IS KITTY MUNCHIES, BUT I FORGET WHICH IS WHICH
11-18
© 1978 PAWS, INC. All Rights Reserved.
WHAM!
JIM DAVIS

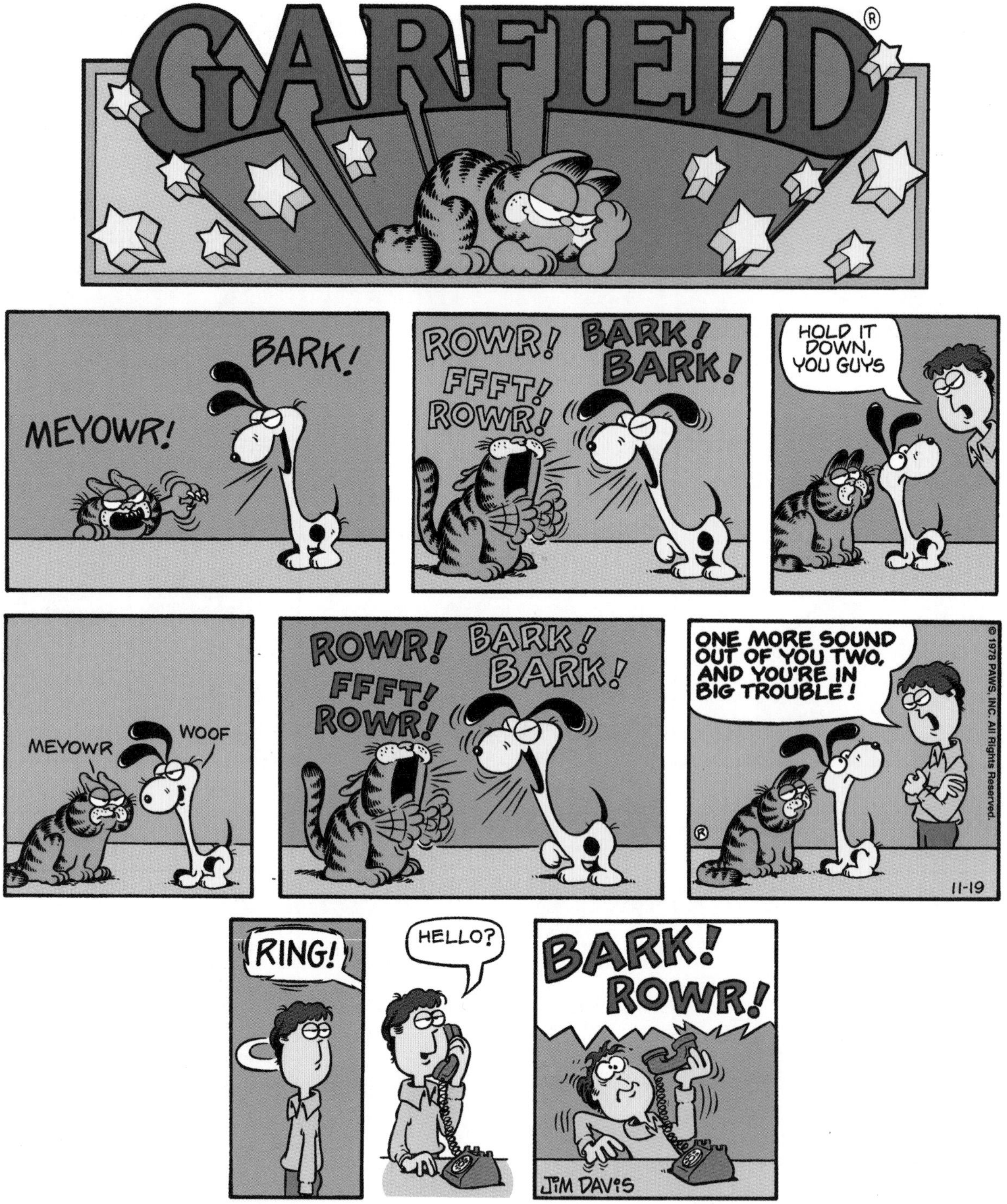
GARFIELD
MEYOWR!
BARK!
ROWR!
FFFT!
ROWR!
BARK!
BARK!
HOLD IT DOWN, YOU GUYS
MEYOWR
WOOF
ROWR!
FFFT!
ROWR!
BARK!
BARK!
ONE MORE SOUND OUT OF YOU TWO, AND YOU'RE IN BIG TROUBLE!
© 1978 PAWS, INC. All Rights Reserved.
11-19
RING!
HELLO?
BARK!
ROWR!
JIM DAVIS

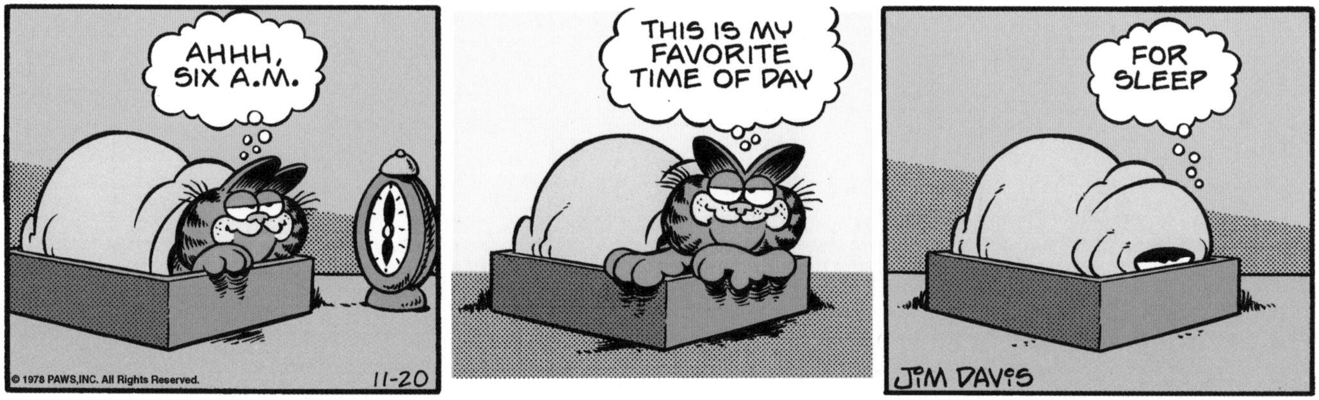
AHHH, SIX A.M.
THIS IS MY FAVORITE TIME OF DAY
FOR SLEEP
© 1978 PAWS,INC. All Rights Reserved.
11-20
JIM DAVIS

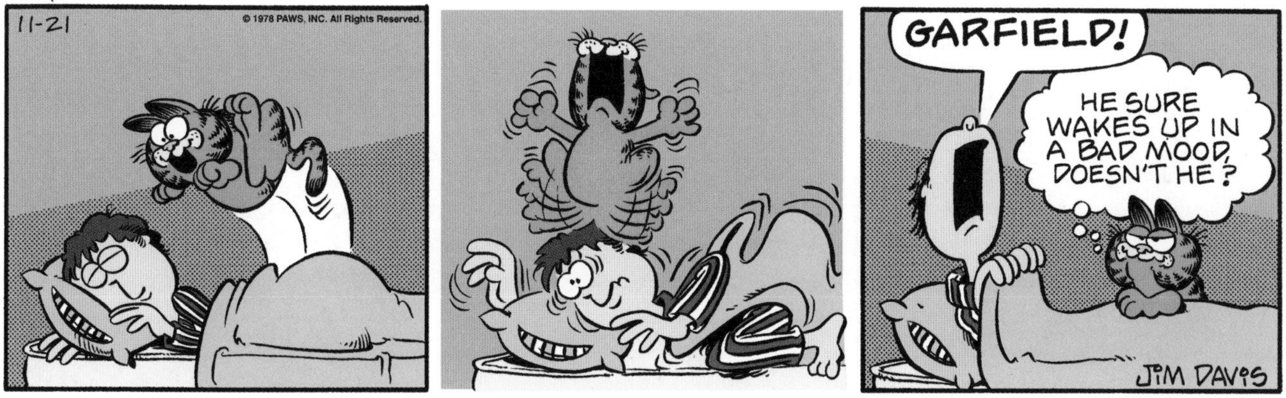
11-21
© 1978 PAWS, INC. All Rights Reserved.
GARFIELD!
HE SURE WAKES UP IN A BAD MOOD, DOESN'T HE?
JIM DAVIS

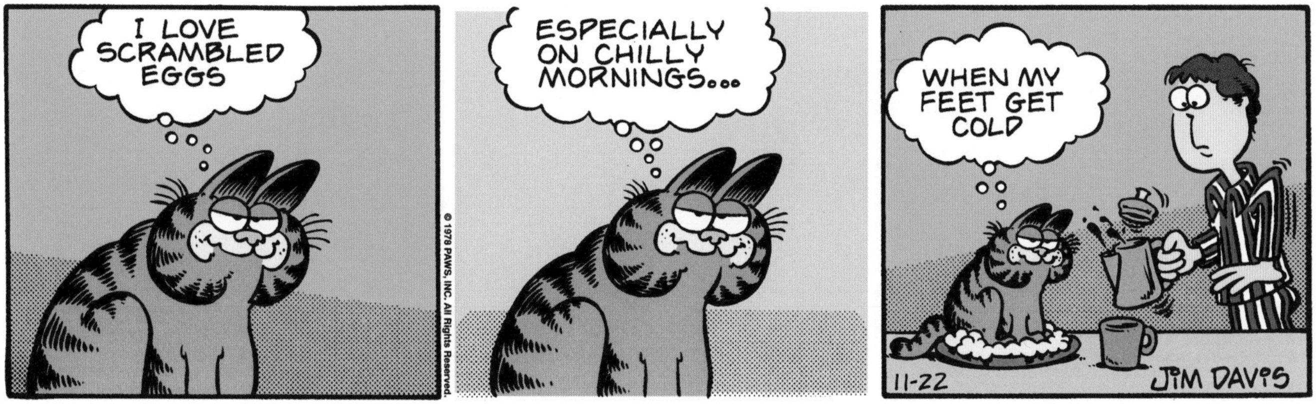
I LOVE SCRAMBLED EGGS
© 1978 PAWS, INC. All Rights Reserved.
ESPECIALLY ON CHILLY MORNINGS...
WHEN MY FEET GET COLD
11-22
JIM DAVIS

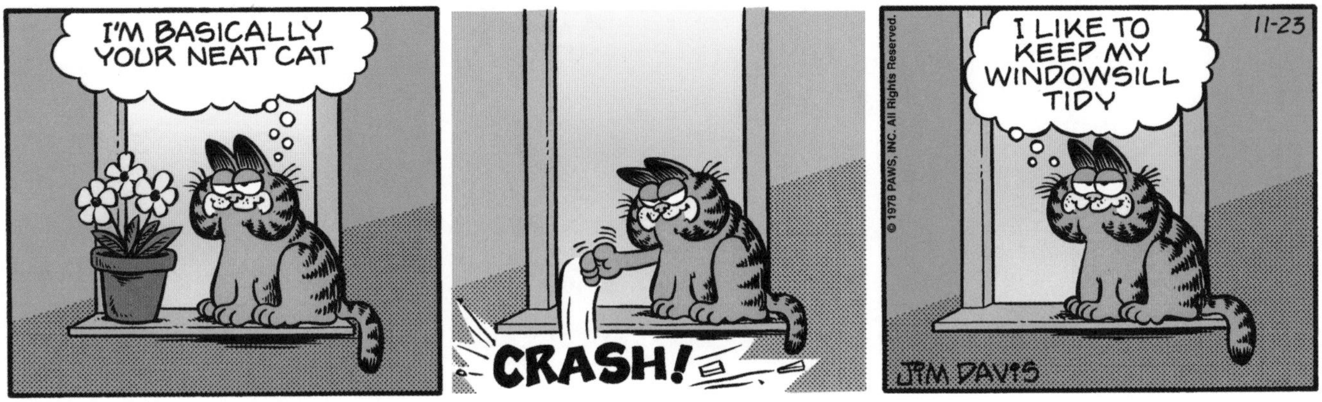
I'M BASICALLY YOUR NEAT CAT
CRASH!
I LIKE TO KEEP MY WINDOWSILL TIDY
© 1978 PAWS, INC. All Rights Reserved.
11-23
JIM DAVIS

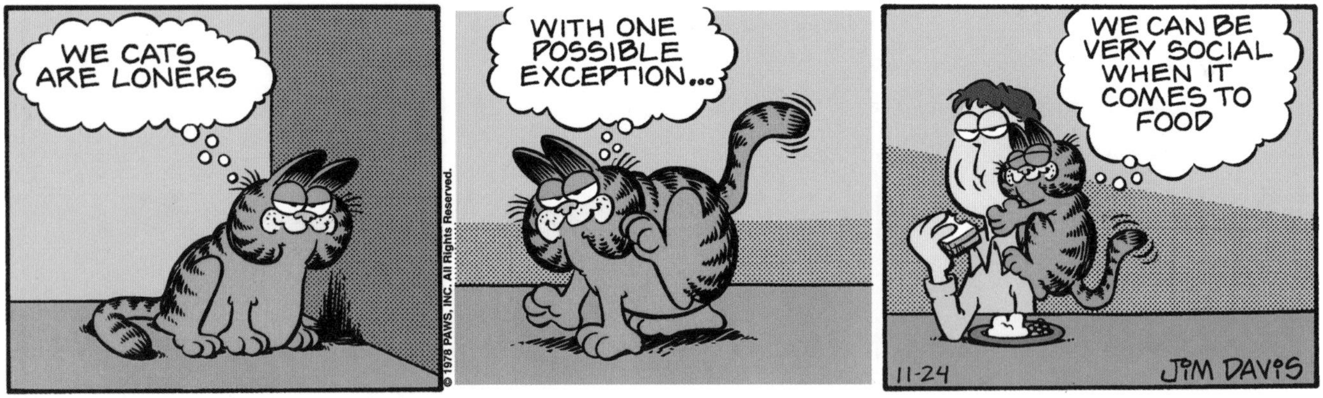
WE CATS ARE LONERS
© 1978 PAWS, INC. All Rights Reserved.
WITH ONE POSSIBLE EXCEPTION...
WE CAN BE VERY SOCIAL WHEN IT COMES TO FOOD
11-24
JIM DAVIS

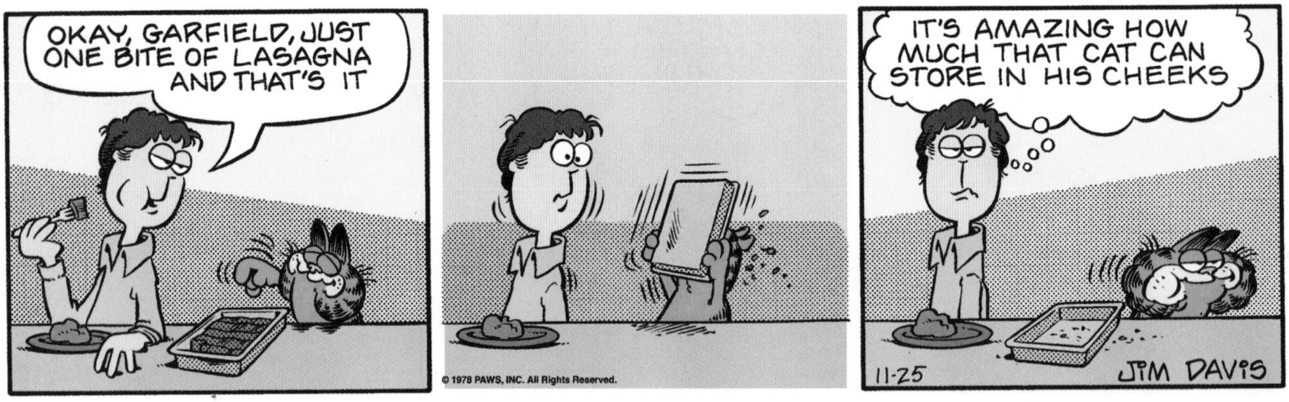
OKAY, GARFIELD, JUST ONE BITE OF LASAGNA AND THAT'S IT
© 1978 PAWS, INC. All Rights Reserved.
IT'S AMAZING HOW MUCH THAT CAT CAN STORE IN HIS CHEEKS
11-25
JIM DAVIS

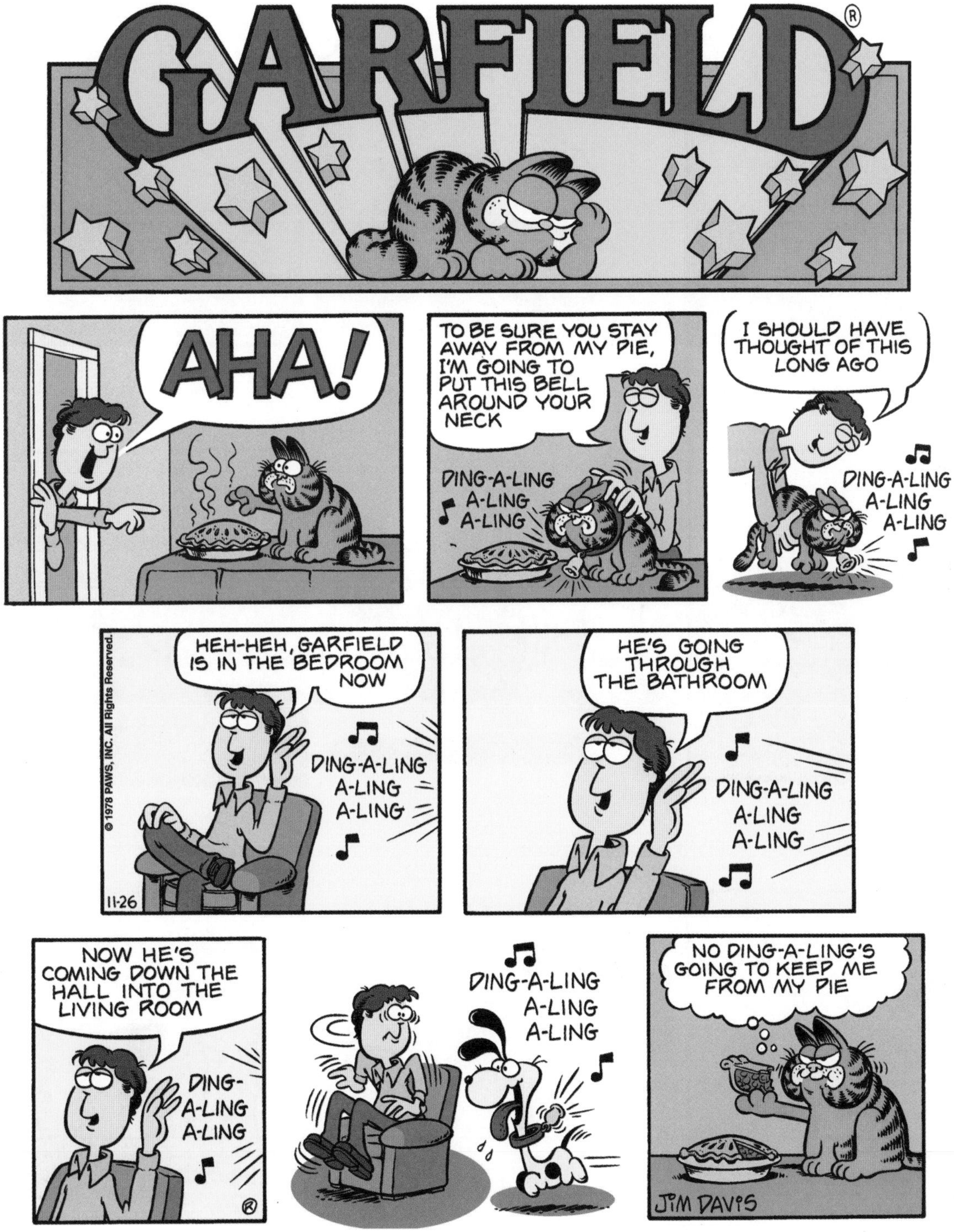
GARFIELD®
AHA!
TO BE SURE YOU STAY AWAY FROM MY PIE, I'M GOING TO PUT THIS BELL AROUND YOUR NECK
DING-A-LING A-LING A-LING
I SHOULD HAVE THOUGHT OF THIS LONG AGO
DING-A-LING A-LING A-LING
HEH-HEH, GARFIELD IS IN THE BEDROOM NOW
DING-A-LING A-LING A-LING
© 1978 PAWS, INC. All Rights Reserved.
11-26
HE'S GOING THROUGH THE BATHROOM
DING-A-LING A-LING A-LING
NOW HE'S COMING DOWN THE HALL INTO THE LIVING ROOM
DING-A-LING A-LING
DING-A-LING A-LING A-LING
NO DING-A-LING'S GOING TO KEEP ME FROM MY PIE
JIM DAVIS

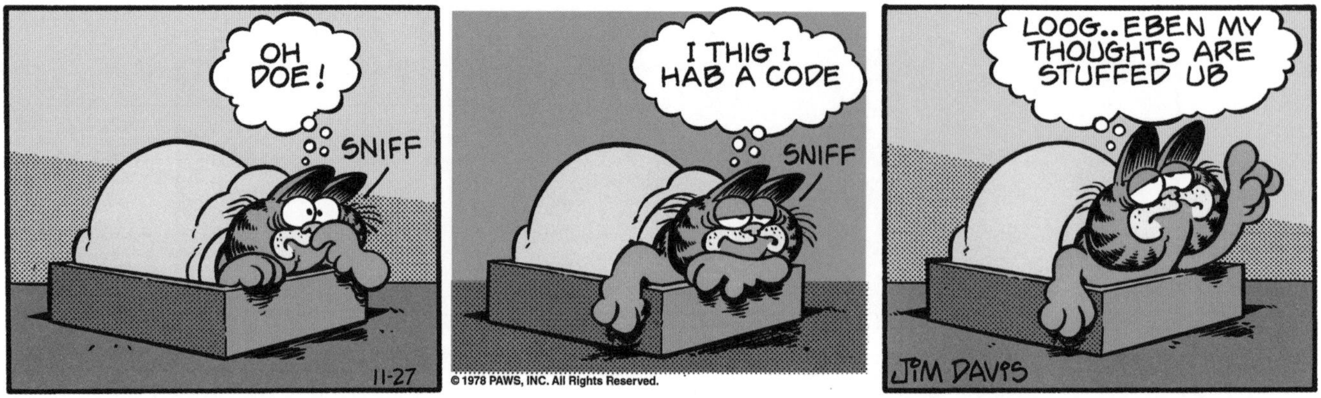
OH DOE!
SNIFF
11-27
I THIG I HAB A CODE
SNIFF
© 1978 PAWS, INC. All Rights Reserved.
LOOG.. EBEN MY THOUGHTS ARE STUFFED UB
JIM DAVIS

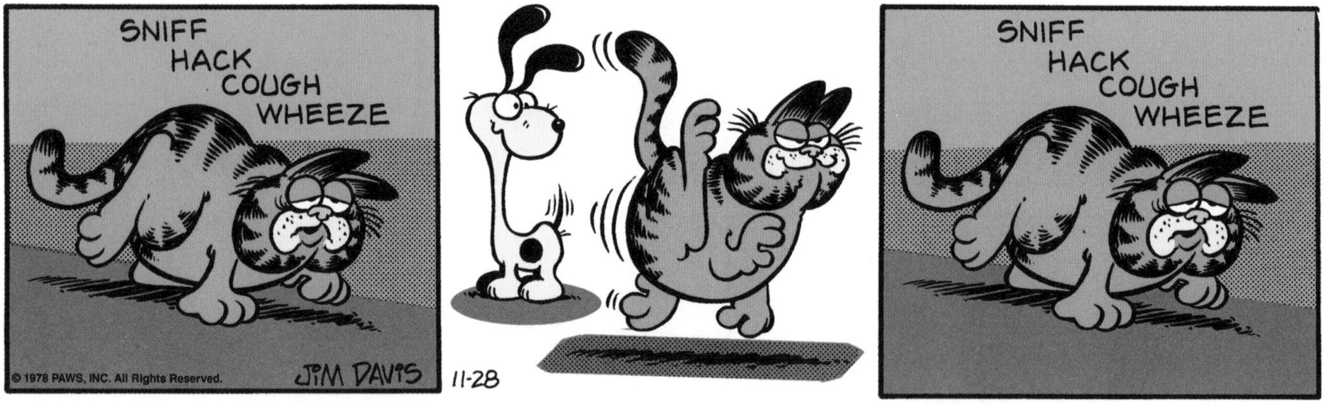
SNIFF
HACK
COUGH
WHEEZE
© 1978 PAWS, INC. All Rights Reserved.
JIM DAVIS
11-28
SNIFF
HACK
COUGH
WHEEZE

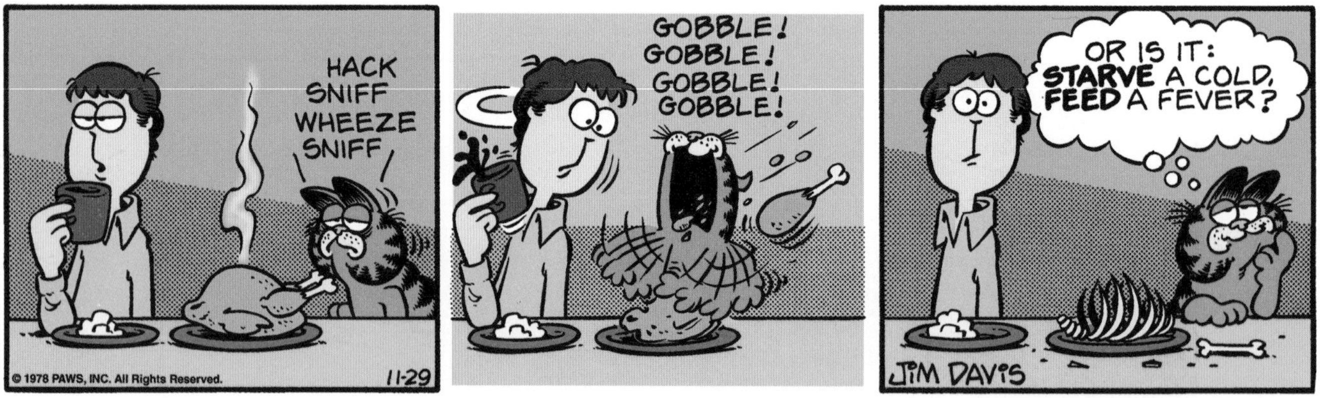
HACK
SNIFF
WHEEZE
SNIFF
© 1978 PAWS, INC. All Rights Reserved.
11-29
GOBBLE! GOBBLE! GOBBLE! GOBBLE!
OR IS IT: STARVE A COLD, FEED A FEVER?
JIM DAVIS

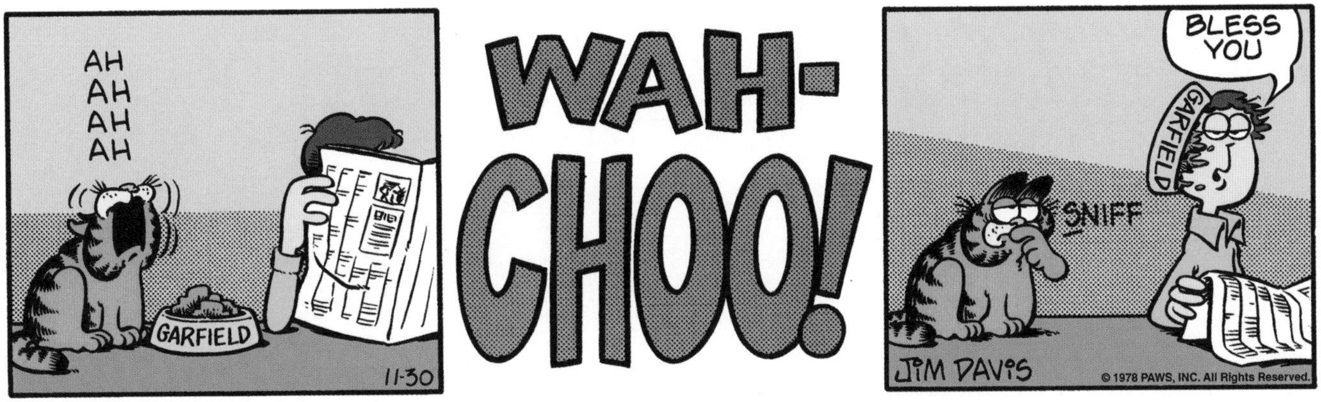
AH AH AH AH
GARFIELD
11-30
WAH-CHOO!
BLESS YOU
SNIFF
GARFIELD
JIM DAVIS
© 1978 PAWS, INC. All Rights Reserved.

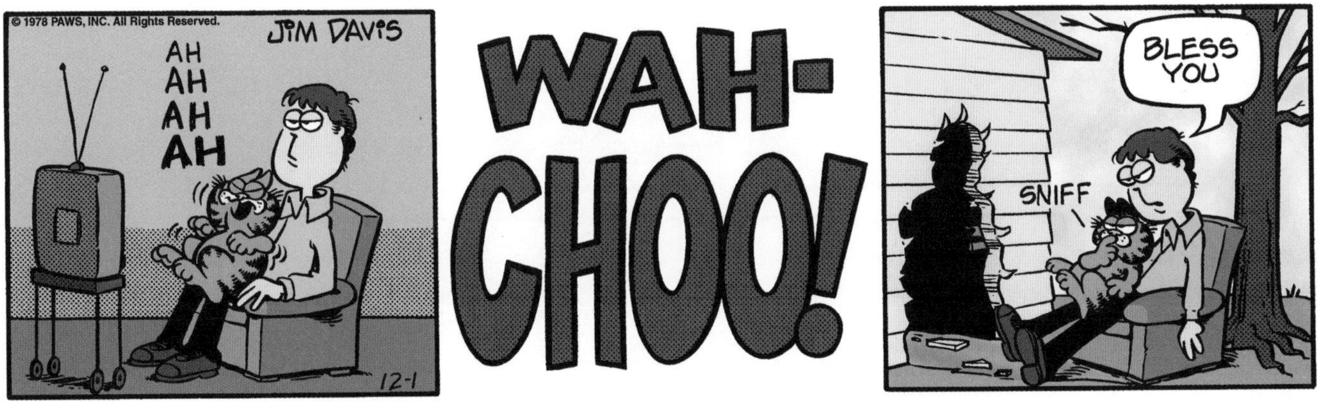
© 1978 PAWS, INC. All Rights Reserved.
JIM DAVIS
AH AH AH AH
12-1
WAH-CHOO!
BLESS YOU
SNIFF

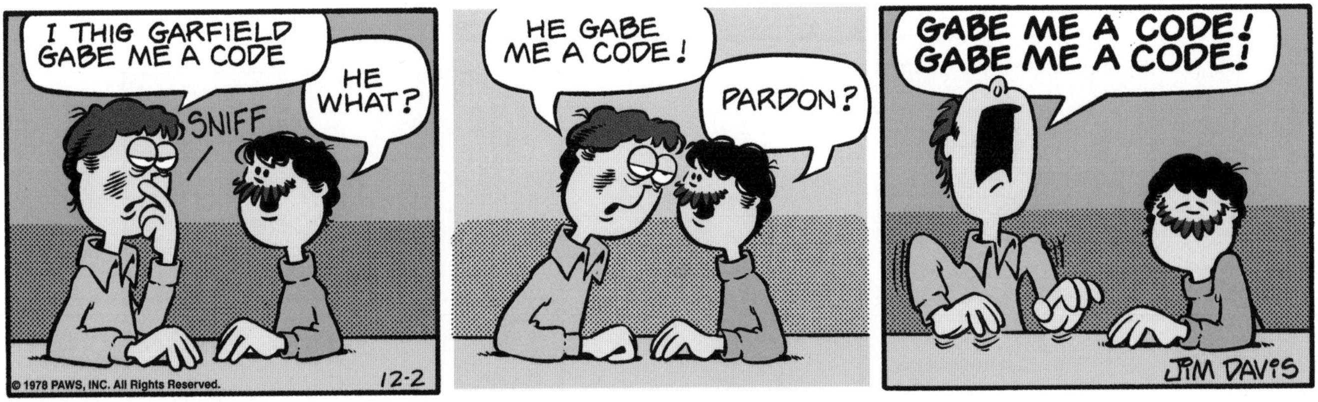
I THIG GARFIELD GABE ME A CODE
SNIFF
HE WHAT?
© 1978 PAWS, INC. All Rights Reserved.
12-2
HE GABE ME A CODE!
PARDON?
GABE ME A CODE! GABE ME A CODE!
JIM DAVIS

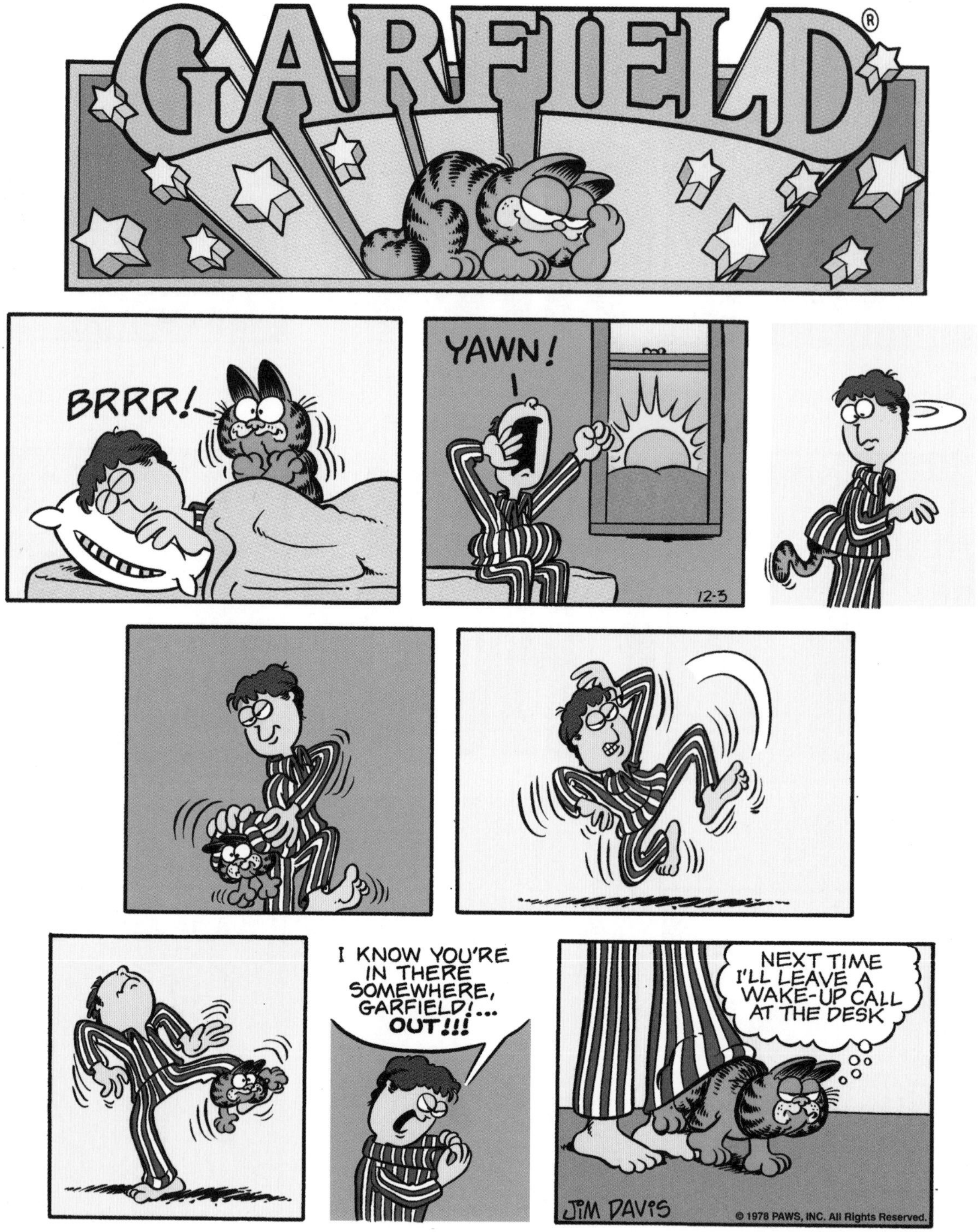
GARFIELD®
BRRR!
YAWN!
12-3
I KNOW YOU'RE IN THERE SOMEWHERE, GARFIELD!... OUT!!!
NEXT TIME I'LL LEAVE A WAKE-UP CALL AT THE DESK
JIM DAVIS
© 1978 PAWS, INC. All Rights Reserved.

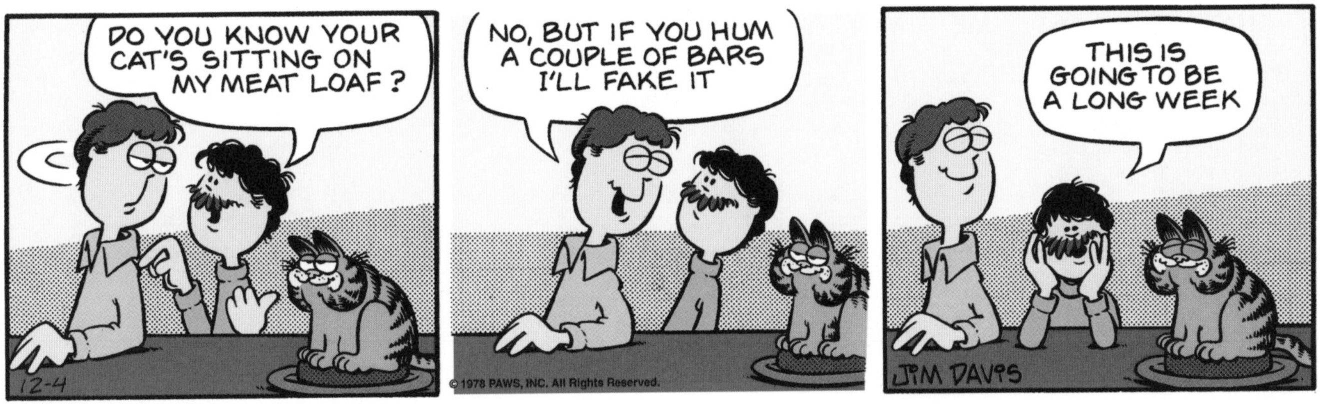
DO YOU KNOW YOUR CAT'S SITTING ON MY MEAT LOAF ?
12-4
NO, BUT IF YOU HUM A COUPLE OF BARS I'LL FAKE IT
© 1978 PAWS, INC. All Rights Reserved.
THIS IS GOING TO BE A LONG WEEK
JIM DAVIS

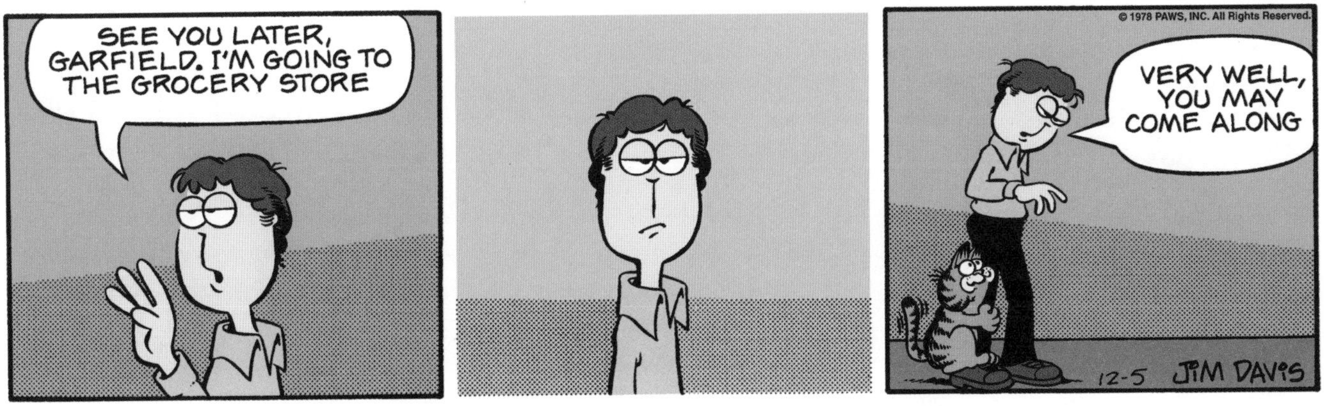
SEE YOU LATER, GARFIELD. I'M GOING TO THE GROCERY STORE
© 1978 PAWS, INC. All Rights Reserved.
VERY WELL, YOU MAY COME ALONG
12-5
JIM DAVIS

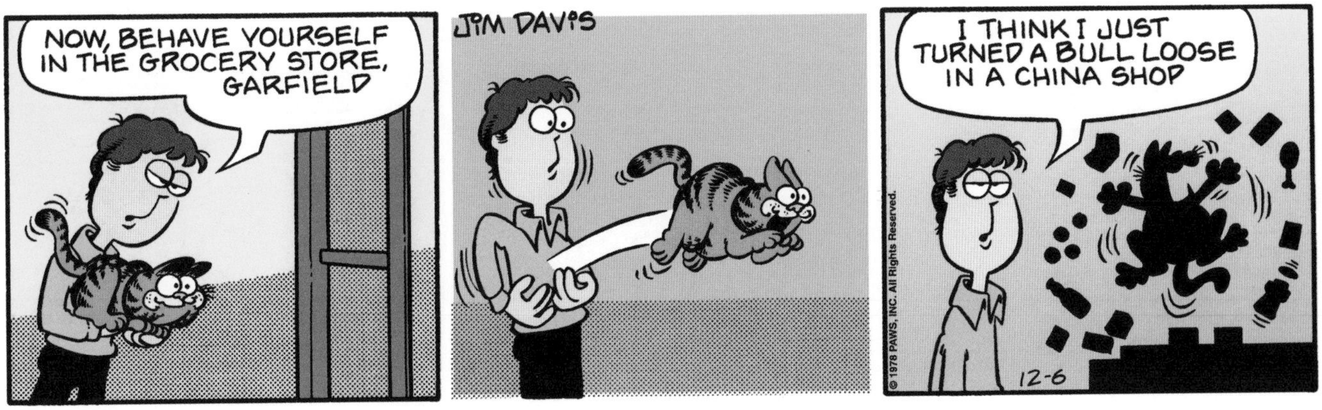
NOW, BEHAVE YOURSELF IN THE GROCERY STORE, GARFIELD
JIM DAVIS
© 1978 PAWS, INC. All Rights Reserved.
I THINK I JUST TURNED A BULL LOOSE IN A CHINA SHOP
12-6

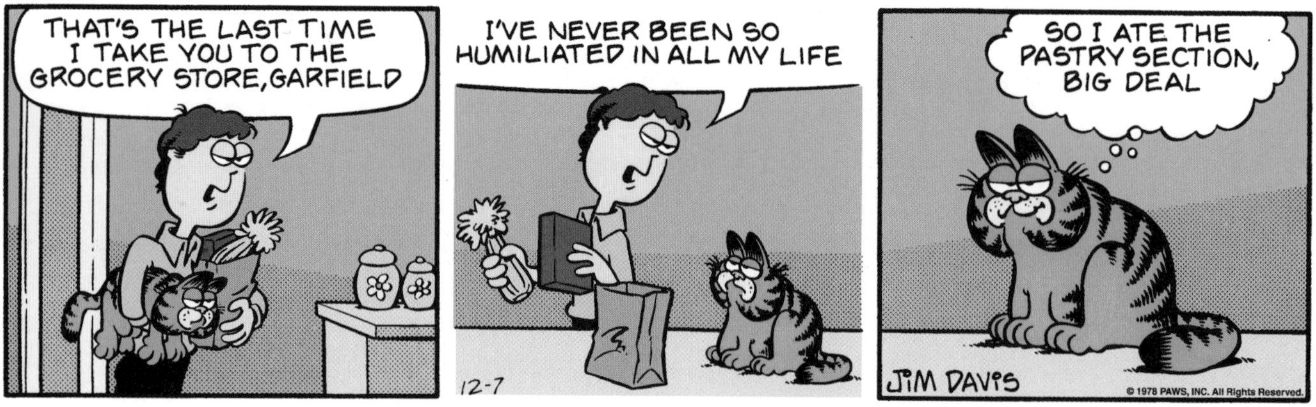
THAT'S THE LAST TIME I TAKE YOU TO THE GROCERY STORE, GARFIELD
I'VE NEVER BEEN SO HUMILIATED IN ALL MY LIFE
12-7
SO I ATE THE PASTRY SECTION, BIG DEAL
JIM DAVIS
© 1978 PAWS, INC. All Rights Reserved.

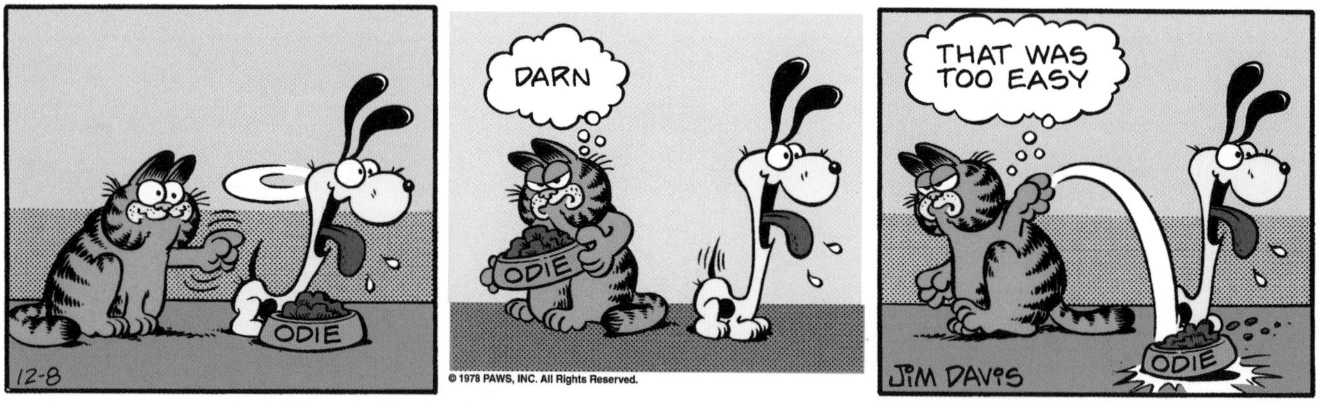
ODIE
12-8
DARN
ODIE
© 1978 PAWS, INC. All Rights Reserved.
THAT WAS TOO EASY
ODIE
JIM DAVIS

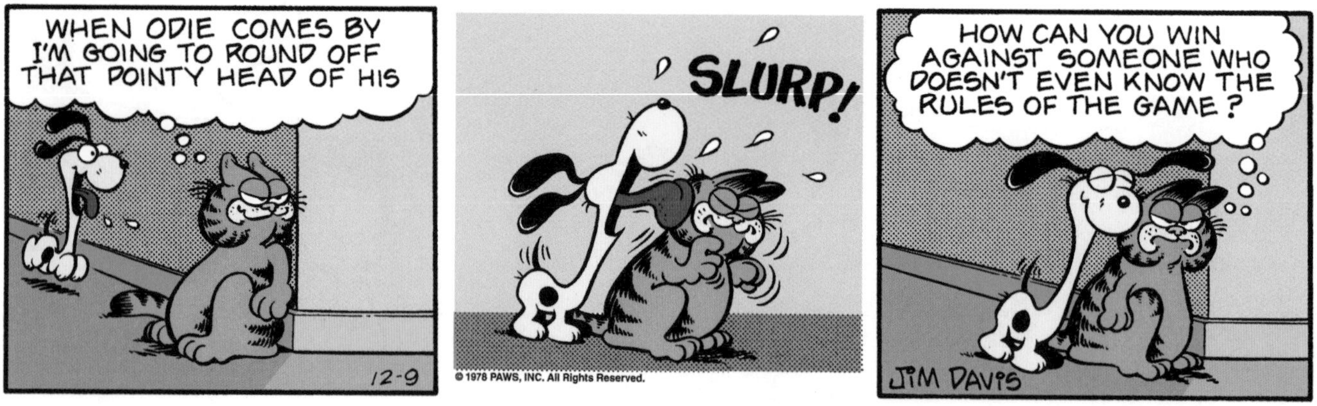
WHEN ODIE COMES BY I'M GOING TO ROUND OFF THAT POINTY HEAD OF HIS
12-9
SLURP!
© 1978 PAWS, INC. All Rights Reserved.
HOW CAN YOU WIN AGAINST SOMEONE WHO DOESN'T EVEN KNOW THE RULES OF THE GAME?
JIM DAVIS

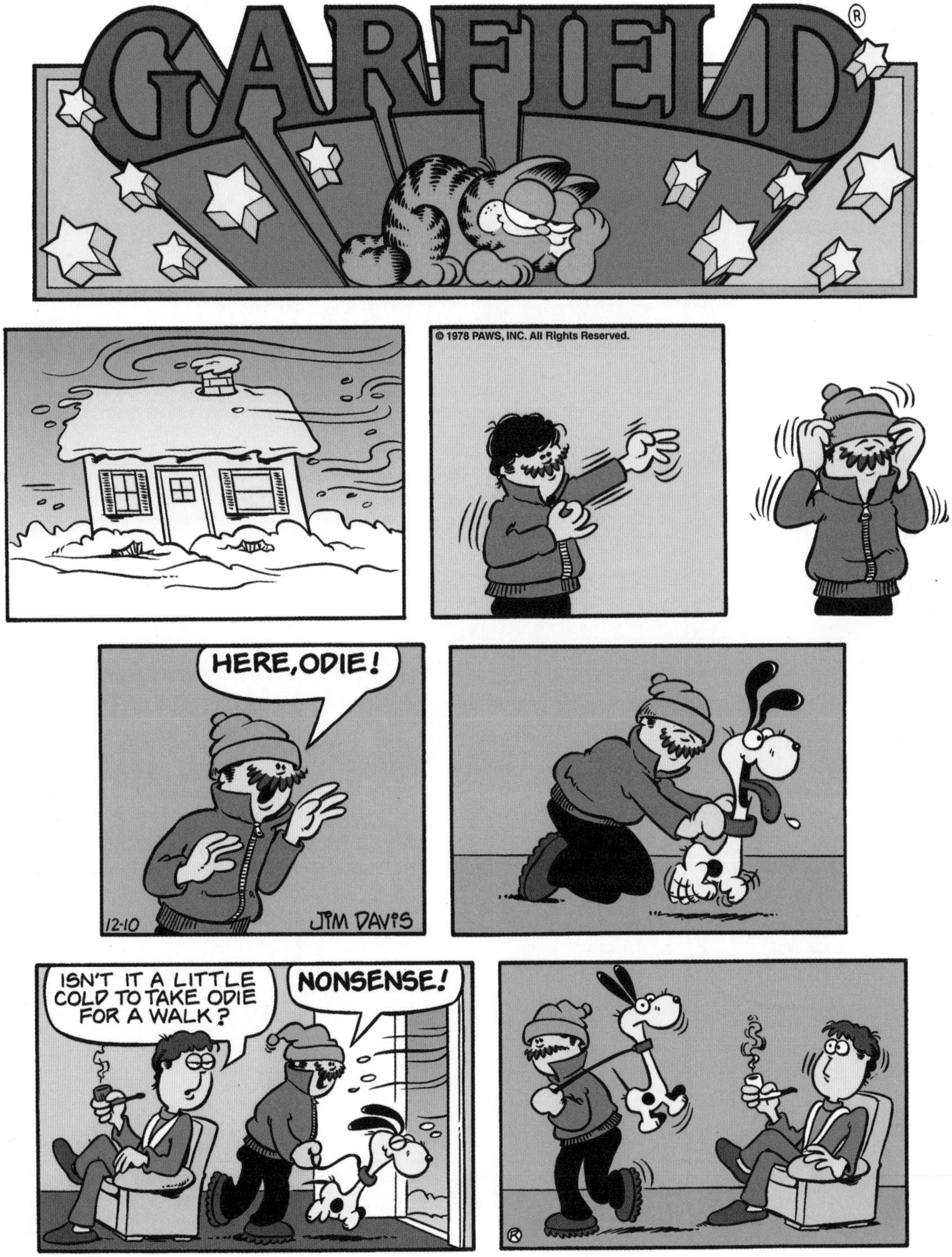
GARFIELD®
© 1978 PAWS, INC. All Rights Reserved.
HERE, ODIE!
12-10
JIM DAVIS
ISN'T IT A LITTLE COLD TO TAKE ODIE FOR A WALK?
NONSENSE!

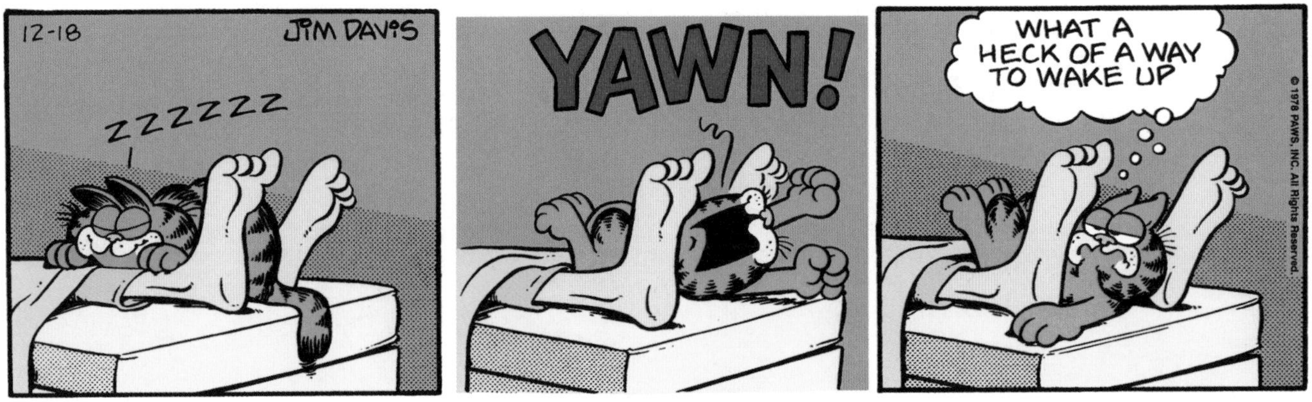
12-18
JIM DAVIS
ZZZZZZ
YAWN!
WHAT A HECK OF A WAY TO WAKE UP
© 1978 PAWS, INC. All Rights Reserved.

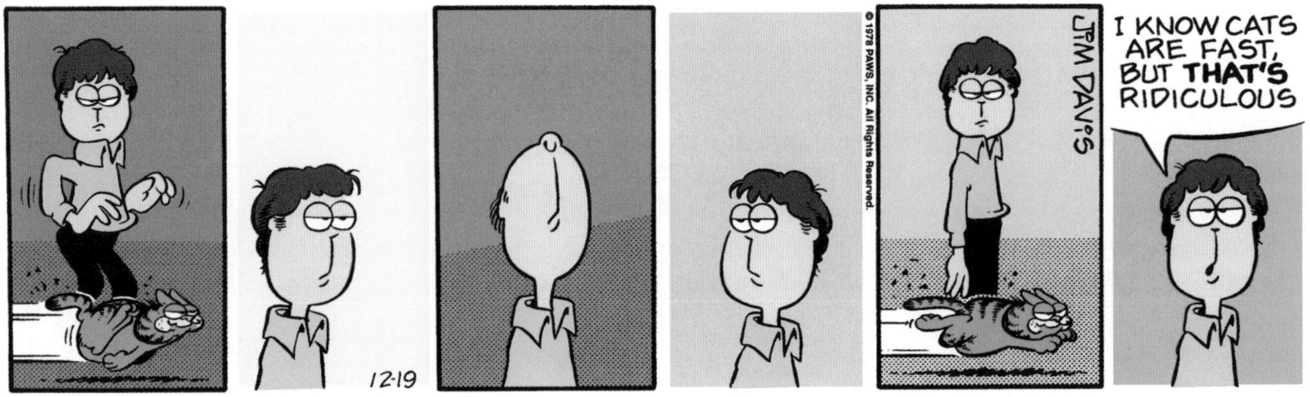
12·19
© 1978 PAWS, INC. All Rights Reserved.
JIM DAVIS
I KNOW CATS ARE FAST, BUT **THAT'S** RIDICULOUS

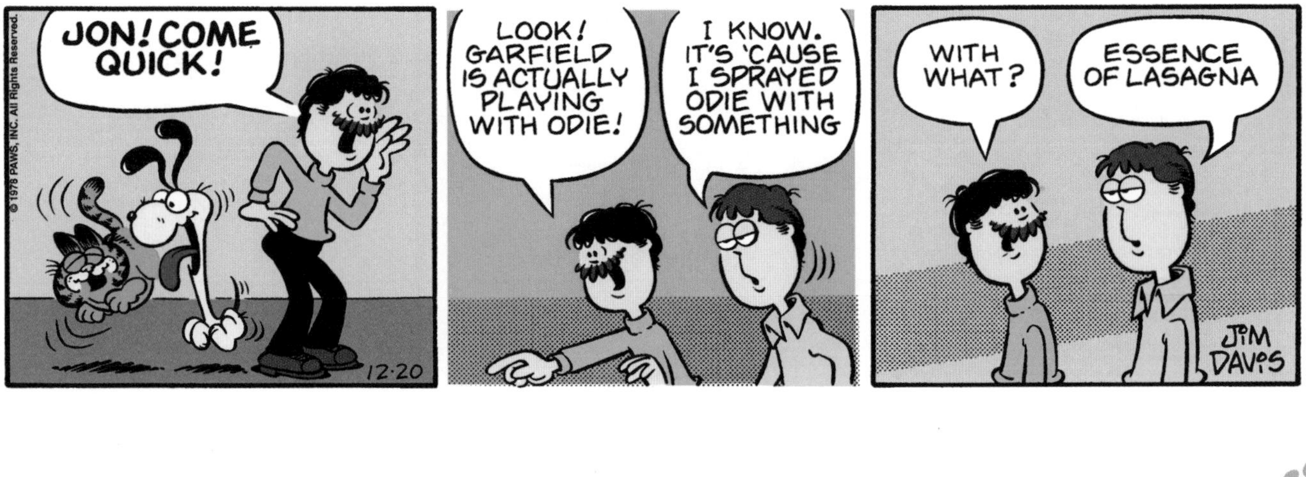
© 1978 PAWS, INC. All Rights Reserved.
JON! COME QUICK!
12·20
LOOK! GARFIELD IS ACTUALLY PLAYING WITH ODIE!
I KNOW. IT'S 'CAUSE I SPRAYED ODIE WITH SOMETHING
WITH WHAT?
ESSENCE OF LASAGNA
JIM DAVIS

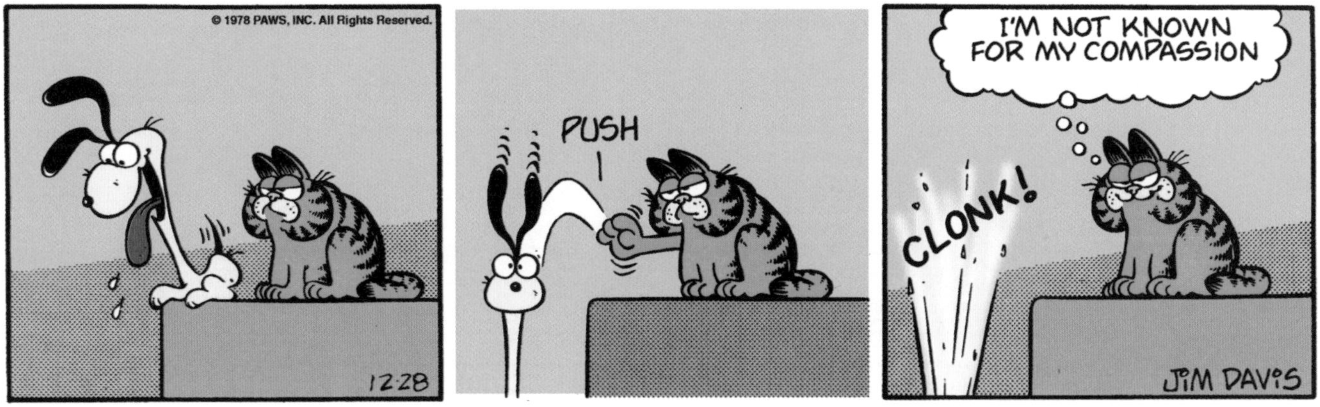
© 1978 PAWS, INC. All Rights Reserved.
12·28
PUSH
CLONK!
I'M NOT KNOWN FOR MY COMPASSION
JIM DAVIS

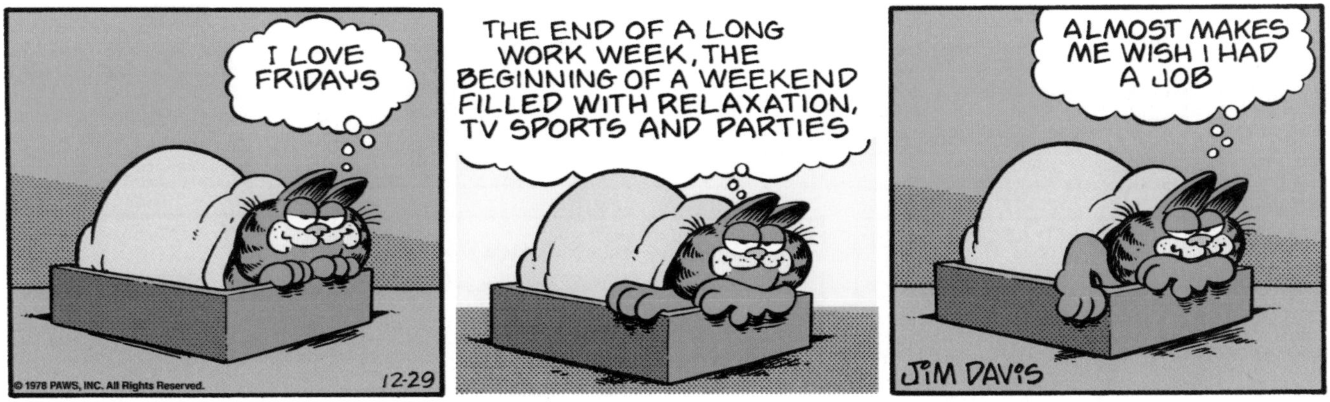
I LOVE FRIDAYS
© 1978 PAWS, INC. All Rights Reserved.
12·29
THE END OF A LONG WORK WEEK, THE BEGINNING OF A WEEKEND FILLED WITH RELAXATION, TV SPORTS AND PARTIES
ALMOST MAKES ME WISH I HAD A JOB
JIM DAVIS

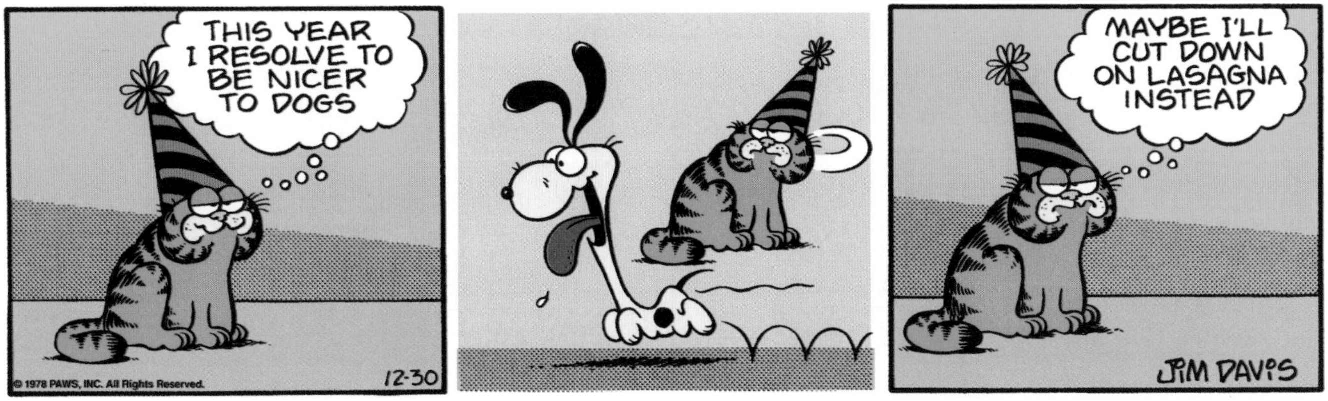
THIS YEAR I RESOLVE TO BE NICER TO DOGS
© 1978 PAWS, INC. All Rights Reserved.
12·30
MAYBE I'LL CUT DOWN ON LASAGNA INSTEAD
JIM DAVIS

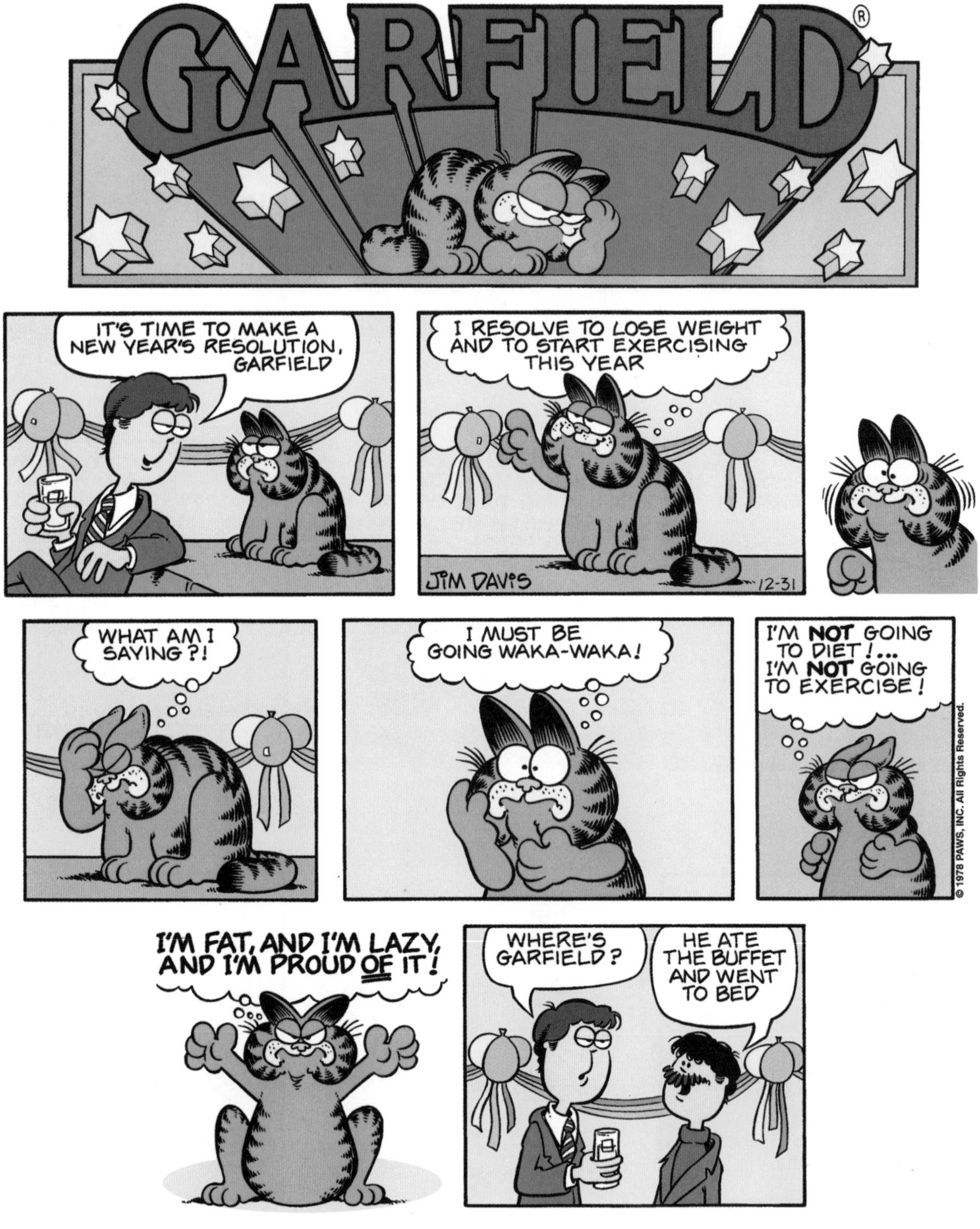
GARFIELD®
IT'S TIME TO MAKE A NEW YEAR'S RESOLUTION, GARFIELD
I RESOLVE TO LOSE WEIGHT AND TO START EXERCISING THIS YEAR
JIM DAVIS
12-31
WHAT AM I SAYING?!
I MUST BE GOING WAKA-WAKA!
I'M NOT GOING TO DIET!... I'M NOT GOING TO EXERCISE!
© 1978 PAWS, INC. All Rights Reserved.
I'M FAT, AND I'M LAZY, AND I'M PROUD OF IT!
WHERE'S GARFIELD?
HE ATE THE BUFFET AND WENT TO BED

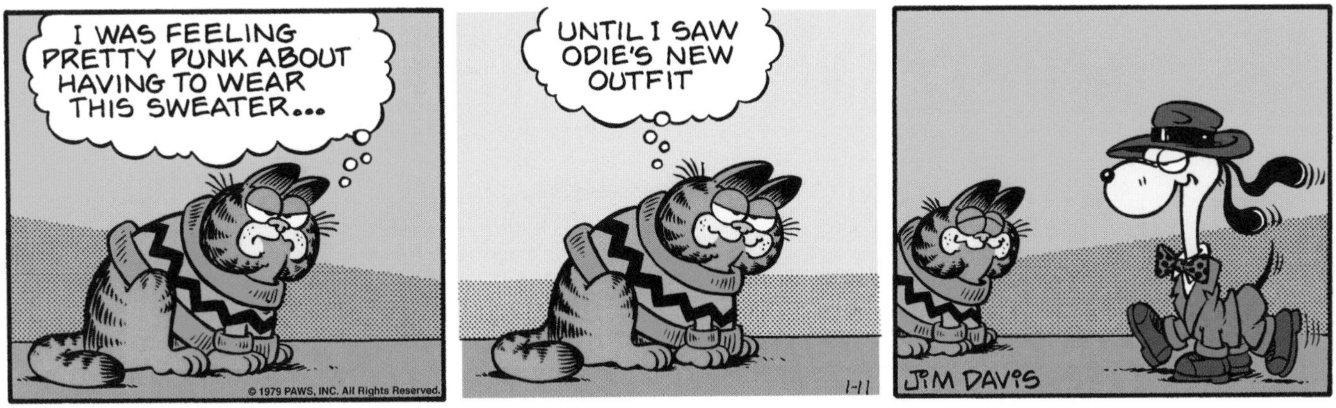
I WAS FEELING PRETTY PUNK ABOUT HAVING TO WEAR THIS SWEATER...
© 1979 PAWS, INC. All Rights Reserved.
UNTIL I SAW ODIE'S NEW OUTFIT
1-11
JIM DAVIS

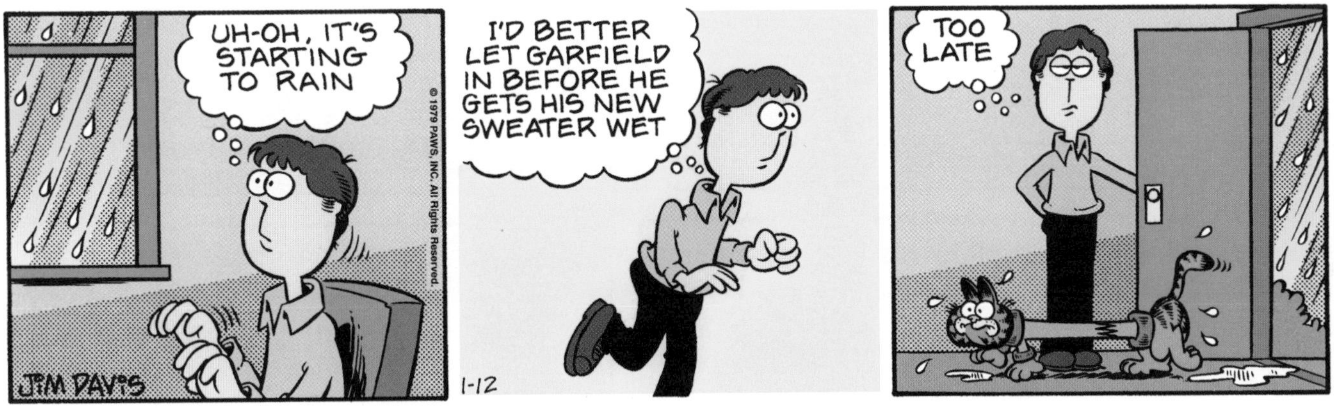
UH-OH, IT'S STARTING TO RAIN
© 1979 PAWS, INC. All Rights Reserved.
JIM DAVIS
I'D BETTER LET GARFIELD IN BEFORE HE GETS HIS NEW SWEATER WET
1-12
TOO LATE

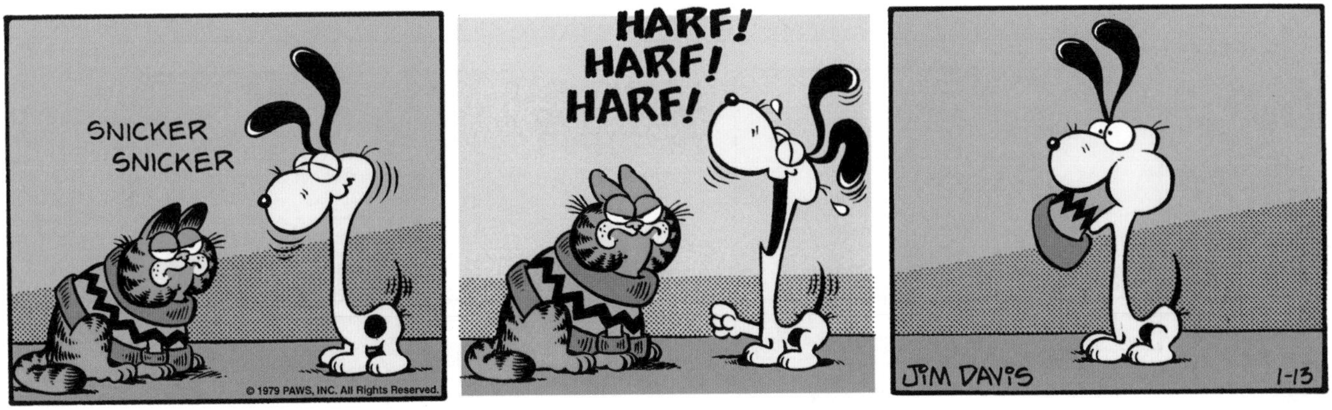
SNICKER SNICKER
© 1979 PAWS, INC. All Rights Reserved.
HARF! HARF! HARF!
JIM DAVIS
1-13

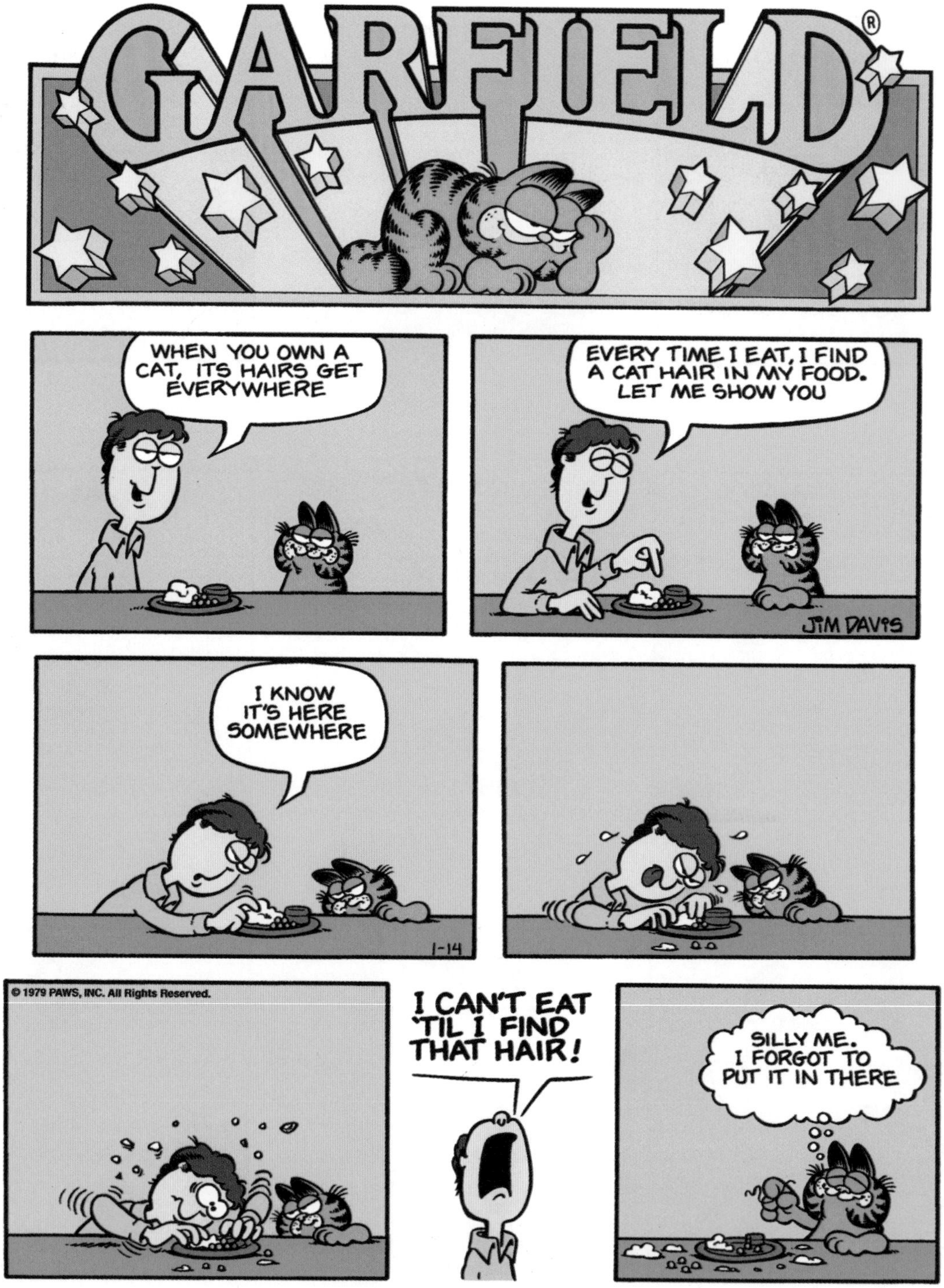
GARFIELD®
WHEN YOU OWN A CAT, ITS HAIRS GET EVERYWHERE
EVERY TIME I EAT, I FIND A CAT HAIR IN MY FOOD. LET ME SHOW YOU
JIM DAVIS
I KNOW IT'S HERE SOMEWHERE
1-14
© 1979 PAWS, INC. All Rights Reserved.
I CAN'T EAT 'TIL I FIND THAT HAIR!
SILLY ME. I FORGOT TO PUT IT IN THERE

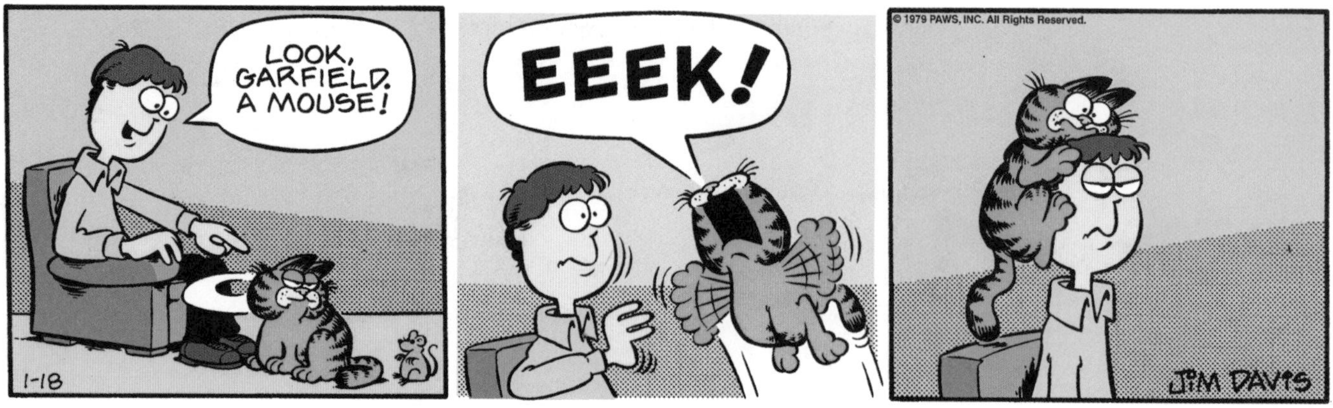
1-18
LOOK, GARFIELD. A MOUSE!
EEEK!
© 1979 PAWS, INC. All Rights Reserved.
JIM DAVIS

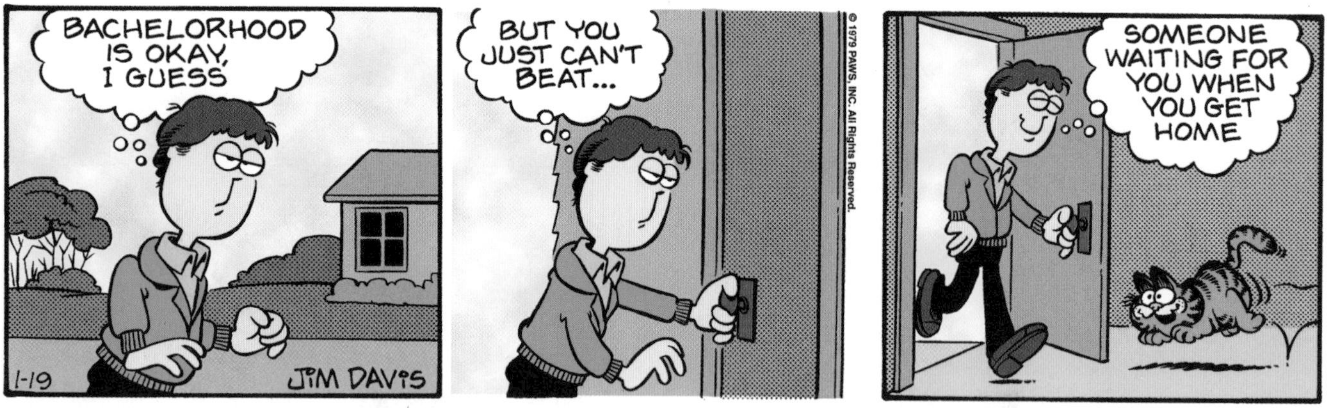
1-19
BACHELORHOOD IS OKAY, I GUESS
JIM DAVIS
© 1979 PAWS, INC. All Rights Reserved.
BUT YOU JUST CAN'T BEAT...
SOMEONE WAITING FOR YOU WHEN YOU GET HOME

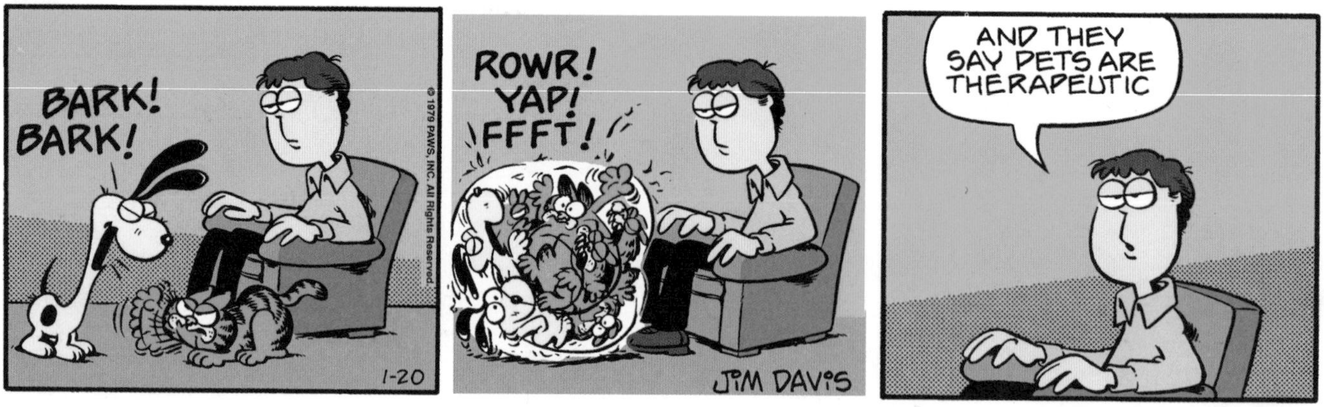
BARK! BARK!
© 1979 PAWS, INC. All Rights Reserved.
1-20
ROWR! YAP! FFFT!
JIM DAVIS
AND THEY SAY PETS ARE THERAPEUTIC